This book examines and compares the two maj[o]
institutionalist thinking in economics: the "old"
of Veblen, Mitchell, Commons, and Ayres, and t]
tionalism developed more recently from neoclass[i]
sources and including the writings of Coase, W[i]
Schotter, and many others. The discussion is org[...]
set of key methodological, theoretical, and normative problems
that necessarily confront any attempt to incorporate institutions
(defined to include organizations, laws, and social norms) into
economics. These are identified in terms of the issues surrounding
the use of formal or non-formal analytical methods, individualist
or holistic approaches, the respective roles of rational choice and
rule-following behaviour, the relative importance of the spontaneous evolution and deliberative design of institutions, and questions concerning the normative appraisal of institutions. The old
and the new institutionalism have often been paired on opposite
sides on each of these issues, and the issues themselves presented
in a series of sharp dichotomies. Professor Rutherford argues,
however, that matters are both more complex and more challeng-
ing. Each tradition contains a variety of positions, and there are
significant points of contact between the more moderate representatives of each group. Although each tradition embodies fascinating insights into the study of economic institutions – their
functioning, evolution, and impact on human welfare – neither
has as yet provided fully satisfactory answers to the problems
identified.

Institutions in economics

Historical Perspectives on Modern Economics

General Editor: Professor Craufurd D. Goodwin, Duke University

This series contains original works that challenge and enlighten historians of economics. For the profession as a whole it promotes better understanding of the origin and content of modern economics.

Other books in the series:

William J. Barber: *From New Era to New Deal: Herbert Hoover, the Economists, and American Economic Policy, 1921–1933*

M. June Flanders: *International Monetary Economics, 1870–1950*

Lars Jonung (ed.): *The Stockholm School of Economics Revisited*

Kyun Kim: *Equilibrium Business Cycle Theory in Historical Perspective*

Gerald M. Koot: *English Historical Economics, 1870–1926: The Rise of Economic History and Mercantilism*

Don Lavoie: *Rivalry and Central Planning: The Socialist Calculation Debate Reconsidered*

Philip Mirowski: *More Heat than Light: Economics as Social Physics, Physics as Nature's Economics*

Mary S. Morgan: *The History of Econometric Ideas*

Takashi Negishi: *Economic Theories in a Non-Walrasian Tradition*

Karen I. Vaughn: *Austrian Economics in America: The Migration of a Tradition*

E. Roy Weintraub: *General Equilibrium Analysis: Studies in Appraisal*

E. Roy Weintraub: *Stabilizing Dynamics: Constructing Economic Knowledge*

Institutions in economics
The old and the new institutionalism

Malcolm Rutherford
University of Victoria

CAMBRIDGE
UNIVERSITY PRESS

Published by the Press Syndicate of the University of Cambridge
The Pitt Building, Trumpington Street, Cambridge CB2 IRP
40 West 20th Street, New York, NY 10011-4211, USA
10 Stamford Road, Oakleigh, Melbourne 3166, Australia

First published 1994
Reprinted 1995
First paperback edition 1996

Printed in the United States of America

Library of Congress Cataloging-in-Publication Data is available.

A catalog record for this book is available from the British Library.

ISBN 0-521-45189-2 hardback
ISBN 0-521-57447-1 paperback

For Frances and Sarah

Contents

viii   **Contents**

Preface and acknowledgements

This book is a product of my long-standing interest in questions relating to institutions and their role in economic life. Initially, this interest took me to the study of the American institutionalist tradition (now often called the "old" institutional economics, or OIE) and to a series of articles on Veblen, Commons, Mitchell, and Ayres (Rutherford 1980, 1981, 1983, 1984, 1987), a line of work I have continued to pursue (1990a, 1990c, 1992a, 1992b). These pieces are written from the point of view of a sympathetic critic; I do not now think of myself, and never have done so, as an adherent of any of the major research programs contained within the OIE. I am sympathetic to the overall aim of incorporating institutions within economics, and I find certain of the ideas and arguments of old institutionalists of great interest, but I have not discovered within the OIE any approach or model that I could wholeheartedly adopt as my own.

In recent years a new literature on institutions has emerged from more neoclassical, Austrian, and game-theoretic sources, a literature that has become known as the "new" institutional economics, or NIE. Accordingly, I turned my attention to the NIE, and particularly to the comparison of the new institutionalism with the old (Rutherford 1989a, 1989b). My impression of the NIE, however, is that it contains problems almost as severe as, but opposite in kind to, those found in the OIE. I am sympathetic to its overall objective of more rigorously analyzing institutions and institutional change, and I find many particular arguments and models of great interest, but, again, I cannot fully align myself with any of its principal research programs.

My major objectives in this book stem from this somewhat ambivalent position. They are, first, to provide a discussion of the *general* problems inherent in any attempt to deal with institutions; second, to outline the strengths and weaknesses of the ways in which the OIE and NIE deal with each of these problems; and third, to offer a few suggestions for a more adequate treatment of institutions than either the old or the new currently provide. In working toward these objectives I am also endeavouring to cut through the mutual hostility and suspicion that has characterized much of the relationship between the old and the new institutionalist (see, for example, Dugger 1983, 1989a). Both approaches are concerned about including institutions within economics, and although they differ significantly in philosophical and methodological orientation, as well as in theoretical direction and normative predilection, the differences between the two have often been simply assumed to be dichotomous and irreconcilable. In contrast, I claim that the differences between the old and the new are often *not* dichotomous in nature, but rather related to matters of emphasis and focus. This leads on to the possibility that some of the contributions of each might be complementary in nature and might indicate different aspects of a problem that should be incorporated in any more complete treatment. It is a part of my argument that any adequate treatment of institutions cannot ignore points made by each, and that neither approach has a monopoly over the good or the interesting.

Because of the nature of these objectives I have organized the book around issues rather than in a chronological sequence or a chapter-by-chapter discussion of individual writers. This approach highlights the underlying problems common to both the OIE and the NIE and provides a basis for comparing the various solutions that each has proposed. In this way, too, historical and contemporary ideas are blended. The discussion of the OIE concentrates on the work of the major figures: Veblen, Mitchell, Commons, and Ayres. The contemporary element is found in the treatment of the NIE and in the relevance of the problems to present-day institutional questions.

This book owes a great deal to the advice and encouragement I have received over the years from my teachers and colleagues. I should mention especially Denis O'Brien, Bob Coats, Warren Samuels, and the late Allan Gruchy. Craufurd Goodwin deserves special thanks for his steadfast belief in the ultimate realization of this project. I am also pleased to acknowledge the aid provided to me by a University of Victoria Faculty Research Grant, the invaluable help of my research assistant, Denby Wong, and of Pattie Eccleston in preparing the manuscript.

Several parts of this book have been presented as conference papers, and many useful comments have been received from discussants and others. In addition, Denis O'Brien read and commented on Chapter 2 and Viktor Vanberg on Chapter 4. I remain responsible for any errors or omissions. Other parts incorporate material I have published previously. Sections from "Clarence Ayres and the Instrumental Theory on Value" (1981) appear in Chapter 6. Sections from "J. R. Commons's Institutional Economics" (1983) appear in Chapters 5 and 6. I thank the copyright holder, the Association for Evolutionary Economics, for special permission to reprint this material. Sections from "Thorstein Veblen and the Processes of Institutional Change" (1984) appear in Chapters 3 and 5. I thank the copyright holder, Duke University Press, for permission to reprint this material. Sections from "Wesley Mitchell: Institutions and Quantitative Methods" (1987) appear in Chapter 2. I thank the Eastern Economics Association for permission to reprint this material. Sections from "Some Issues in the Comparison of Austrian and Institutional Economics" (1989a) appear in Chapter 3. I thank the copyright holder, JAI Press, for permission to reprint this material. Sections from "What is Wrong with the New Institutional Economics (and What Is Still Wrong with the Old)?" (1989b) appear in Chapters 3, 5, and 6. I thank Edward Arnold for permission to reprint this material.

Malcolm Rutherford
Victoria, B.C. 1993

CHAPTER 1

Definitions and issues

Throughout the history of economic thought, attempts have been made to incorporate issues relating to institutions[1] and institutional change within the discipline. The most obvious example is that of the American institutionalist tradition of Veblen, Mitchell, Commons, and Ayres. But institutional analysis of various kinds can also be found in the works of classical economists such as Adam Smith and J. S. Mill; members of the German, English, and American historical schools; Marx and other Marxians; Austrian school members such as Menger, von Wieser, and Hayek; Schumpeter; and neoclassicals such as Marshall.

This book concentrates on the two major traditions of institutionalist thought in economics. The first is the American institutionalist tradition that began at the turn of the century and has continued uninterrupted (although with large swings in popularity and prestige) to this day. The second is a more recent development, but one that can be seen as a revival and considerable expansion of the institutionalist elements to be found in classical, neoclassical, and Austrian economics,[2] elements that had fallen into neglect in the intervening period. The former tradition is now often called the "old" institutional economics, or OIE, while the latter is usually called the "new" institutional economics, or NIE.[3]

1.1 The old and the new institutionalism

The old institutionalism consists of that tradition of thought associated with Thorstein Veblen, Wesley Mitchell, John R. Commons, and Clarence Ayres, and with the more recent contributions of Allan Gruchy, Wendell Gordon, Marc Tool, and the many others represented in the pages of the *Journal of Economic Issues*. Despite claims to the contrary (Gruchy 1947, 1972), the OIE does not represent a single well-defined or unified body of thought, methodology, or program of research. Within the OIE there are two research programs of major theoretical significance. The first is associated with Thorstein Veblen, and with the development and modification of Veblen's system undertaken by Clarence Ayres. This program is built around the concept of a fundamental dichotomy between the business or pecuniary and the industrial aspects of the economy. This is also expressed in a more general way as a dichotomy

1

between institutional and technological or between ceremonial and instrumental ways of doing and thinking (Waller 1982; Munkirs 1988). In very sweeping terms, this program focuses on investigating the effects of new technology on institutional schemes, and the ways in which established social conventions and vested interests resist such change. Institutions, then, need not be well adapted to the available instrumentalities, the criterion of judgement usually being some notion of "instrumental value," which in turn is based on a more or less broad definition of "community serviceability." These ideas are often coupled to a view of the structure of the modern economy that emphasizes the political and economic power of large corporate interests.

The second major program within the OIE has its roots in the work of John R. Commons and is now represented by writers such as Warren Samuels and Allan Schmid (Schmid 1978; Samuels and Schmid 1981). This program concentrates on law, property rights and organizations, their evolution and impact on legal and economic power, economic transactions, and the distribution of income. Here, institutions are seen largely as the outcome of formal and informal processes of conflict resolution, the criterion of success being whether the institution has generated a "reasonable value" or "workable mutuality" out of conflict. In some respects, this program is complementary to the Veblen–Ayres approach, which does not explicitly address the judicial and political processes of conflict resolution central to Commons's work, but there are points of tension and even of outright conflict between them. For example, Commons ([1924] 1968: 376, [1934] 1961: 673) himself directly attacks both Veblen's approach and his "cynical antithesis" between business and industry, and this conflict extends into the value concepts used by each (Ramstad 1989). It is also the case that the Commons tradition – owing to its emphasis on transactions, property rights, and organizations – has closer links with the NIE than does the Veblen–Ayres tradition. Nevertheless, as will be seen in later chapters, Commons's approach still differs from anything found in the NIE in significant ways.

It is probably true that the NIE is just as disparate as the old (Coats 1986; Maki 1987; Andersen and Bregn 1992). One major strand is to be found in the work on property rights (Demsetz 1967; Alchian and Demsetz 1973) and common law (Posner 1977, 1981). Another strand is that concerned with public choice processes, including those involving rent seeking and the activities of distributive coalitions (Olson 1982; Mueller 1989). A third important element deals with organizations and includes the agency theory developed from Jensen and Meckling (1976), and work on transactions costs stemming from Coase (1937) and utilized extensively by Oliver Williamson (1975, 1985). Further aspects are provided by game theorists, some of whom use game theory primarily to model action within given institutional situations (Shubik 1975), while others use it in a more ambitious attempt to explain the evolution of the social institutions themselves (Schotter 1981). Many of these elements can be found combined in the institutional economic history of Douglass North (1981, 1990). The new institutionalism has also been defined to include Austrian and neo-Schumpeterian efforts to explain various types of institutional development in invisible-hand or evolutionary terms (Hayek 1967, 1973, 1979; Nelson and Winter 1982; Langlois 1986a).

As with the OIE, in some respects these programs complement each other, but differences and disagreements do exist. Douglass North criticizes both those who take a *purely* rent-seeking approach to government activity and those who limit their analysis to alterations in contracts occurring *within* a given basic institutional framework. North also argues forcefully for a much fuller recognition of the importance of notions of fairness and ideology in institutional change (North 1984, 1986). Agency theory and the transactions cost approach of Williamson have differences too. Williamson (1987a, 1990) points to differences in the basic unit of analysis and in the ex ante focus of agency theory as opposed to the ex post approach of transactions cost economics. Most agency theorists are also more orthodox in their assumptions concerning maximizing behaviour than is Williamson. More fundamentally, Langlois (1986b) argues that the NIE *should* concentrate more on spontaneous, invisible-hand, processes. He claims that certain key problems with the NIE stem from its "neoclassical core," and argues that the NIE should move in a more Austrian direction (Langlois 1989: 291–294). It is certainly possible to distinguish between a more neoclassical and a more Austrian "wing" to the NIE. The vast majority of the work in the NIE belongs in the former category (Eggertsson 1990). The latter would include Langlois's outline of a program, Hayek's work on institutions, Nelson and Winter's neo-Schumpeterian evolutionary economics, and, possibly, some of the work in game theory.[4]

Given the nature of these bodies of work, one might question the usefulness of the simple two-way division into old and new institutionalisms. Indeed, in some cases it will be necessary to make finer distinctions – into Veblen–Ayres, Commons, neoclassical, and Austrian divisions, for example – but for many purposes the Veblen–Ayres and Commons traditions can be grouped together in contrast to both the neoclassical and Austrian. This can be seen most clearly in the criticisms that each levels at the other. The new institutionalist, whether neoclassical or Austrian, complains of the old institutionalists' lack of theory; tendency to argue in holistic terms rather than in individualistic terms; use of a "behaviouristic" rather than a rational choice (or intendedly rational choice) framework; failure to give sufficient emphasis to *economizing* as "the main case"; and failure to appreciate the importance of unintended and evolutionary processes in institutional development, as opposed to processes of collective decision making and institutional design (Seckler 1975; North 1978; Schotter 1981; Coase 1984; Williamson 1987b; Ault and Ekelund 1988). The OIE is thus portrayed as descriptivist and anti-formalist, holist, behaviourist, and collectivist. Old institutionalists also reject individualistic welfare criteria and are more interventionist, favouring greater government involvement to correct institutional failures. Of course, some of these labels apply better to some old institutionalists than to others, but it is hard to deny all truth to the characterization, particularly when old institutionalists willingly apply many of the same labels to themselves (Gruchy 1947; Wilber and Harrison 1978; Dugger 1979a). It seems that what new institutionalists see as faults, the old claim as virtues.

The old institutionalists, and those more sympathetic to their position, make the opposite set of criticisms of the new. They argue that its theory is often too abstract and formal; that it sometimes adopts an extreme, reductionist, version of individualism; that the individual is seen as an overly rational and overly autonomous being, constrained, but not otherwise influenced by, his institutional and social setting; that orthodox welfare criteria are not appropriate for appraising institutional change, and that a complacent attitude prevails concerning the efficiency characteristics of markets and of institutions that emerge spontaneously (Mirowski 1981; Field 1981, 1984; Dugger 1983; Dow 1987; Hodgson 1988). The NIE is thus portrayed as more formalist (particularly in its neoclassical and game theoretic manifestations), individualist, reductionist, orientated toward rational choice and economizing models, and generally anti-interventionist. Again these labels apply more to some than to others, but again they are labels that new institutionalists have willingly applied to themselves, in part in order to clearly distinguish their work from the OIE (Coase 1984; Langlois 1986a).

1.2   Dichotomies and problems

Despite the disparity that exists within both the OIE and the NIE, it appears that the OIE and NIE can be usefully distinguished. This is not to suggest, however, that the old and the new therefore sit on opposite

CHAPTER 2

Formalism and anti-formalism

Formalism is defined here as the use of an abstract language such as mathematics or symbolic logic in place of natural linguistic or literary methods of presentation. Formal systems were originally developed to investigate the rules of deductive inference, and for this purpose the exact meaning to be attached to the primitive terms employed is unimportant. For economics, however, the interpretation and economic meaning of terms is important, and the use of formal methods usually involves the construction of a "model" that both embodies a formal structure and provides the basis for interpreting the symbolism.

Using the terminology of formal and natural languages may give the impression that it should be possible to translate one into the other without much difficulty. It is true that some arguments can be translated from one language into another with relatively little difficulty or alteration of the content, but this is far from always the case. To formalize a theory is not simply to make it more precise; rather, some aspects of the theory are singled out to produce a highly idealized representation of it. In this, the ambiguity of natural language may be overcome, but at the cost of losing much of its richness and suggestiveness.

Although formalism can be traced far back in the history of economics, it is associated in particular with the development of neoclassical economics. Early neoclassical contributors such as Walras, Jevons, and Edgeworth drew on the example of physics and adopted the mathematics of constrained maximization (Mirowski 1989, 1991). Despite Marshall's more eclectic approach,[1] mathematical formalism has since become one of the hallmarks of neoclassical economics. The chief advantage claimed for this mathematical formalism has always been that it increases the clarity and precision with which theoretical arguments can be stated. Formalism encourages the more explicit statement of assumptions, including initial conditions and behavioural hypotheses, and makes the derivation of implications not only more exact but also much more visible and open to examination. Although less frequently commented upon, another of its advantages is that it promotes the elaboration of sequences of models, with each model representing some development or modification to the assumptions or derivations.

In both of these respects, neoclassical economics has had considerable success. In particular, formalization has enabled theorists to build upon and rapidly develop the work of their predecessors. Of course, formalization tends to bring with it an increased degree of abstraction from the particularities of a historical or institutional type. This high degree of abstraction has, however, traditionally been seen as more of a benefit than a cost, allowing the theorist to focus attention on those factors thought to be most important or of the most *general* relevance. Thus, abstracting from many of the complexities of the real world has frequently been seen as a necessary means of gaining insight into its functioning.

Those who have criticized formalism have usually done so on the grounds that the available formalisms are inappropriate or insufficient for the explanation of certain classes of social phenomena. It is often claimed that formal methods direct inquiry to those topics, or to the use of those particular assumptions, that are mathematically tractable. Equilibrium analysis based on the assumption of maximizing behaviour is a great deal more tractable than the analysis of sequential processes of change based on adaption, and it is not surprising that those traditions that have stressed the importance of process and raised questions concerning the use of maximizing assumptions have also been sceptical of the use of formal methods. Moreover, the same high degree of abstraction that creates generality may cause indeterminacy, indicating that the outcome reached in any particular case may depend on the specifics of the situation omitted from the model. For reasons such as these, those who reject formal methods tend to utilize more literary forms of theorizing, often (but not always) combined with studies of a historical, institutional, or case study nature.

The debate between formalists and anti-formalists has been a staple of methodological dispute in economics, often over the realism and relevance of economic theory. It is closely related to, but not identical with, the long-running debate over induction versus deduction. Formalism is identified with the study of deductive inference, and those classed as inductivists have generally been anti-formalists. Nevertheless, as the Austrian tradition demonstrates, a commitment to deductive methods need not imply the use of highly formal methods of inference. Although the induction/deduction distinction is one that is often found in the literature on the OIE, many of the issues involved have had much more to do with the appropriate degree of formalism than with induction or deduction as such. When the distinction is seen in these terms, it becomes apparent that members of the OIE and NIE have more concerns in common than is usually thought.

2.1 Formalism and anti-formalism in the OIE

According to Langlois (1986a: 5), one of the central difficulties with the work of "early institutionalists" is that "they wanted an economics with institutions but without theory." A similar argument, but in harsher terms, is made by Coase (1984: 230): "American institutionalists were not theoretical but anti-theoretical. . . . Without a theory they had nothing to pass on except a mass of descriptive material waiting for a theory, or a fire." This view of the OIE as primarily descriptive and non- or even anti-theoretical in nature is by no means uncommon. It takes support particularly from Wesley Mitchell's statistical work on business cycles and John R. Commons's vast documentation of the history of the labour movement, but the impression of the OIE as anti-theoretical or purely descriptive is quite misleading. Even the work of Mitchell and of Commons contains theoretical underpinnings and theoretical purposes (Rutherford 1983, 1987). What is true is that old institutionalists reject the more orthodox neoclassical forms of theory and model building as overly formal, abstract, and narrow. The methodological dispute here is less over theory versus description than over the appropriate degree of abstraction to be used in the analysis of a complex evolving system. Since Allan Gruchy's (1947) first major book, old institutionalists have frequently characterized the issue in terms of the less formal "cultural" or "holistic" perspective of the OIE versus the formalism of economic orthodoxy (Wilber and Harrison 1978; Gruchy 1987). Although not explicitly expressed in these terms, the criticisms of orthodox theorizing made by earlier contributors to American institutionalism are not dissimilar.

2.1.1 From Veblen to Clark

Veblen is perhaps best known for his stinging criticism of the psychological preconceptions of neoclassical and Austrian economics.[2] In Veblen's view, both adopted the hedonistic view of man as a "lightning calculator of pleasures and pains," a "homogeneous globule of desire of happiness" (Veblen 1898: 73). This comment of Veblen's raises a number of issues, some of which will be examined in more detail in later chapters. Within the present context, what is most significant is Veblen's argument that the assumption of the rational "hedonic calculus" combined with an assumption of a *given* institutional situation (including the "natural right of ownership") leads to an economic theory that is nothing more than the detailed and rigorous deduction of the "rational response to the exigencies of the [given] situation in which man is placed" (Veblen [1909] 1961: 234–236). Such an economics lends itself to formal methods of presentation. The theory is a theory of the "normal" case, a highly refined and developed theory of equilibrium states, but one that simply excludes the issues of evolutionary institutional change ([1900] 1961: 164–165). Veblen even characterizes the so-called dynamic neoclassical theory not as a treatment of the underlying "phenomena of change," but at most as a discussion of the "rational adjustment to change which may be supposed to have supervened" ([1909] 1961: 232). As a result, whenever any institutional phenomenon "is involved in the facts with which the theory is occupied, such institutional facts are taken for granted, denied, or explained away" ([1909] 1961: 233).

In place of this orthodox type of theory, Veblen wanted to substitute an inquiry into the evolution of institutions and their impact on human conduct. In this, he made repeated references to Darwin and to evolutionary biology as a model of "modern science." By "modern science" he meant a focus on sequential, continuous, change explained in causal (as opposed to intentionalist) terms, and without any presumption of a final term or consummation (Veblen 1898). This institutional economics was not to be purely descriptive. He criticized the German historical school for having produced nothing more than a "narrative survey of phenomena" (1898: 72). What Veblen wished to produce was a "genetic account of an unfolding process,"[3] a treatment of institutional evolution as a process of "cumulative causation." For Veblen, this cumulative process was based less on rationalistic calculation than on habituation to material conditions and constraints:

The growth of culture is a cumulative sequence of habituation, and the ways and means of it are the habitual response of human nature to exigencies that vary incontinently, cumulatively, but with something of a consistent sequence in the cumulative variations that so go forward, – incontinently, because each new move creates a new situation which induces a further new variation in the habitual manner of response; cumulatively, because each new situation is a variation of what has gone before it and embodies as causal factors all that has been effected by what went before; consistently, because the underlying traits of human nature . . . by force of which the response takes place, and on the ground of which the habituation takes effect, remain substantially unchanged. ([1909] 1961: 241–242)

The issue of habituation versus rational choice will be discussed in more detail later, but Veblen's notion of cumulative causation raises two other important points. The first is the claim that a proper treatment of institutional evolution should consist of more than a treatment of adjustment to a series of exogenously given shocks. Much of the NIE fails this test, dealing not with the internal dynamic of the system but only with the rational (or intendedly rational) responses to exogenously given changes in population, technology, trading opportunities, or ideology. The second, and related, point is that Veblen's discussion of cumulative causation involves a clear idea of path dependency. History matters in the sense that what happens next depends critically on the details of the existing state of affairs, which in turn is the outcome of the pre-existing situation. Small differences in initial conditions can make for widely differing outcomes. There is, in this, the idea of the openness of the evolution of a complex system. From similar starting points different cultures will develop in different ways; Veblen ([1908a] 1961: 230) talks of the "exuberant uncertainties of cumulative change." Of course, the process is not unconstrained, and one can develop theories about the overall evolutionary processes at work and provide an analysis of institutional history. However, no particular historical or institutional development can be explained without referring to the details of the actual historical circumstances involved. As in evolutionary biology, the theory need not be able to predict the next step in evolution in order to claim explanatory value. The explanations of particular events must combine the theory with a great deal of concrete information. This is what Wesley Mitchell (1927: 54) called "analytic description." Theory is by no means excluded. Even highly formal theory can play a role in such a program, but any attempt to understand the actual course of institutional history cannot be limited to highly abstract formal models.

Veblen's own work is almost always a blend of theory with a discussion of the related historical sequence of events. Veblen does not test his theories against the factual and historical information he presents, but weaves the two into an analytic description of the process of cumulative causation. Veblen's main concern in his methodological essays, however, is to emphasize the evolutionary approach based on the idea of cumulative causation. He provides little by way of more detailed methodological guidelines and many parts of his work are open to empirical criticism. Veblen's tendency to ignore the job of critically examining his conclusions is one remarked upon by Wesley Mitchell (1929: 29).

Wesley Mitchell's own discussion of methodology also centers on the issue of the complexity of many economic phenomena.[4] In his study of business cycles, Mitchell remarks on the vast number of competing theories, each of which focuses on a small number of causal factors and many of which seem to have at least some empirical support. For Mitchell, this "multiplicity of explanations" arose from the "complexity of the problem itself." Business activity "depends upon the smoothly coordinated functioning of many processes" and "any of the factors or processes can be made to yield a plausible theory of business cycles, provided some investigator can show that it is an independent source of recurrent fluctuations in the activity of trade" (Mitchell 1927: 48).

Mitchell's aim was to produce a "thoroughly unified explanation of business cycles," but to achieve this end he rejected the standard method of abstract model building as one that made it too easy to neglect "phenomena which do not fit neatly into preconceived schemes" (1927: 49). Mitchell's critique of the standard methodology successfully isolates a number of its major weaknesses. First, the empirical work may simply be neglected and the theory never tested (Burns and Mitchell 1946: 8). Second, the need for theoretical simplicity may result in simplifying assumptions which give a theory only a "problematical relation" to the actual world and may render it, in practical terms, untestable (Burns and Mitchell 1946: 8–9). Third, even if the theory is testable, "the worker who tries to verify it must examine the processes on which it centres attention." The test is therefore "superficial" as it is quite possible that many competing theories could all be similarly verified (Burns and Mitchell 1946: 9). This problem is compounded to the extent that the investigator is "prone to adduce only the evidence and arguments that seem to prove his explanation" (Mitchell 1927: 181). Fourth, Mitchell argues that the behaviour of economic agents is often more complex than it appears in arguments that proceed by deducing behaviour from a few assumptions such as the importance of profit for the businessman. That business is conducted for profit "is not a simple matter" that enables the theorist to deduce results with any degree of certainty. Describing his own view, Mitchell put the point as follows: "There is much in the working of business technique which I should never think of if I were not always turning back to observation. And I should not trust even my reasoning about what businessmen will do if I could not check it up" ([1928] 1936: 415).

Mitchell's conclusion was that to overcome these problems and to capture the full extent of the complexity of economic phenomena, observations should play a greater role, but he neither denied that some conceptual apparatus and working hypotheses were necessary to guide enquiry nor accepted the usual empiricist notion of induction from an objective empirical base ([1927] 1936: 59, n. 2). He considered the scientific method to consist of "the patient processes of observation and testing – always critical testing – of the relations between the working hypotheses and the processes observed," as contrasted with the method of orthodox economics of "trying to think out a deductive scheme and then . . . verifying that" ([1928] 1936: 413–415). Mitchell's method does not dispense with theorizing, but, as he put it, the place for it is "inside the investigation" ([1928] 1936: 413). His aim was to bring factual research and theorizing into the closest possible contact.

Care is required, however, in interpreting Mitchell's concepts of working hypotheses and testing. For Mitchell, working hypotheses included definitions, measurements, and low-level empirical hypotheses, as well as explanatory hypotheses concerning behavioural or causal relationships. In parts of Mitchell's work, the first three types predominate, but not because he was only interested in arriving at empirical generalizations, but rather because of his views on the weakness of standard empirical verifications and his desire to arrive at a more meaningful testing procedure. At the same time, Mitchell's "critical testing" did not go so far as to imply a Popperian search for falsifiers or any abandonment of the basic verificationist idea that defines a successful test in terms of corroboration. What Mitchell rejected was the extremely uncritical process of searching for, and usually finding, only verifications, not verificationism itself. To be meaningful, a verification should take the form of empirical investigation that is at least open to the possibility of finding contrary evidence, or, what is often more important, evidence that the theory is incomplete.

Mitchell thus came to argue that empirical work should be directed at discovering new information by examining in detail the process or phenomenon to be explained within an overall conceptual framework and utilizing existing theories as working hypotheses to help guide inquiry in a close interplay between the working hypotheses and empirical findings. In this fashion Mitchell hoped to discover both the strengths and weaknesses of existing hypotheses and to define more clearly, in terms of what had to be explained, the task remaining to the theorist (Mitchell 1927: 58,[1931] 1950: 409; Burns and Mitchell 1946: 9–10). Only in this way did Mitchell think that the investigator could arrive at a full understanding of the complex interactions of the many causal elements that both produced business cycles and gave rise to their differences over time.

Commons, too, was deeply concerned with the issue of how to analyze the operation of a complex evolving whole. Commons did not want to abandon entirely the insights of orthodox theory, but he did want to build them into a more complete institutional political economy, one that would give collective action, both in the sense of collective organizations such as firms and unions and in the sense of the collectively enforced rules of custom and law, its proper place in economics. In Commons's ([1934] 1961: 5–6, 161–162, 439–440) view, orthodox theory had failed to do this for a number of reasons. First, it assumed harmony of interests instead of conflict of interests, and thus failed to bring out the need for institutionalized rules to constrain individual behaviour. Second, orthodox theory tended to substitute given psychological propensities for what were actually customary (and evolving) modes of behaviour. And third, orthodox theory confused physical materials with the institutional aspects of property rights and thus led to the conflation of materials and ownership.

To overcome these problems and to include all relevant factors, Commons realized he would have to find a way to analyze the enormous complexity of the evolving legal and economic system. To help organize his efforts, Commons ([1934] 1961: 94) utilized what he called "principles" or "similarities of action," and "formulas" or "relations between the parts and the whole."[5] In terms of the legal/economic system as a whole, the major principles utilized by Commons are "Efficiency," "Scarcity," "Custom," "Sovereignty," and "Futurity" (or forward lookingness). These principles interrelate according to such formulas as that of "Limiting and Complementary Factors" ([1934] 1961: 627, 737–738). When dealing with politics as a whole, the principles become "Personality," "Political Principle," "Organization," "Jurisdiction," "Rationing," "Stabilization," and "Justification" ([1934]: 753). It is this approach that gives Commons's work its flavour of being little more than a loose and often confusing conceptual framework. Commons's work does contain general ideas concerning the nature of the evolutionary processes at work (which will be discussed later), but much of his intellectual effort was directed at the testing, modifying, and policy application of his hypothesized principles and formulas. For Commons, a "theory" was "a complex activity of analysis, genesis and insight, actively constructed by the mind in order to understand, predict and control the future" ([1934] 1961: 102):

> The method of analysis consists in breaking up the complexity into all the supposed similarities of behavior, and then giving to each similarity a name which designates it as a proposed scientific principle to be tested by investigation. The method of genesis consists in the discovery of changes which have occurred in the past as explanations of why the present situation exists as it is. The method of insight consists in understanding the ways of leadership and followship. ([1934] 1961: 753)

In this activity, Commons made extensive use of the collection of relevant documents and pioneered the use of interviews, particularly with key negotiators and decision makers. His "prime method of investigation" was the "constructive method of interviewing" ([1934] 1961: 106). Commons's case studies and his involvement in institutional reform display this methodology in action. Through his own case studies, and those conducted by his students, Commons continually modified and refined his conceptual apparatus of principles, developed his explanations of the various factors that shaped the present situation, and sought to uncover the "negotiational psychology" he could apply in each case in order to bring about change or resolve a dispute (Biddle 1990b).

Of the earlier writers in the OIE tradition, J. M. Clark represents an interesting case. Clark was certainly more theoretically inclined than most other old institutionalists, and he made significant contributions, such as the accelerator (Clark 1917), to economics in general. Despite his greater theoretical orientation and willingness to use formal methods, Clark was especially concerned with extending economics into the realm of the dynamic analysis of economic phenomena and institutions. Clark considered this shift to dynamic analysis to be of fundamental importance:

The key to statics, as we have seen, is a problem: that of levels of equilibrium. . . . The key to dynamics is a different problem: that of processes which do not visibly tend to any complete and definable static equilibrium. The importance of this shift from the search for levels to the study of processes can hardly be overemphasized; it is not less significant than the change from static to dynamic conditions. (Clark [1927] 1967: 203)

Clark made many references to Veblen's work and it is clear that he regarded "dynamics" as having to do with process and cumulative change. He also argued for more "inductive" work designed to develop appropriate premises and an understanding of the phenomena to be explained. Clark's (1923, 1961) own work on overhead costs and the dynamics of competition are good examples of his blending of theoretical and empirical investigation into an informal dynamic analysis.

While Clark was of the view that "the complexities of these dynamic realities could not be compressed into conventional geometric or algebraic models" (Markham 1968), and argued for the development of a "non-Euclidian" economics (Clark 1921), he did not reject static or more formal models entirely. Indeed, Clark was significantly kinder to more orthodox theory than other old institutionalists. Even "in the pursuit of dynamic analysis" Clark ([1927] 1967: 226) thought that "certain aspects of static analysis will find a place." A complete dynamic analysis may not always be possible, and a more simplified static approach may be necessary to penetrate the complexities involved. In addition, static analysis may provide a point of departure for dynamic analysis, or a benchmark for the appraisal of the impact of dynamic forces ([1927] 1967: 726–728).

Despite their variety, none of the methods discussed above can be regarded as having been entirely successful. Veblen's approach resulted in broad cultural histories and interpretations of sometimes highly doubtful validity.[6] In contrast, Mitchell and Commons, in their different ways, often allowed their emphasis on concrete detail to obscure their more general theoretical ideas and purposes. Clark, perhaps, had most theoretical success, but he is best known for work that is closest in nature to orthodox analysis, and even within the OIE his "dynamics" has had relatively little impact. At the same time, they were all struggling with the problem of how to analyze a system that is not simple, stable, and recurrent but complex, highly interrelated, and evolving over time. This problem still faces writers in both the old and the new traditions of institutionalism, and it is a problem with no obvious or easy solution.

2.1.2   *Pattern models and participant-observation*

Within the OIE, the more recent literature has closely associated the "cultural" or "holistic" outlook of old institutionalists with the idea of a "pattern model" borrowed from Abraham Kaplan (1964) and Paul Diesing (1971). This is most obvious in the work of Wilber and Harrison (1978), Wilber and Jameson (1983), Ramstad (1986), and Gruchy (1987).

Kaplan (1964: 332) describes the "pattern model of explanation" as the idea that "we know the reason for something when we can fit it into a known pattern." Thus, "according to the pattern model . . . something is explained when it is so related to a set of other elements that together they constitute a unified system" (1964: 333). Kaplan's work, however, does not place the pattern model entirely in opposition to deductive models, his argument being that "both may serve a useful purpose in methodology" (1964: 333). Diesing's (1971: 137) position is quite similar, but he does see the pattern model and its related methods as particularly suitable for "studying a whole human system in its natural setting." As this seems to have a close correspondence with the objectives of the OIE, Diesing's position deserves closer analysis.

Diesing's argument begins from the proposition that "human systems tend to develop a characteristic wholeness" or unity that "manifests itself in nearly every part" (1971: 137). This is then taken to imply that the characteristics of any part and its functioning are "largely determined by the whole to which it belongs and by its particular location in the whole system." Further, the techniques of investigation and concept development *should* be such as to "somehow capture and express this holistic quality" (1971: 138). These techniques and concepts must not "distort" the subject matter by abstracting too much. The concepts used must be "relatively concrete and particularized, close to the real system being described" (1971: 139–140). More specifically, he outlines a method of investigation that uses data collection, interviews, and, most important, the technique of the "participant-observer" (1971: 144–155).

The notion of the participant-observer lies at the heart of Diesing's method. The method begins with a case study in which the investigator is to "become part of the community or group he is studying." He must "allow himself to be socialized and accept the point of view and ideology of his hosts" (1971: 144). Through this process of socialization into the group, the investigator hopes to "be impressed by recurrent themes that reappear in various contexts" (1971: 145). These themes are then developed, interpreted, and tested by "contextual validation," that is, by the use of several sources and kinds of evidence in a process of "cross checking" (1971: 146–149). Out of many themes and concepts developed in this way the researcher gradually builds a "pattern model," the end result being "a model or account of the whole system being studied" (1971: 157). Out of many such case studies, and by use of the comparative method, a more general theory or model can gradually be constructed (1971: 182–196).

Diesing's discussion of the participant-observer method is clearly based on the methods of field research in anthropology and sociology, and on the kinds of models found predominantly in functionalist anthropology and sociology. Diesing's case study is the method of the anthropologist studying some isolated society by joining the group and becoming a part of it, or of the industrial sociologist studying the sociology of the factory floor by joining a work group and gradually becoming accepted as a member of it. Two related questions now arise: is Diesing's method suitable for the study of large-scale systems such as the economy of a modern industrialized nation, and is Diesing's method the method of the OIE?

On the first issue, Diesing's emphasis on the participant-observer *becoming* a member of the group in fact restricts this method to small groups or relatively simple social systems. Diesing (1971: 7) himself is quite clear on this point, stating that the most successful examples of his technique involve "studies of simple non-literate societies or small formal organizations." Studies of larger complex systems, he argues, require the use of a variety of methods: "Attempts to study the U.S. or world economy have necessarily involved great reliance on statistics and thus have moved toward the survey research method, which is much better suited to a large subject matter" (1971: 7). He further points out that the old institutional economists' objective of studying "the total set of institutions in which a particular economy functions, seen in historical perspective," involves great difficulty owing to the "size and complexity of its subject matter" and goes on to express the view that while there is not currently any single institutionalist methodology, "if a unified institutionalist method is ever fully developed it will probably be some amalgam of clinical-historical, survey research, and even formal methods" (1971: 7).

In contrast to Diesing, Wilber and Harrison argue that the participant-observer method is also *the* institutionalist method: "Clearly institutionalists have been participant-observers in the sense used by Diesing" (Wilber and Harrison 1978: 75). Ramstad is more cautious, doubting that there is *an* institutionalist methodology, but claiming that "many or most" institutionalists have followed the method outlined by Wilber and Harrison, and that Commons, in particular, is an "exemplar" of that approach (Ramstad 1986: 1068–1069). The opinions expressed by Wilber and Harrison and Ramstad, however, suggest some confusion between participant-observation as Diesing means it, where the investigator *becomes* a member of the group being studied, and the broad participation of American institutionalists in economic policy making and in all kinds of agencies, commissions, and associations. This is obviously *not* the kind of participation Diesing is thinking about. The claim that Diesing's method applies in a general way to old institutionalists is simply false. Veblen, Mitchell, Clark, and Ayres do not fit at all,[7] and Commons, who probably comes closest to being a participant-observer in Diesing's sense, and who utilized interview techniques and completed vast numbers of case studies, qualifies only in part. More recent work in the OIE provides no evidence that participant-observation is in common use, or indeed, that old institutionalist writings are distinguished by the use of *any* techniques "not 'allowed' in mainstream economics"; what does distinguish the old institutionalists is that "they do *not* use certain techniques such as mathematical modelling and 'advanced' econometrics" (Lind 1993: 8).

None of this should be taken as denying that there are some aspects of Kaplan's and Diesing's discussion that apply to the OIE. Leaving out the specific method of participant-observation, the overall idea of the pattern model does seem to capture some key elements of the approach found in the OIE. For example, in the OIE business behaviour is not formally deduced from a set of axioms, but rather related, less formally, to a general conceptual apparatus and an understanding of the surrounding institutional context. Observation is not focused so narrowly on the testing of the particular predictions of a formal model, but has a larger, although less well defined, role. It is the broad range of business behaviour that is to be explained by demonstrating its consistency with the pattern of established business goals and existing institutional constraints and incentives. Inconsistencies might raise questions about the underlying concepts or, more commonly, the understanding of the institutional context contained in the pattern model, or about the observational evidence and its interpretation. Much of the work of Veblen, Commons, Galbraith, and other old institutionalists can be seen in this way. Of course, there is often much in pattern models that could be expressed more formally, but greater formalization is not a goal that most old institutionalists have adopted. Although Radzicki (1988: 636) has argued that "a method for adding precision, rigor, and structure to pattern modeling must be devised," and Wisman and Rozansky (1991) claim that some old institutionalists (notably Gruchy and Samuels) might have sympathy with the view of pattern modeling as a first step to the development of a more sophisticated body of theory, it is clear that the majority of old institutionalists find pattern models entirely appropriate to the subject matter of economics.

Unfortunately, the idea of pattern model explanation does have its difficulties. It is very open to uncritical "validation," particularly as a pattern containing broadly defined elements that work in opposite directions, such as the Veblenian dichotomy of institutions vs. technology, may be made compatible with almost any set of observations. Pattern modeling also encourages one to resort to functionalism or other forms of argument that run along holistic lines. However, many of the most serious problems to be found in the methodology of the OIE lie not so much in the pattern model in and of itself, but in the almost total rejection of any and all formal techniques, even where these could play an illuminating role (as in the case of game theory),[8] and in the overly empiricist view of the way in which pattern models should be developed and constructed. This is evident in the attempt to adopt Diesing's participant-observer method, despite the fact that Diesing explicitly applies his method only to simple systems and small groups.

Another way of expressing this problem is to ask what is to be understood by statements such as Diesing's that the "holistic quality" of a system should be captured or Wilber and Harrison's that "social reality must be studied as a whole" (1978: 79). If they mean simply that the part should always be analyzed within its broader context and that those factors that create the organization, structure, and evolution of the whole should be objects of study, then the claim is not objectionable, but also not necessarily inconsistent with the use of abstract or formal techniques. Alternatively, the statements can be interpreted as the argument that the social scientist should be trying to capture the whole in its *total* complexity. Strictly speaking, it is not possible to study a whole in the sense of a *totality* (Popper 1961: 76–78), but the idea that one should try to limit the amount of abstraction and formalism in theory and stay as close to the complex concrete reality as possible is one that has influenced many institutionalists, including Mitchell and Commons. The appropriateness of the approach, *especially* when applied to complex systems with many interdependencies, is rarely explicitly discussed within the OIE. The shortcomings of the available formal techniques are emphasized, but the opposite problems created by less formal approaches are simply glossed over. It is difficult not to agree with Diesing that the subject matter of institutionalism is such as to require a mix of techniques, not excluding (but equally not limited to) more formal ones, or to endorse Lind's (1993: 14) argument that institutionalists should apply a pluralist methodology in which "interviews, surveys, and participatory observation are put to systematic and sophisticated use together with the methods of mainstream economics."

2.2   Formalism and anti-formalism in the NIE

The various streams of thought that make up the NIE have a common emphasis on the need for more explicit theoretical content than is usually found in the OIE. However, the exact nature of the theoretical content, and the desirable degree of formalism, are seen in very different ways by different groups of writers.

Perhaps the most formal part of the NIE is to be found in certain agency models of organization. Not all agency theory is so formalist,[9] but as agency theory represents the "neoclassical response" to certain questions concerning organizational behaviour (Levinthal 1988), it is not surprising that the formalism of most neoclassical theorizing has been brought into this area. Much of the theory of agency rests upon standard neoclassical assumptions concerning self-interested rationality. Agency theory is designed to deal with "the problems posed by limited information and goal conflict within organizations," but it has done so by retaining a narrow view of rational self-interest and postulating very high degrees of "sophistication and cognitive capabilities" on the part of all individuals (Levinthal 1988: 154, 181). These assumptions certainly help in retaining the ability to utilize formal mathematical methods of presentation[10] but have left the theory open to criticism for its artificiality and largely ahistorical nature. Indeed, in many areas of the NIE there has been a significant movement away from models based solely on maximizing behaviour and toward a more evolutionary point of view.

The other highly formalized area of the NIE is to be found in the mathematical institutional economics of game theorists (Shubik 1975; Schotter 1983). Both Shubik (1975: 546) and Schotter (1983: 675) criticize neoclassical general equilibrium theory on the grounds that it is "static," "tightly coupled," and "error free" and lacks any "behavioral or strategic complexity or interest." Game theory can be used to model interaction within given rules of the game interpreted as institutions and conventions. It is, however, important to realize that institutional detail is often required in order to obtain a deterministic solution to a game. The more generally a game is represented, the more the possible strategies, and thus the more the possible solutions. Game theory can also be used to model "invisible-hand" processes of institutional development through the device of the repeated game or supergame (Schotter 1981), but several limitations exist. Game theorists sometimes claim that they can show how institutions can emerge *purely* out of the self-interested behaviour of individuals. As will be seen below, this is a highly questionable claim. Moreover, it has been pointed out that game theory cannot deal adequately with institutional *change* as it requires "three assumptions of constancy": the constancy of the players, the constancy of the basic rules, and the stability of the objectives and the environment. These assumptions are required for the mathematical formalism and the solution concepts employed. Thus, "contrary to the claims often made in the literature on supergames, those models cannot encompass historical change" (Mirowski 1986: 252–255; see also Mirowski 1981; Field 1979, 1984).

Among other contributors to the NIE, there are varying degrees of attachment to highly formal techniques. In a recent paper De Alessi (1990: 11) argues that the NIE can be divided into a formalist and a "literary" branch and claims to find a "growing bifurcation" between the two. This division within the NIE reflects some of the same issues that led to the separation of the OIE from the neoclassical mainstream. On the one hand, the desire to deal with more of the complexities of institutional history leads to less formal approaches, but they bring conflict with the widely accepted emphasis on rigour. On the other hand, concentrating on rigorous formal modelling means confining attention to more simple and idealized models that obviously fail to capture important elements of institutional history. De Alessi himself comments on the benefits of formalism in terms of greater rigour, but also notes "the drift of neoclassical economic theory into irrelevance and an emphasis on formalism for its own sake" (1990: 12).

De Alessi places writers such as Alchian, Coase, Demsetz, and Williamson in the literary group. One might add others such as Douglass North. Of course, the literary group do not dispense with standard economic analysis, but they present it non-mathematically and closely bound to a discussion of particular institutions or institutional history. They also tend to be more willing to relax the strict adherence to the assumption of universal optimization than is normally the case in neoclassical economics.

Examples of the above can be found in the work of Coase, North, and Williamson. Coase's (1984: 230) theorizing uses virtually no mathematical methods of presentation. He argues that what is distinctive about the NIE is that it does use "standard economic theory to analyse the working of . . . institutions and to discover the part they play in the operation of the economy," but he goes on to modify his support of standard neoclassicism by claiming that the assumption that "man is a rational utility maximizer" is both "unnecessary and misleading." He concludes that "modern institutional economics should study man as he is, acting within the constraints imposed by real institutions" (1984: 231). This, of course, sounds very much like the views of the old institutional economists, and is certainly one that would seem to militate against formalism, as least to the extent that is found in most neoclassical economics or in game theory. At times Coase has even sounded a little like Wesley Mitchell. Commenting on Williamson's studies, he argues for more empiricism: "An inspired theoretician might do as well without such empirical work, but my own feeling is that the inspiration is most likely to come through the stimulus provided by the patterns, puzzles, and anomalies revealed by the systematic gathering of data, particularly when the prime need is to break our existing habits of thought" (1988: 71). Coase still looks forward to formalization, but he sees the first stage as involving more empirical investigation: "once we begin to uncover the real factors affecting the performance of the economic system, the complicated interrelations between them will clearly necessitate a mathematical treatment . . . and economists like myself, who write in prose, will take their bow" (1992: 719).

A similar emphasis can be found in the work of transaction cost theorists such as North and Williamson. North (1990) has been a consistent advocate of the use of neoclassical theory but has also admitted limitations. He argues that ideology and changes in ideology play a vital role in secular change and that most secular change cannot be explained simply in terms of "the strictly neoclassical constraint of individualistic, rational purposive activity" (1981: 58). Although some aspects of North's work can be formalized (Eggertsson 1990: 318–326), his own work is not formal, but an analytic discussion of institutional history, and one that recognizes the many interdependencies involved (North 1990: 7–9). Williamson (1975, 1985) also modifies standard neoclassical approaches by adopting the assumption of bounded rationality together with a more evolutionary perspective. Williamson admits that most transaction cost economics is "crude" and its models "primitive." He points to greater formalization as a goal, but expresses the view that formalism can result in losses and "is not wanted at any cost." He argues that his own research enterprise is broadly consistent with Morishima's view that economists should move toward the "institution-alization of economics, in the sense of slowing the speed of all develop-ment toward mathematization and developing economic theory in accordance with knowledge of economic organizations, industrial struc-ture and economic history" (1985: 386, 390–391). It is noteworthy that Williamson has been criticized for his lack of formalism by more neoclassically oriented economists, although some, such as Baumol (1986), modify their complaint by recognizing that a large part of the difficulty lies "in the nature of the subject matter chosen for analysis" (Baumol 1986: 285).

Other interesting cases involve the work of Nelson and Winter and those belonging to, or influenced by, the Austrian tradition. Nelson and Winter explicitly link the high mathematical formalism of neoclassical economics with the adoption of a maximizing and equilibrium frame-work. These they reject in favour of notions of decision rules and evolutionary change. Given the nature of their thinking, they use simulation methods rather than the more usual modelling techniques. They argue that while "critics of orthodox theory can be accused of not appreciating the importance of a coherent theoretical structure and of underestimating the resiliency and absorptive capacity of prevailing orthodox theory, the defenders of orthodoxy can be accused of trying to deny the importance of phenomena with which orthodox theory deals inadequately and at the same time overestimating the potential ability of models within the orthodox framework somehow to encompass these phenomena" (Nelson and Winter 1982: 48).

Many Austrians and neo-Austrians also reject mathematical formal-ism. Ever since Menger, Austrians have pursued a non-formal approach, based on their subjectivist view of knowledge, the importance they attach to process, and their stress on the complexity of systems of social order. Despite this rejection of formalism, they have consistently em-phasized general theoretical conceptions and have rejected historical and empirical approaches. This non-formal but deductive approach can be found in the work of Mises (1949), Hayek (1945, 1978: 23–34), and others influenced by Austrian ideas such as James Buchanan. Buchanan emphasizes subjectivism in particular, and he criticizes the formalism of orthodox economics as leading to the idea that an optimum or efficient solution is objectively definable and a matter of computation only. Thus:

It is indeed hard for almost anyone trained in economics almost anywhere in this part of our century to exorcise the false constructions and presuppositions that characterize the mathematical perspective. It is not easy to give up the notion that there does, indeed, exist an efficient resource allocation "out there," to be conceptually defined by the economist, and against which all institutional arrangements may be tested. Despite the emerging emphasis on process as opposed to end-state philosophizing, economists will only reluctantly give up major instruments of their kit of tools. (Buchanan 1988: 129–130)

The Austrian emphasis on subjectivity has links with J. R. Commons (Perlman 1986), but, more broadly, there is a clear similarity between the views of old institutionalists and the process orientation of Austrians. This leads both groups away from standard equilibrium models to non-deterministic evolutionary economics. In the words of O'Driscoll and Rizzo (1985: 5):

A process economics differs from one incorporating dynamic states insofar as the former is not deterministic. There is no stable endpoint toward which the process must lead, nor a single path that it must follow. At least on a general level, our view shares much in common with that of Nelson and Winter (1982), who have developed a non-deterministic evolutionary economics. In their approach, as in ours, error and the correction of error are important facets in the dynamic process. In counter-distinction to the neoclassical approach, however, these errors do not wind down to a determinate equilibrium state. Thus, we have process or evolution without traditional equilibria.

Although virtually all of the NIE is more formal in its theory than the OIE, the degree of formalism within the NIE varies widely. It is at its greatest in some areas of agency theory and in game theory. Works that contain a more explicitly evolutionary perspective and that relax traditional concepts of maximizing tend to exhibit less formalism. Whatever their strengths, the highly formal methods presently in common use cannot, on their own, provide an adequate approach to an institutional economics, at least to one capable of dealing with institutional evolution and historical change.

2.3   Conclusion

The standard techniques of formal analysis have significant limitations in their ability to handle complex evolving systems. The degree of abstraction and the type of simplification required does obvious violence to the subject matter, and this has been a matter of concern to many economists, including many writers in both the OIE and the NIE. The similarity in the basic criticisms of the standard formalism is quite striking. New formalist techniques are being developed and have attracted interest in both traditions, but their usefulness remains to be seen.[11]

Within the mainstream of neoclassical economics, however, and despite Marshall's concerns, formalism has proceeded with surprisingly little serious thought being given to its limitations. Perhaps partly because of this, dissident traditions such as the OIE entirely abandoned the methodology of neoclassicism, but they, too, have paid little serious attention to the difficulties faced by their less formal methods in disentangling a highly complex and evolving world. It is a sad fact that in the face of complexity *all* available methods fall prey to greater difficulties. It is an even sadder fact that methodological allegiances commonly act to prevent communication, even between those who are vitally interested in similar issues and problems. As Diesing (1971: 11) observes:

Communication and co-operation occur primarily within the boundaries of a method, not within a field. Thus, clinical psychologists and anthropologists have co-operated closely for thirty years now, but clinical and experimental psychologists in the main maintain a cold reserve. . . . Formal and institutional economists have little [that is] polite to say to each other, but some institutionalists can work with anthropologists and sociologists who deal in problems of social institutions and cultures.

This lack of communication has particularly severe consequences in thwarting progress toward an improved institutional economics. It is not hard to agree with the critics of the OIE that their theorizing is often too informal and imprecise and has sometimes been obscured by a wealth of concrete information, and that their approach must be responsible, at least in part, for their obvious lack of theoretical advancement. At the same time, orthodox neoclassical theorizing has often sacrificed the understanding of real institutions and institutional history to highly formal models that are usually cast in structural and ahistorical terms and are difficult to apply to the concrete events of institutional history. The NIE is not as guilty of this sin, by force of its subject matter and Austrian influences, as most neoclassical economics, but it still tends to exaggerate the potential of certain formalisms and to deride the contribution that can be made by informal approaches and by the study of particular institutional histories. In this connection it is worth restating Alfred Marshall's view that "economic theory is . . . as mischievous an imposter when it claims to be economics *proper* as is mere crude unanalysed history" (Stone 1966: 19),[12] and to draw attention to two recent restatements of the same opinion: one by Alexander Field (1979), a supporter (although not an unqualified supporter) of the OIE; and the other by Basu, Jones, and Schlicht (1987), adherents (although not uncritical adherents) of the NIE.

In Field's view, any attempt to incorporate institutions *totally* within the explanatory reach of formal models is misguided. Such models are analytic but not fully explanatory in that the theory cannot explain exactly when and in what form phenomena such as cooperation, cartels, or social norms will emerge. Such phenomena "have to be approached on a case by case basis." The "hope that rule structures can, in principle, be made totally endogenous using economic models, thus avoiding the sort of research which Commons and his students undertook, is a chimera." Case studies are also necessary to provide the empirical information required for adequate theorizing: "The best theoretical work has always been that which combines a detailed knowledge of the subject under investigation with the ability to abstract and interrelate its essential features" (Field 1979: 67). Not dissimilarly, Basu, Jones, and Schlicht (1987) draw a distinction between the structural, model-building approach, and the historical approach to institutions. They argue that institutions suffer from a degree of "inertia" that means that the details of history cannot be ignored:

NIE tends to be structural, explaining an institution as an optimal institutional solution without reference to the past. This is the opposite of what historians tend to do. We urge . . . that both structural and historical explanations are needed in economic history, and that these are complementary rather than exclusive. (Basu, Jones, and Schlicht 1987: 2–3)

The recognition of this complementarity is important. As argued by Field, it is only with the general acceptance of the value of both types of work that "we may be able to effectively address the challenge" of developing an adequate institutional economics (Field 1979: 67). That is, we may be able to develop an institutional economics that is both theoretically compelling and historically relevant.

CHAPTER 3

Individualism and holism

The methodological problems associated with individualism and holism are particularly difficult to discuss. The terms have been at the centre of a long-running controversy in the social sciences, yet there is no agreed upon set of definitions. What is meant by "individualism" or "holism" often seems to vary with the writer, and, as will be seen later in the chapter, what the old institutionalist means by these terms does not always coincide with what the new institutionalist means. A great deal of effort, therefore, must be spent on defining more precisely the various positions taken.

Another difficulty is that the debate covers a number of separate but closely interrelated issues. The literature dealing with the more general methodological questions merges into that on the merits of specific approaches to social science, such as functionalism, game theory, and Marxism (Harsanyi 1968; Cohen 1982; Elster 1982; Roemer 1982), and on the use of the maximizing model of man as opposed to the more sociological, rule-following model (Meckling 1976; Brunner and Meckling 1977; Brunner 1987; Vanberg 1988). In order to isolate the main issues of concern here, this chapter will not deal with arguments relating specifically to Marxism. In addition, a discussion of the maximizing versus the rule-following model will be postponed to the next chapter.

3.1   Individuals and institutions

A great deal of confusion surrounds the debate over methodological individualism and holism. Methodological individualism is usually associated with the reductionist claim that all theories of social science are reducible to theories of individual human action. Put another way, this means that the only allowable exogenous variables in a social science theory are natural and psychological givens (Boland 1982). All social or collective phenomena, such as institutions, are to be endogenized and explained in terms of individual human action. The emphasis is therefore on how individual action gives rise to institutions and institutional change. By contrast, holism is concerned with the social influences that bear on individual action. The individual is seen as socialized, as having internalized the norms and values of the society he inhabits. The holist focuses attention on how social "forces" (institutions, social conventions, etc.) condition individual behaviour. This may even be taken to the point where such social forces appear to be almost autonomous entities with distinct functions, purposes, or wills of their own. Whether or not the argument is taken to this extreme, the holist would certainly deny the reductionist claim that all social phenomena can be explained through theories of individual behaviour alone.

The principal distinction between reductionist methodological individualism and holism, then, is to be found in the primacy given to the individual actor in the former as opposed to the primacy given to the social or institutional whole in the latter. These two approaches are usually seen as mutually incompatible, although this supposed dichotomization has come under increasing challenge.

3.1.1   Methodological holism

Methodological holism (MH) is an approach associated with sociology and anthropology more often than with economics, but, as already noted, many writers within the OIE have used the term to describe their own position (Gruchy 1947; Wilber and Harrison 1978; Ramstad 1986).

The holist approach can be summarized as follows:

MH(i)   The social whole is more than the sum of its parts.
MH(ii)   The social whole significantly influences and conditions the behaviour or functioning of its parts.
MH(iii) The behaviour of individuals should be deduced from macroscopic or social laws, purposes, or forces that are *sui generis* and that apply to the social system as a whole, and from the positions (or functions) of individuals within the whole.[1]

These statements are arranged in order from the weakest and least controversial to the strongest and most controversial. The first two statements have to do with the nature of social reality. The third pertains to a program of research. MH(iii) is *not*, however, a simple logical consequence of MH(i) and (ii), despite some suggestion to the contrary. MH(i), which states that the social whole is more than the sum of its parts, is an affirmation of the idea that society is more than a mere aggregation of autonomous individuals. Societies have a coherence, order, and structure that makes them more than just groups of independently acting individuals. Of course, this idea, taken alone, can be and has been attacked for its triviality: no one rejects it, and it applies not just to social groups but to a vast number of assemblages. To use Popper's (1961: 82) example, even three apples arranged in a certain way on a plate are more than just a haphazard heap of apples and plate. Nevertheless MH(i) does serve to point to the undeniable importance of the history and traditions of a social group in giving it coherence and its own special character. Thus, despite usually being seen as an individualist, and despite his criticisms of other aspects of holism, Popper (1961: 17–18) has argued that

the social group is *more* than the mere sum total of its members, and it is also *more* than the mere sum total of the many personal relationships existing at any moment between any of its members. . . . A group can easily retain its character intact if it loses some of its less important members. And it is even conceivable that a group may keep much of its original character even if *all* of its original members are replaced by others. But the same members who now constitute the group might possibly have built up a very different group, if they had not entered the original group one by one, but founded a new one instead. The personalities of its members may have a great influence on the history and structure of the group, but this fact does not prevent the group from having a history and a structure of its own. Nor does it prevent this group from strongly influencing the personalities of its members.

This quotation, with its emphasis on the history and traditions of a social group and on the influence of history and tradition on individuals, links MH(i) with proposition MH(ii). MH(ii), which states that the social whole influences or even, to some extent, determines the behaviour of the individuals who make it up, has sparked a great deal of controversy. Sociologists would take this to mean that social rules enforced by external sanctions do more than merely *constrain* the individual. Individuals are brought up to accept established norms. As they internalize the norms, they become socialized personalities. In this, "a person's willingness to abide by norms becomes independent of external sanctions and, instead, becomes part of a person's character" (Vanberg 1988: 5).

Those who accept positions such as MH(ii) tend to criticize individualists, including most orthodox economists, for ignoring the importance of the established social rules and ethical norms of behaviour. Talcott Parsons (1968: 314) claims that "individualists" have "either not recognized at all, or have not done justice to" the fact that economic action takes place "within the framework of a body of rules, independent of the immediate individual motives of the contracting parties." Similarly, Geoff Hodgson (1988: 53–54) argues at length that "the key element in the classic statements of methodological individualism is a refusal to examine the institutional or other forces which are involved in the moulding of individual preferences and purposes." Opinions such as these are based on statements made by numerous more orthodox economists. For example, Harsanyi objects to Parsons's use of the social norm as a "not-analyzed basic constituent" of his theory, claiming that Parsons's position means "giving up any possibility of explaining the existence of these social norms themselves in terms of the personal objectives and interests of the individual members of society" (Harsanyi 1968: 313). More strongly still, Meckling (1976: 552) argues that "if behaviour is determined by acculturation, then choice, or purpose, or conscious adaptation are meaningless." Thus, "sociological man is con-formist and conventional," his behaviour being "a product of his cultural environment." Meckling claims that cultural factors are *reflected* in human behaviour. They are factors that enter into the choices individuals make, but should not be thought of as *determining* human behaviour.

These criticisms of MH(ii) suggest, however, that internalization and socialization mean the individual has no choice but to completely and unconditionally adopt established social norms. As Brunner (1987: 375) puts it, man is "fully programmed by his social context." It is true that one can find many examples of this "over-socialized" concept of man, particularly in sociology (Wrong 1961; Granovetter 1985), but it is far from clear that all those who accept MH(ii) interpret the statement as implying more than a *conditional* acceptance of or *disposition* to follow social rules. This would represent a position not incompatible with many versions of individualism. Popper (1961: 158), for example, finds nothing amiss in the idea that "'human nature' varies considerably with the social institutions," and Watkins ([1957] 1973: 172) agrees that "methodological individualism allows the formation, or cultural conditioning, of a widespread disposition" provided that it is explained "only in terms of other human factors and not in terms of something *in*human, such as an alleged historicist law which impels people willy-nilly along some pre-determined course."

Watkins's argument brings us to MH(iii), the programmic statement that the behaviour of individuals is to be explained in terms of social or historical laws, forces, functions, or purposes that are not themselves explicable as the intended or unintended outcomes of the decisions and actions of individuals. This argument has always been the subject of vehement attack by individualists of all stripes. It is the primary object of Popper's (1961) famous criticism of Historicism, and of Watkins's ([1957] 1973: 168–169) insistence on the principle that "no social tendency exists which could not be altered *if* the individuals concerned both wanted to alter it and possessed the appropriate information," or that "no social tendency is somehow imposed on human beings 'from above.'" It is also the major point at issue in the recent discussion and criticism of the functionalist approach to sociology. Thus, Harsanyi (1968: 314) attacks Parsons's attempt to explain social norms "in terms of their social functions." For Harsanyi, Parsons's functionalist explanation "is no explanation at all unless Parsons can also specify the actual social *mechanisms* through which the functional needs of the society are translated into the appropriate social norms – that is, unless he can specify the personal *incentives* that individual members of the society have to establish and maintain these social norms in accordance with the best interests of the society as a whole." Many others, including Jon Elster, have taken a similar line of argument. For Elster (1982: 454), the principal difficulty with the usual functionalist explanation is that it postulates "*a purpose without a purposive actor.*" The same point could be made against historicist and organicist versions of holism.

While many holists find merit in some of these criticisms of historicism and functionalism, they counter with the argument that there are many types of "social laws," not all of which involve "global laws of directional change" or overarching social purposes (Mandelbaum [1957] 1973). Furthermore, holists doubt that individual behaviour can be explained without reference to social conditions. For holists:

> The explanation of individual actions themselves . . . may often have to be given partly in societal terms, employing laws that link individual behavior with types of social conditions. They deny, however, that this commits them either to organicism or to historicism. For *sui generis* social laws can be of various logical types. They need not be organic, in the sense of relating the parts of the social system in a way that makes society self-regulating or self-maintaining, nor need they be developmental. There is thus no necessary connection between methodological holism and the dismal conclusion that men are caught up in some inexorable process that possesses something like a life of its own. (Dray 1967: 54)

All versions of holism give primary importance to the social whole. This social whole is seen as influencing and conditioning individual behaviour. However, the *strength* with which the social is seen as conditioning or determining the behaviour of the individual varies substantially between holists. So, too, does the interpretation given to notions such as social laws and functions. In some cases, holists do seem to imply that macro or social entities have some sort of agential power of their own, but this is by no means a universal characteristic of the genre.

3.1.2 *Methodological individualism*

As in the case of methodological holism, the key propositions of methodological individualism (MI) can be summarized in three statements:

MI(i)   Only individuals have aims and interests.

MI(ii)   The social system, and changes to it, result from the actions of individuals.

MI(iii) All large-scale sociological phenomena are ultimately to be explained in terms of theories that refer *only* to individuals, their dispositions, beliefs, resources, and interrelations.[2]

As before, these statements are arranged in order of their strength and the amount of controversy they have engendered, with MI(i) being the weakest and least controversial. Again, the first two statements are about the nature of social reality, while the third defines a program of research. MI(i) reflects the individualists' fundamental idea that any institution, society, or collective entity, cannot possess its own distinct aim or purpose. This is not to say that individuals may not behave as if such aims and purposes exist: "An institution may have aims and interests only when people *give it an aim*, or act in accord with what *they consider should be its interest*; a society or an institution cannot have aims and interests of its own" (Agassi 1960: 247). It should be noted that MI(i), in and of itself, says nothing about how an individual's aims and interests are formed. It does not positively endorse the idea of social conditioning, but neither is it inconsistent with this idea.

Statement MI(ii) takes the same line of argument slightly further. MI(ii) makes the claim that social institutions and norms, and changes to them, arise as the (intended or unintended) result of the decisions and actions of individuals. It repudiates the idea of inexorable social laws, purposes, or forces that determine the nature of society and its evolution regardless of what individuals, singly or jointly, may do. MI(i) and (ii) taken together express the individualists' insistence on the priority of individual actors over the social whole. Individuals are the only real actors; the social whole is the creation of the actions undertaken by individuals. Not without justice, holists often see this idea as a denial of the social influence over individuals. The holist tends to emphasize the priority of the social over the individual. He stresses that the Human Being is a social product, rather than that society is the product of human beings. As already mentioned, some individualists seem to have great difficulty recognizing that the social system has influence over the individual, but, for other individualists, such as Watkins and Popper, the key point in MI(i) and (ii) is simply that "it is *people* who determine history, however people themselves are determined" (Watkins [1955] 1973: 179).

More recently, the term "supervenience" has been proposed to indicate the priority of the individual over the social while allowing for the social conditioning of individuals. The "supervenience thesis" states that "whatever complex and reciprocal relations there are between social entities and individuals, it is the totality of individual facts which determines the totality of social facts" (Currie 1984: 345). The social is thus said to be supervenient upon the individual. Of course, it is not just the totality of individual facts at a particular time, t, that determines the totality of social facts at t. The social significance of the actions of individuals at a particular time also depends on previously established institutions and norms, on the history of the society up to that time. The modified thesis is that "if two worlds are such that they have the same individual histories up until t, then their social states at t will be the same" (Currie 1984: 350). This version of the thesis is what Currie calls "global supervenience." Global supervenience is obviously not incompatible with much of what the holist would argue concerning the social influence over the individual. What global supervenience does maintain, however, is the priority of the individual over the social in a particular, if fairly weak, sense: although identical individual histories will result in identical social states, the reverse does not hold. There are two parts to this argument. First, the claim that identical individual histories will give rise to identical social states does *not* imply that a given social state can only emerge out of one particular history of the actions and beliefs of individuals. The same social state may arise despite some difference in individual thoughts and actions. Second, the argument that the same social state may be compatible with different individual-level histories implies that the state of all individuals cannot be supervenient upon the social history up to that time. That is, because "many different combinations of individual thoughts and actions may realize the same social state," it is "possible for worlds that have the same social histories up to t to be in distinct individual states at t" (Currie 1984: 352). To claim otherwise would be to deny the compositional "plasticity" of social states.

The supervenience thesis is one of the weakest versions of individualism, and, as such, would seem to be inconsistent with only the most extreme versions of historical or cultural determinism. Methodological individualism, however, is usually thought of as making much stronger claims concerning individualistic theory and the acceptable type of explanation of social phenomena. These claims, and the debates that have surrounded them, come from certain interpretations of statements such as MI(iii). MI(iii) is frequently taken to mean that the only "rock-bottom explanations of . . . large-scale [social] phenomena" are those "deduced . . . from statements about the dispositions, beliefs, resources, and interrelations of individuals" (Watkins [1957] 1973: 168), or that "facts about society and social phenomena are to be explained solely in terms of facts about individuals" (Lukes 1968: 120), or that "all true theories of social science are *reducible* to theories of individual human action, plus boundary conditions specifying the conditions under which persons act" (Nozick 1977: 353), or that "all sociological laws are bound to be such as can ultimately be reduced to laws of individual behavior" (Dore 1973: 77). These interpretations contain two related claims: (i) that "social theories are reducible to individualist theories," and (ii) that any "fully adequate explanation of social phenomena must refer solely to individuals, their relations, dispositions, etc." (Kincaid 1986: 493). Consider, first, the debate over the reductionist claim.

Within the individualist literature, reduction is often presented as a simple consequence of statements such as MI(i) and MI(ii). Reducibility is seen as grounded in the arguments that only people have aims and purposes and that the social system is the outcome of the actions of individuals.[3] This is equivalent to arguing that the supervenience of the social on the individual implies the reducibility of the social to the individual (Mellor 1982: 70). This argument fails for reasons partly alluded to earlier. Supervenience does *not* require or imply that a given social state can only arise out of one particular history of individual-level behaviour. But reduction *does* require "biconditional bridge laws connecting primitive terminology of social theories with terminology of individualist theory" (Kincaid 1986: 494):

Reduction requires equivalences between social and individual terms. However, if one social term refers to an event or entity that can be realized by many different configurations of individuals, then no single individualist term will be forthcoming for any given social term. In short, one side of the required biconditional will fail. (Kincaid 1986: 497)

Reduction, therefore, is not a simple consequence of, or firmly grounded upon, propositions such as MI(i) and (ii).

More serious is the fact that the same point concerning multiple realizations is also one of a number of closely related arguments that indicate the extreme difficulty, if not impossibility, of completely eliminating social predicates and successfully expressing social theory in purely individualistic terms. First, as already mentioned, social terms such as "class" or "bureaucracy" do not define a single particular set of individual relations, states, and beliefs. Second, individual actions take their meaning from their surrounding context, and these contexts usually involve social institutions and norms, which must also be described individually. This, however, simply raises the same two problems of multiple realizations and social context all over again (Kincaid 1986: 498).[4] Third, there is the related problem raised by descriptions of behaviour that utilize the notion of social roles. An individual's behaviour is commonly explained by reference to his role as, for example, teacher, doctor, or judge. Applying terms such as these involves an implicit reference to a vast range of social norms and institutions that surround and define each role. To express all of this in purely individualistic terms seems an unimaginable task (Mandelbaum [1955] 1973; Lukes 1968). Fourth, these arguments can be given a historical dimension. Existing institutions "affect the opportunities available to people, and they shape people's utility functions" or dispositions (Nozick 1977: 357). Thus, an individual's present behaviour cannot be explained without referring to the existing institutions in which he is operating. These existing institutions can be explained as the outcomes of the actions of individuals in the past, but those past actions can only be explained by referring to the set of institutions that existed at that time, and so on. As argued by Agassi (1960: 255), "this regress will be an unsuccessful attempt to eliminate statements about institutions from our own explanation unless we assume that there was at least one moment in the society's history in which only material environment and human nature determined rational action" (see also Nozick 1977: 359).[5] Taken together, these arguments indicate the great improbability of successfully completing the reductionist program.

The claim that "fully adequate" explanations of social phenomena must be given in purely individualistic terms is similarly doubtful. If the argument is that there is "an explanation in solely individualist terms" for "each kind of social event or entity," then this requires the reduction of theories already seen to be very unlikely (Kincaid 1986: 504). It could be argued that individualist explanation only requires the explanation of every *particular* social event or entity on a case-by-case basis rather than the explanation of *kinds* of social events or *types* of social entities. That such explanations can be given is a consequence of the supervenience thesis, but it is difficult to accept such explanations as fully adequate:

Supervenience of course insures that we can describe what individuals did, for example, in bringing about the French Revolution and we might go on to invoke laws of psychology or other laws about individuals to say why they behaved as they did. Such a story would be explanatory, but it surely would fall far short of being a full explanation. We would have no way to understand this event as a kind and, in particular, as a social kind. (Kincaid 1986: 507)

The position that fully adequate explanations must run in *purely* individualist terms is thus extremely difficult to justify. Moreover, even if the reduction of theories were possible, it would still not follow that one would wish to pursue such a reduction in practice. Reduction may be difficult, or result in unwieldy theories, or add nothing to practical predictive ability. It also does not follow that social science must be done individualistically and that theories about social phenomena must always be built up from individualistic theory rather than the other way around. As pointed out by Nozick (1977: 361), the argument that the only "*proper* way to construct a social theory is to *start* with the theory of human action, and to work one's way up *from* it" is not a necessary consequence of the "thesis of methodological individualism."

The stronger claims of methodological individualism, that social theories can be reduced to individualistic theories or that any fully adequate theory of social phenomena must run solely in individualistic terms, do not seem to be supportable. The notion of global supervenience does provide some limited support for the priority of the individual over the social, and statements such as MI(i) and (ii) alone can provide the basis for the individualist critique of historicism, functionalism, or any other type of holistic argument that fails to provide the specification of the mechanisms through which individual actions affect the social. As Kincaid (1986: 510) argues, it is the "explanation of how social wholes and events are connected to individual behavior" that constitutes a significant part of "the intuitive appeal of individualism." The individualist can "plausibly claim that any social explanation which makes no reference to individuals, in particular to mechanisms involving individuals which bring about social events, has not given a *complete* or *full* explanation." This, however, need involve neither reduction nor the elimination of all social terminology.

3.1.3   *Individualism versus holism?*

If holism necessarily involves the idea that social wholes have their own purposes or aims, then holism is in conflict with the individualist's basic rejection of such holistic aims and purposes. If individualism necessarily involves reduction or the idea that all social terminology both can and should be eliminated from explanations of social events and entities, then holism, with its basic emphasis on the irreducibility of the social whole to its individual parts is in fundamental conflict with individualism. However, as argued earlier, many self-professed holists do not accept that institutions or social wholes have aims or purposes of their own, and some may even be able to accept the supervenience thesis, at least in its global form. Similarly, some individualists, notably Popper and Agassi, make no claim that theories must be reduced or all social terminology eliminated. This opens up a methodological middle ground where it is recognized that the social whole is more than a simple aggregation of individuals, and that the social context influences and conditions individual behaviour, while at the same time insisting that "full" explanations in social science should contain a specification of the mechanisms through which individual behaviour generates the social phenomena in question. In terms of the various statements outlined earlier, MH(iii) and MI(iii) are in conflict, but MH(i) and (ii) and MI(i)

(which may be more or less compatible with new technological insight) and in the interests of decision makers (which may be more or less compatible with new innovation). Technology has institutional consequences by altering material circumstances and the methods, patterns, and habits of life and thought of individuals. Thus, even "for purposes of a genetic theory" Veblen is concerned with individual conduct, at least insofar as "this individual conduct is attended to in those respects in which it counts toward habituation, and so toward change (or stability) of the institutional fabric, on the one hand, and in those respects in which it is prompted and guided by the received institutional conceptions and ideals on the other hand" (1909: 243). The difficulty with Veblen's approach to institutional change is that he often seems to fail to follow his own advice. In some instances he fails to analyze properly exactly *how* technological changes alter the situations and goals of individuals or exactly *how* altered individual ideals actually bring about changes in social conventions and laws, preferring instead broad statements asserting the (eventual) determining power of technology over institutions:

The material exigencies of the state of industry are unavoidable, and in great part unbending; and the economic conditions which follow immediately from these exigencies imposed by the ways and means of industry are only less uncompromising than the mechanical facts of industry itself.... So that, in due course, the accredited schedule of legal and moral rights, perquisites and obligations will also presently be brought into passable consistency with the ways and means whereby the community gets its living. ([1919] 1964: 32–33)

More often it is the case that Veblen does discuss the processes involved, but in highly questionable terms. In his work on the possible demise of the business system, he seems to suggest that experience with machine industry will bring about profound changes in the thinking of industrial workmen, including the rejection of natural rights and conventional justifications for private property and the adoption of more socialistic ideals ([1904] 1975: 302–373). This "moral" or ideological shift comes about not because of the workman's relative pecuniary position but because of his working environment, which shapes his habits of thought: "It is a question not so much of possessions as of employments; not of relative wealth, but of work" ([1904] 1975: 348). It is arguments such as these that represent the behaviourist aspects of his thinking, but not all his analysis of institutional change is of this nature. Veblen discusses the adoption of warlike ways by primitive herdsmen in terms of the situation faced when competition over grazing land leads to conflict ([1914] 1964: 165), and his writings on the transition from handicraft to business contain passages that deal with the altered logic of the situation created by the growth of the market and new technological conditions, and the craftsman's response to these changes ([1914] 1964: 278–79). Other examples could be given, but it is unfortunately the case that Veblen does not consistently give explanations of institutional change in terms that adequately or convincingly connect altered material situations to altered individual ideals and objectives, and these, in turn, to altered social institutions and norms.[6]

These methodological difficulties with Veblen's work are not unlike those that crop up in Galbraith's *The New Industrial State* (1971). Galbraith tends to present many aspects of government policy – for example, full employment, price stability, education, defense, international relations, and so on – as having the principal function of meeting the needs of the technostructure and the large corporations it manages, but these policies may have such a function without that function serving as an adequate *explanation* of the policy. Galbraith (1971: 312, 319) does attempt to provide some support for his view in terms of a "complex two-way flow of influence," but involving primarily the "adaption of public goals to the goals of the technostructure." How this process occurs is not made terribly clear, however, and the argument often degenerates into a strong version of functionalism in which the only explanation given for almost every social and economic policy considered is simply that it is what the mature corporation of the industrial system "needs."

These problems are compounded in the writings of Clarence Ayres and some other recent contributions to the OIE. In Ayres's work, the individual level of analysis, which is usually present (even if unsatisfactorily) in Veblen's discussions of institutional change, is almost entirely displaced by an analysis of broad cultural "forces," particularly those of the dynamic and progressive "technological continuum" and the inhibitory institutional or "ceremonial" system of conventional norms and practices.[7] For Ayres (1962: 112), "the whole analysis must proceed on the level of generalization of culture rather than of individuality." Ayres does agree that "the functions, factors, and forces into which culture is resolved by analysis do not 'act' as men act," but he goes on to argue that "they do constitute a causal nexus the analysis of which is the problem of the social sciences, and in this analysis of social causes and effects the acts of individual men are not at issue" (1962: 97). Within the Ayresian tradition, technology, or more exactly, technological progress, is commonly presented as "a cultural process governed by its own inherent dynamic" (Hill 1989: 466), one that has very little to do with economic incentives, social need or the "creative genius of individual inventors" (Hill 1989: 466; Gordon 1980: 42). The argument tends to dwell on a battle of social forces, as in Wendell Gordon's (1980: 17) notion that institutionalized "behavior norms" will "continue to prevail until an outside power," primarily that of the inherently dynamic technological continuum, "comes along to force their change."

It is sometimes difficult to know whether such arguments are merely a way of emphasizing the cultural whole and its influence over individuals without denying that all social forces must arise out of the actions and decisions of individuals, or whether they represent a deliberate holistic determinism in which the individual is seen as entirely subordinate to social forces operating according to *their own internal* dynamic, and not explicable in terms of individuals and their actions given their situations. Both interpretations exist even within the OIE itself (Hill 1989; Mayhew 1987). Hill talks critically of Ayres's "cultural determinism," while Mayhew (1987: 50), in defending the concept of culture, points out "it is obvious that culture is necessarily a creation of people and that this is so even if we also accept that people are creations of their culture."

The work of other institutionalists raises similar problems of interpretation. Wesley Mitchell's work on business cycles, for example, involves the extensive use of statistical aggregates. Mitchell ([1925] 1950: 25–26) argues that the analyst need not begin with the theory of the individual but can start with the observation and analysis of "mass phenomena." Rutledge Vining, in his defense of Mitchell against the methodological criticism of Tjalling Koopmans (1947), takes the argument much further. Vining (1949: 79) claims that "trade fluctuations" involve "an entity that is not a simple aggregate of the economizing units of traditional theoretical economics"; that "we need not take for granted that the behavior and functioning of this entity can be exhaustively explained in terms of the motivated behavior of individuals who are particles within the whole"; and that "the aggregate has an existence apart from its constituent particles and behavior characteristics of its own not deducible from the behavior characteristics of the particles." There is little doubt that Mitchell shares Vining's suspicion of the orthodox theory of optimizing agents, but there is much reason to doubt that Mitchell shares Vining's idea of the aggregate having a separate existence and behaviour characteristics of its own that are, in principle, not derivable from the behaviour of individuals. Mitchell's view of matters is that mass or aggregate-level phenomena are the outcome of the standardized behaviour patterns generated by institutional norms and constraints (see Rutherford 1987). Business cycles are to be understood as an unintended, and perverse, consequence of the behaviour patterns created by society's monetary, business, and other institutions (Mitchell 1927). This position obviously involves the rejection of any version of individualism that seeks to eliminate reference to the significance of institutions and their influence over individuals, but not of positions such as institutional individualism or methodological structurism. Of course, even in these terms Mitchell did not succeed in developing an adequate theory of business cycles, but it can be argued that this was his ultimate objective. He thought that the connection between institutions and observable aggregate economic phenomena would increasingly lead quantitative investigators into a critical analysis of that "complex of institutions known as the money economy" (Mitchell [1925] 1950: 30).

Somewhat less difficult to interpret is the position of John R. Commons. Commons's approach is clearly holistic in the limited sense that he accepts and emphasizes propositions such as MH(i) and (ii). There is, however, very little doubt that Commons did *not* analyze institutional evolution in terms of social forces, functions, or distinct holistic purposes or aims. In both *Institutional Economics* ([1934] 1961) and *The Economics of Collective Action* (1950), Commons places great stress on the need to carefully analyze whole–part relations. He argues "'society' is not a *sum* of isolated individuals . . . it is a *multiple* of cooperating individuals" (1950: 132). Individuals are members of organizations, citizens of the state, participants in a society, and "in the process of organization the whole is greater than the sum of its parts" (1950: 132). Further, the individual is both constrained by institutionalized rules enforced by a variety of sanctions and also socialized into a set of "habitual assumptions." The individual is, to a significant extent, an "Institutionalized Mind":

Individuals begin as babies. They learn the custom of language, of cooperation with other individuals, of working towards common ends, of negotiations to eliminate conflicts of interest, of subordination to the working rules of the many concerns of which they are members. They meet each other . . . as prepared more or less by habit, induced by the pressure of custom, to engage in those highly artificial transactions created by the collective human will. . . . Instead of isolated individuals in a state of nature they are always participants in transactions, members of a concern in which they come and go, citizens of an institution that lived before them and will live after them. ([1934] 1961: 73–74)

Commons's reference here to the "collective human will" might suggest more than an emphasis on the institutional, and the adoption of that extreme holism that is concerned with autonomous social entities. This interpretation has been taken by Langlois (1986a: 4, n. 2), but most commentators find that, on closer examination, Commons's references to the "collective will" indicate nothing more than the outcome of individual and collective (particularly political and judicial) processes of decision making, and are *not* supposed to imply that society as a whole has a distinct purpose or will of its own.[8] It can be argued that Commons's methodological position is an excellent example of the "middle way" outlined above.

3.3   Individualism and holism in the NIE

Just as holism is the professed methodology of the OIE, so individualism is the professed methodology of the NIE; and just as the holism of old institutionalists varies, so does the individualism of new institutionalists. In a few cases the specification of the exact individual-level mechanisms is so lacking that, ironically, the argument becomes purely functionalist in nature. In some cases the version of individualism pursued is highly reductionist, but in many others no attempt is made to eliminate references to all institutional givens or to provide arguments that run in individual terms only.

Examples of functionalism, although presumably functionalism by neglect rather than by design, can be found in some parts of the neoclassical literature on property rights and common law. Alchian and Demsetz (1973: 16), for example, argue that rules and customs serve to "resolve conflicts that arise in the use of scarce resources," while Demsetz (1967: 348) states "a primary function of property rights is that of guiding incentives to achieve a greater internalization of externalities." In both cases the authors argue that property rights will tend to respond to cost–benefit considerations, but exactly how such changes are brought about, and what it is about the mechanisms of change that tends to give rise to such results, is left quite unclear. Demsetz is particularly guilty of this failing. He states his thesis that "property rights develop to internalize externalities when the gains of internalization become larger than the cost of internalization" (1967: 350), and illustrates it with examples such as the development of private property in land among the Indians of the Labrador Peninsula. But the process through which these changes in rights actually came about, whether an invisible hand or a collective decision-making process, is nowhere made explicit. Alexander Field makes a similar point concerning the work of Posner on "basic" (i.e., common law) rules. According to Field (1981: 175), Posner's work suggests that the basic rules

have been selected as if they had been chosen so as to maximize the net social surplus: Like technologies, the prevailing basic rule structures exist because they are efficient. In some way "the market" has somehow selected the customs or rules which at the same time circumscribe and define it.

Jon Elster (1982: 459) agrees with Field's interpretation, adding that "Posner and his school" tend to the "strong functional paradigm," which is the extreme position that "all institutions or behavioral patterns have a function that explains their presence."[9]

Within the NIE many attempts have been made to deal with institutions and institutional change in a way that is not simply functionalist.

Some of these attempts pursue a reductionist method. As noted earlier, Harsanyi (1968) criticizes both the functionalist explanation and any explanation that takes social norms as givens. He argues that "*social norms* should not be used as basic explanatory variables in analyzing social behavior, but rather should be themselves explained in terms of people's individual objectives and interests" (1968: 321). This is the program adopted by those who aim to endogenize institutions within an expanded neoclassical framework, and by some game theorists such as Andrew Schotter.

A strictly neoclassical approach to endogenizing institutions would see institutions and institutional changes as the (intended or unintended) outcome of the optimizing decisions of individuals operating in the face of changing technological, demographic, and other exogenously given constraints (Boland 1979). According to Alexander Field (1981: 184), neoclassical approaches to institutions attempt to "explain one of the four categories of traditionally exogenous variables" (institutions) "by reference to the other three" (endowments, technology and preferences). This program can be found expounded by Eggertsson (1990) and pursued by Douglass North (North and Thomas 1973; North 1981, 1990). Eggertsson (1990: xiii) explains the procedure of successive endogenization as follows:

At the first level, the structure of property rights and forms of organization are explicitly modeled but are treated as exogenous, and the emphasis is on their impact on economic outcomes. At the second level, the organization of exchange is endogenized, but the fundamental structure of property rights remains exogenous. Exchange within firms, across formal markets, and in nonmarket situations is organized by means of contracts that constrain economic agents. For instance, the firm is defined as a network of contracts. At the third level, attempts are made to endogenize both social and political rules and the structure of political institutions by introducing the concept of transaction costs.

The question that arises is whether *all* social rules can be successfully endogenized within such a framework. The efforts of Douglass North to complete the third level of this program of endogenization are especially illuminating.[10] North and Thomas (1973) adopt an efficiency approach. They treat institutions as if

selected from a book of organizational blueprints, given endowments, technologies, and preferences *but no exogenously specified rules*. . . . The social problem, at each moment, is to choose the rule set which maximizes output net of overhead costs. Changes in the prevailing rules are . . . to be understood as resulting from the aggregation of the decisions of economic agents maximizing short-term individual interests in response to changes in the underlying parameters of the economic system, as reflected in the changing explicit or implicit prices they face. . . . In North and Thomas, there is no omniscient social maximizer who performs these calculations. But the authors imply . . . that the political and economic processes function as if there were such a maximizer. (Field 1981: 184–185)

However, North and Thomas run into considerable difficulties. Given that they are concerned with actual historical change, it is not surprising that at many points they have to abandon an efficiency explanation and refer to the conservatism of existing institutions (Field 1981: 184–193). For example, North and Thomas (1973: 23) explain that in the case of the development of exclusive ownership rights, "the customs of the manor . . . slowed down the changes that could be made in existing property rights." In this case "the inherited structure of land use gave those who currently under the customary law had access to the land . . . an incentive to oppose the development of such property rights." In the case of the development of free labour, "existing fundamental institutional arrangements, the customs of the manor, assured that the new secondary institutional arrangements would be piecemeal steps rather than a once-and-for-all jump to a 'free' labour force" (1973: 24). The reversion to direct labour services is explained as a result of the costs of "a complete break with tradition, the governing law of the manor." Thus, "to avoid costly complications the alteration in payment had to be set within the framework of existing customs" (1973: 60; see also Field 1981: 189–190). In this way North and Thomas admit that existing institutions are real constraints on the pace and direction of further institutional change, but in doing this "the authors wreak havoc with their research objective." By appealing whenever necessary "to this conservative principle to explain why a given set of expectations (in this case, 'traditions, the governing law of the manor') are not challenged, then the implicit model of institutional change is shattered" (Field 1981: 190).

In his more recent work, North has abandoned the exclusive use of efficiency explanations. He first developed a treatment of government that involved rulers devising property rights in their interests (North 1981). This, together with transactions costs, accounts for "the widespread existence of property rights throughout history . . . that did not produce economic growth" (1990: 7). More recently this explanation has been supplemented by a discussion of the interactions between organized interests and institutions and the "feedback process by which human beings perceive and react to changes in the opportunity set" (1990: 7). Ideas such as these have led North to see institutional evolution as path dependent, but path dependence means that history matters, and the explanation of any given institutional change will have to take other, pre-existing, institutions as given. Furthermore, North has come to stress the importance of "ideology" as a motivator of human action, a motivator that often resists explanation in strictly neoclassical terms. In his 1981 book North argues that a purely neoclassical model of self-interested individuals cannot explain why "people obey the rules of society when they could evade them to their benefit" (1981: 11). Similarly, neoclassical theory cannot explain why individuals sometimes act to try to alter institutions in line with their ideals at great personal cost. In his most recent book, he argues that he knows of "no way to explain the demise of slavery in the nineteenth century that does not take into account the changing perception of the legitimacy of one person owning another" (1990: 24). Thus, "change and stability in history require a theory of ideology to account for these deviations from the individualistic rational calculus of neoclassical theory" (1981: 12). North does not provide such a theory, so that his treatment of institutional change and stability now rests on the change or stability of a factor that is, in significant part, exogenously determined.[11] Ideology, however, contains many norms and conventions (of fairness and distribution) that can themselves be seen as institutions. What North has done is to make exogenous one part of the institutional framework of society (certain consensus institutions) in order to explain the stability or change of other parts of that framework. These two considerations mean that North's program of successive endogenization is likely to remain incomplete.

In contrast to North, certain game theorists claim that they *can* explain the emergence of cooperative behaviour on the part of self-interested individuals even under circumstances that have traditionally been seen as inimical to cooperation. Such game theorists would claim to be able to solve at least one of North's problems by explaining how cooperative behaviour might emerge without having to refer to an exogenous ideology. Andrew Schotter (1981) places his analysis of how cooperation might emerge within an institutional state of nature, which, as noted above, is supposed to avoid all reference to other institutional givens. The state of nature is not presented as having ever actually existed, but as a useful analytic device. It is, however, a device that is necessary to the reductionist program.

In the present context the key part of Schotter's argument is that even in a prisoners' dilemma, where in a single play of the game each individual has strong incentives to defect (non-cooperation), cooperative strategies can emerge if the game is repeated.[12] This is possible provided the game is played an infinite (or indefinite) number of times. In this case each player faces the possibility that non-cooperation on his part in the present "round" will result in a non-cooperative response from the other player in the next round. Each player can effectively punish non-cooperation by the other player by withdrawing

his own cooperation, and reward cooperation with his own cooperation. As mutual cooperation provides benefits to both players in excess of those of mutual non-cooperation, incentives exist for developing and sustaining a situation of mutual cooperation. This type of
argument, together with computer experiments such as Robert
Axelrod's (1984), which demonstrate the ability of simple "tit-for-tat"
strategies to result in cooperative behaviour in repeated prisoners'
dilemma games, has often led to enthusiastic responses, heralding this
work as the basis for a new individualistic social science (Brunner
1987).

The difficulty with the game theoretic argument is that it does not,
in fact, avoid the necessity of specifying some exogenously given rules,
institutions, or basic norms of behaviour. To take the example of a
repeated prisoners' dilemma, the emergence of a cooperative solution depends critically on the game actually being repeated. This, in
fact, requires that no party to the game can simply exit the game or
inflict catastrophic damage on others that prevents retaliation. As argued by Field, the situation of a repeated prisoners' dilemma game
already assumes "an overall structure of rudimentary non-betrayal interaction" (Field 1984: 699). According to Field, game theorists often
lose sight of what must be presupposed, which is "the arena in which
the players are to compete or cooperate." Analysis of the prisoners in
the prisoners' dilemma cannot explain "why escape or insurrection is
not part of the strategy space" (1984: 703). To explain cooperative
interaction of the sort discussed by North, it is still necessary to postulate some prior, given, set of shared beliefs or norms. Game theory
cannot successfully reduce all such items to the outcomes of individual interaction motivated solely by self-interest. A similar point can be
made about the contractarian literature. Here, some basic constitutional rules are supposed to emerge from the voluntary agreements of
free (non-institutionalized) rational individuals. The problem is that,
on examination, these individuals are found to have already accepted
many of the most fundamental norms of civilized discourse and behaviour. Speaking of John Locke, Commons ([1934] 1961: 50) puts
the point as follows:

The fallacy of Locke's reasoning was the historic fallacy of Inverted Sequence.
. . . He projected into primitive times intellectual beings like himself. . . . He
projected backward the practices, to which he was accustomed and which he
wished to see perpetrated, into an eternal reason binding upon men hence-
forth without change. . . . Thus he transposed to an original state of nature the
voluntary agreements which centuries of strong government and a king's
judiciary had made the common law of England.

The Austrian tradition of thought, too, is sometimes associated with reductionist versions of individualism (Nozick 1977). The clearest example of this is probably to be found in the work of von Mises. Mises (1949: 21) insists that "the ultimate judgements of value and the ultimate ends of human action are given for any kind of scientific inquiry." He does discuss the fact that most individuals take over their goals and patterns of behaviour from the society that surrounds them, but goes on to argue that the common man "chooses to adopt traditional patterns or patterns adopted by other people because he is convinced that this procedure is best fitted to achieve his own welfare," and "is ready to change his ideology and consequently his mode of action whenever he becomes convinced that this would better serve his interests" (1949: 46).

Not all participants in the NIE pursue a reductionist program. Indeed, reductionism has been explicitly rejected by writers such as Langlois (1986b) and Basu, Jones, and Schlicht (1987). It is also the case that many Austrian and neoclassical contributors have actually pursued research strategies that implicitly adopt something like Agassi's institutional individualism. Within the Austrian tradition the work of Friedrich von Wieser ([1927] 1967) is most noteworthy. Wieser strongly criticizes both holistic "organic" approaches and "naive" individualism. Organicism is at fault for ignoring the fact that it is individuals who are "the sole possessors of all consciousness and of all will," while naive individualism is in error for ignoring the power of institutions over individuals and for treating individuals as "entirely independent." Thus, "one must hold himself aloof from the excesses of the individualistic exposition, but the explanation must still run in terms of the individual" (Wieser [1927] 1967: 154). Menger is less easy to interpret. His criticism of the holism of the historical school is well known, as is his insistence that social theory should start at the level of the individual actor (Menger 1883: 93–94). But Menger's discussion of the evolution of money, for example, does not start from a pre-institutional state of nature. Rather, it takes as given an already well-established system of private property and barter exchange ([1871] 1950: 260). It has also been argued that in his theory of consumption Menger worked with "an assumption about consumer tastes akin to that used by U. S. institutionalists" (Endres 1984: 898). In addition to this, Hayek (1967: 70), following his evolutionary perspective, argues that the "overall order of actions in a group" is "more than the totality of regularities observable in the actions of individuals and cannot be wholly reduced to them." The whole is a particular relationship of parts and these relations "cannot be accounted for wholly by the interaction of the parts" but also has to make reference to the "selection process of evolution" that operates on "the order as a whole" (1967: 71). Hayek also argues that the individual's psychology should not be thought of as exogenous to his cultural and institutional context. Hayek's view is that "Mind" has "developed in constant interaction with the institutions which determine the structure of society" (1973: 17) and that "culture and reason develop concurrently" (1979: 155) – a point that might easily have been made by Veblen or by Wesley Mitchell in their discussions of the effect of pecuniary institutions on rationality (see Chapter 4). In addition, Langlois (1986b: 237, 247–252) makes reference to Agassi's institutional individualism and quite explicitly rejects the reductionist objective. For Langlois, institutions emerge in an invisible-hand fashion, but, at the same time, each agent's situation is defined and bounded by a variety of existing social institutions that affect his behaviour.

Starting from a more neoclassical perspective, Basu, Jones, and Schlicht (1987) argue that Field's criticisms of "neoclassical institutional economics" outlined above apply only to the "extreme form." They agree with Field that "some rules must be presupposed in any economic analysis and model building" (1987: 2, 4), but point out that what exactly should be left exogenous and what made endogenous depends on the problem and "involves substantive hypotheses about the subject matter rather than taste for a particular intellectual tradition" (1987: 19). Despite this, and their criticism of the tendency in the NIE to explain institutional change in narrow efficiency terms, they argue that the NIE is on the "right track" in attempting to endogenize institutions, particularly as it aims to "give an adequate account of the process, instead of assuming some parametric variation in things both cultural and economic which are essentially endogenous" (1987: 8). One can add that this is quite consistent with the work of Oliver Williamson and many others within the NIE. Williamson (1985: 22) does endogenize organizational forms, but he takes as given much of the surrounding institutional system. Williamson is also sensitive to the variety of ways in which institutions affect behaviour. This is particularly evident in his discussion of the problem of "atmosphere" that arises from the fact that individuals desire a "satisfying exchange relationship." Atmosphere implies that changes to exchange relationships can encourage or discourage altruism, trust, and cooperativeness, and that "organizational effectiveness" has to "be viewed more broadly than the usual efficiency calculus would dictate" (1975: 37–39). Unfortunately, Williamson has not expanded on these observations.

3.4   Conclusion

In Chapter 2 it was argued that what was required was *both* formalist *and* non-formalist methods, or both structural *and* historical methods. In this chapter what is being argued is not that both holism and individualism are required but that what is reasonable in each can and should be combined into a middle way that, for convenience, will be called by Agassi's term "institutional individualism." The types of holism that imply that social wholes have their own aims or purposes or can act as agents are taken to be unacceptable. The types of individualism that attempt to eliminate all reference to institutional givens are similarly unappealing. Such reductionist programs are unlikely to succeed and, in any case, appear to be quite unnecessary for the provision of fully acceptable explanations of social phenomena.

Within the OIE, examples of arguments that run in terms of apparently autonomous social forces can be found. Similarly, examples of reductionism can be found within the NIE. In both traditions the lack of well-specified mechanisms relating the individual to the social has resulted in functionalism. Nevertheless, there are large bodies of work within both traditions that take institutions and institutional change as the outcome of the actions of individuals, while, at the same time, maintaining that the existing institutions constrain and affect the situations and goals of individuals. Implicitly, if not explicitly, institutional individualism is the method that has been followed by many institutionalists both old and new. Institutional individualism, however, only provides very broad methodological parameters and, appropriately, leaves many questions, such as the nature and roles of rule following and rational choice, the exact mechanisms that link individual choices to social outcomes, the tendency of institutions to conform to the requirements of economic efficiency or social benefit, entirely open. It is to these questions that we now turn.

CHAPTER 4

Rationality and rule following

The discussion of individualism and holism in Chapter 3 touches on several points concerning the extent to which man should be conceptualized as a "rule follower," who develops habits and routines and, more important, adopts social norms and conventions, as opposed to a rational maximizer, who adjusts his behaviour to changes in his circumstances and opportunities in such a way as to maximize his net benefits. Just as individualism and holism have often been dichotomized, so have these two conceptions of man. In Jon Elster's (1989a: 97) words:

One of the most persistent cleavages in the social sciences is the opposition between . . . *homo economicus* and *homo sociologicus*. . . . The former adapts to changing circumstances, always on the lookout for improvements. The latter is insensitive to circumstances, sticking to the prescribed behavior even if new and apparently better options become available. The former is easily caricatured as a self-contained, asocial atom, and the latter as the mindless plaything of social forces or the passive executor of inherited standards.

Orthodox economists frequently caricature the sociological model, while attempting to argue that their own is not so naive as sometimes thought. Brunner (1987), for example, outlines what he calls the REMM model – resourceful, evaluating, maximizing man – which he associates with economics, and the sociological model of socialized, role-playing, and sanctioned man, or SRSM. Brunner and Meckling (1977: 73) claim that in the sociological model man "is neither resourceful nor an evaluator." His behaviour is "directly determined by social factors and cultural conditions," he is "a conformist enslaved by conventions." By contrast, they are much more generous to the REMM model, which they argue does *not* ignore social norms and conventions. Rather, "in the REMM model acculturation conditions the constraints and preferences of the individual in his coping, groping and interested behavior" (1977: 73).[1]

Brunner and Meckling, nevertheless, raise some key issues that tend to undermine the very dichotomy they are seeking to confirm. Within orthodox economics the conditioning role of social norms and institutions is commonly pushed so far into the background as to be entirely lost to view, and hence the notion of *homo economicus* as an asocial atom. However, if it is recognized that "acculturation conditions the constraints and preferences of the individual," then economists cannot avoid serious questions concerning the role of social norms and how they relate to the exercise of rational, evaluative processes. A purely rational maximizer would, presumably, only adopt a norm or follow a rule if doing so were in his or her own interest. One approach then, and one frequently found within the NIE, is to attempt to explain rule following of various types in rationalist terms. This might overcome the dichotomy by reducing rule following to the outcome of a rational choice, but such efforts are not without their difficulties. Alternatively, it may be assumed that at least some rule following cannot be explained in rationalist terms, so that human behaviour is seen as involving *both* rational and non-rational processes. In this case the problem is not that of choosing one model over the other, but of understanding how rationality and rule following relate: what role each performs and how they are combined. As Elster (1989b: 102) argues: "actions typically are influenced both by rationality and by norms," the outcome sometimes is a compromise, sometimes rationality acts to constrain social norms, and sometimes norms act to constrain rationality.

A similar difficulty exists if one begins from the sociological model. Sociologists have had to recognize that man, particularly in his economic and market activity, is rational and evaluative. An obvious response is to claim that rationality itself represents adherence to a social norm, one that is applied especially to market behaviour. This is an argument that can be found quite explicitly in the OIE. However, this leaves "the problem unresolved how somebody who is able to behave like a rational man in the market place can be restricted to non-rational behavior in all other social relations" (Lindenberg 1990: 729).

4.1   Habits, norms, and rule following

In the preceding section no clear distinction was made between different types of rules (habits, routines, social conventions, social norms), or between the implications of rule-guided behaviour and rational choice. These deficiencies will be remedied here.

There are many different types of rules, and they can be categorized in a number of ways. Some rules are entirely personal, with no broader social significance. Certain habits and routines may be of this nature, as may certain rules of personal morality. Such rules are private in the sense of not being supported by any external, legal or social, sanction. Personal habits and routines are maintained by convenience or inertia, rules of personal morality by private conscience. Social rules also vary. Some social rules are of the nature of conventions. Conventions may be self-enforcing in that all individuals have an interest in adhering to the same rule. Legal norms are those rules enforced by a police power and judicial system that will act to punish violators. Social norms are particularly interesting as the category consists of many and various types of rules and observances, rules that are enforced by social approval and disapproval. Rule violation will be punished by criticism and even ostracism by others. Norms are frequently supported by a "metanorm" that sanctions the punishment of someone who fails to enforce a norm (Axelrod 1986). In addition, social norms may become internalized, in which case the external sanction is no longer required for compliance. The norm will be maintained by the individual's own feelings of self-worth. The violation of a social norm may leave an individual feeling guilty or having a troubled conscience. Many types of norms exist, including consumption norms, norms of reciprocity, honour, retribution, distribution, and equality (Elster 1989a: 107–125). Within economics, norms of fairness have received particular attention (Kahneman, Knetsch, and Thaler 1986a, 1986b), but norms can cover everything from core attitudes and beliefs to apparently minor points of etiquette and dress. Some social norms can be seen as solutions to problems of social coordination and cooperation, but many others are intimately bound up with matters of group identity and social status (Coleman 1990). Over the range of human societies, they incorporate a quite remarkable array of rules and associated behaviours.

These various types of rules are sometimes treated together. The dividing line between private and social rules is not a sharp one, and particularly within the OIE it is common to use the term "habit" to denote any rule consistently followed by an individual, including the rules derived from social norms. Thus, socialization is treated as a type of habit formation. In addition, in both the old and new institutionalism social rules are sometimes seen as developing out of practices that were initially private habits or routines. Nevertheless, the distinction between private rules, particularly habits, and social rules, particularly social norms, is significant and will be maintained here.

The fact that individuals develop and follow rules does not, in and of itself, indicate that they are not behaving rationally. For example, the usual game theoretic discussion of the emergence of social conventions out of the situation of a repeated game is an attempt to explain a social rule in a way compatible with standard notions of rational maximization.[2] Even more obviously, it is perfectly rational for an individual to comply with an existing social or legal norm if the costs of non-compliance make adherence to the norm his maximizing choice on each and every occasion (Akerlof 1976). In approaching this issue it is useful to distinguish between "rational case by case adjustment" and "genuinely rule following behavior" (Vanberg 1988: 2–3), and also between maximizing and adaptive notions of rationality. The model of case-by-case adjustment captures the usual notion of rational maximizing behaviour. Such a type of maximization can be consistent with rule following if the structure of incentives in recurrent choice situations is stable. By contrast, *genuine* rule following involves "a disposition to abide by the rules *relatively independently* of the specifics of the particular situational constraints" (Vanberg 1988: 3). The rule is followed "without choosing in each and every situation anew whether or not to obey," so that particular acts of rule following may be non-maximizing (Vanberg 1988: 7). Examples of this may be an individual or firm following a certain decision rule that works reasonably well but sometimes fails to lead to optimal results; an individual holding to a particular consumption pattern despite modest changes in relative prices; an individual taking the time and trouble to vote in an election despite the fact his vote will make no difference and non-voting carries little social disapproval; an individual following a rule of honesty or of "proper" behaviour despite opportunities to violate the rule to his or her own advantage and remain undetected; an individual pursuing a goal of social justice at great personal cost; or individuals following a norm by taking the trouble to express disapproval of a norm violator, despite the fact that they have not been hurt by the violation.

That such genuine rule following behaviour exists is now widely accepted. Too many convincing examples have been amassed for social theorists to believe that all human behaviour is strictly consistent with a process of case-by-case adjustment. However, the question concerning such genuine rule following is whether it, too, can be explained within some type of rational choice framework. It is, of course, true that rationality can be made consistent with virtually any behaviour by suitably adjusting the individual's utility function, but this does not supply a rationalist *explanation* of the adoption of the rule or norm. If an individual is always honest despite opportunities to cheat in an undetectable way, a rationalist explanation demands that it be shown that such behaviour is to the individual's own benefit, that the rule-guided behaviour is an effective *means* to a selfish end. This assumes the individual to be a "rational egoist." To simply incorporate a desire for honesty into the individual's utility function would be to say only that he is honest because he has a taste for honesty. Such a taste could be the result of socialization.

Rationalist explanations, however, need not be maximizing in nature. Most orthodox economics interprets rationality in maximizing or optimizing terms and has attempted to reconcile this with genuine rule following by reference to information costs, cognitive constraints, or advantages of precommitment or reputation effects. Rationality, however, can also be interpreted in adaptive terms. Adaptive rationality still involves an evaluation and decision on the basis of the consequences of alternative courses of action, but it is less demanding of informational and cognitive requirements. It also has an obvious congruence with an evolutionary perspective. Under certain conditions, adaptive models can give similar results to those based on maximization, but this is not a necessary result (Winter 1964; Nelson and Winter 1982). Whether maximizing or adaptive forms of rationality are capable of explaining the full variety of rule-guided behaviour is a widely debated question. Vanberg (1988) and Coleman (1990), among others, suggest a positive answer, arguing that there are a variety of ways in which it can be advantageous for an individual to follow a rule or a norm rather than to attempt to adjust to the specifics of each case. At the same time, a number of writers, including Alexander Field (1984) and Jon Elster (1989a, 1989b), have argued that rule following, particularly the propensity to adopt and uphold social norms, cannot be fully explained in rationalist terms and that a broader treatment of human behaviour is required.

4.2   Rationality and rule following in the OIE

The traditional assumption of rational maximization has long been the subject of attack within the OIE. From the days of Veblen, Mitchell, and Commons down to the present, old institutionalists have insisted that habits, norms, and institutions play an important role in directing human behaviour. On many occasions this caused the OIE to be criticized for downplaying the role of rational choice and economizing behaviour, and for falling into behaviourism by treating behaviour as the outcome of exogenously given habits, norms, and institutions (Seckler 1975; Ault and Ekelund 1988). Yet, virtually no old institutionalist eliminates notions of rationality altogether, and their ideas concerning the formation of habits and social norms are more activist in nature than is generally understood. In some instances an adaptive type of rationality is implied. This is particularly common in the OIE treatment of habit and the adjustment of habit over time. In the case of social norms, the role of rationality, even of an adaptive type, is much less clear. Veblen rejects rationalist approaches, but the instrumentalism of later writers does imply a significant potential role for the instrumental appraisal and adaption of social customs and norms.

4.2.1   *Habits and routines*

A great deal of the discussion concerning rule following within the OIE is conducted in terms of habit and habit formation. The underpinnings of the treatment of habit in the OIE are to be found in the work of the pragmatist philosophers and psychologists, most obviously William James.[3]

James's discussion of habit is illuminating. From the physiological point of view, he defines a habit as a "pathway of discharge formed in the brain, by which certain incoming currents ever after tend to escape" (James 1893: 134). Once established, a habit exhibits resistance to change, but not a total resistance. The pathways in the brain have a high degree of "plasticity," meaning "a structure weak enough to yield to an influence, but strong enough not to yield all at once" (1893: 135). Habits are formed with "extreme facility" but "do not easily disappear" (1893: 137).

This propensity to form habits is seen by James as the result of man being "born with a tendency to do more things than he has ready-made arrangements for in his nerve centres." The number of different performances that men wish to undertake is so enormous that most of them must be studied and practised until habits are formed. "If practice did not make perfect, nor habit economize the expense of nervous and muscular energy, [man] would be in a sorry plight," his whole activity confined to only a few operations (1893: 138). Habit simplifies movements, makes them accurate, reduces fatigue, and "diminishes the conscious attention with which our acts are performed" (1893: 138–139). Even complex activities involving long sequences of actions and considerable amounts of skill can become habitual (1893: 139).

Veblen's discussion of habit, and that of most later old institutionalists, takes all of this for granted. Veblen starts from a critique of the hedonism of orthodox economics, the best-known part of which is his attack on the notion of man as a "lightning calculator of pleasure and pains" ([1898] 1961: 73). In this, Veblen is rejecting two ideas: first, the notion that individuals make instant rational calculations of the optimal solution in each and every case as they encounter it. For Veblen, people develop habits of thought and action, habits that are slow to change in response to new circumstances. Second, the more fundamental notion that people simply react to a given utility function or pleasure–pain calculus. This hedonistic conception, Veblen argues, denies man any real discretion. Thus, "hedonistic man is not a prime mover," he merely reacts to "circumstances external and alien to him"; he is "an isolated, definitive human datum, in stable equilibrium except for the buffets of the impinging forces that displace him in one direction or another" (1898: 73–74). Veblen substitutes a more active view of man, but a view in which man acts through habits. This active conception may seem to be at odds with the notion of habitual action, but Veblen is taking James's point that it is only through the device of habit that man can achieve very much of anything at all. For Veblen, the ideas of man as an active being and as a habit former are perfectly consistent:

It is the characteristic of man to do something, not simply to suffer plea-sures and pains through the impact of suitable forces. He is not simply a bundle of desires that are to be saturated by being placed in the path of the forces of the environment, but rather a coherent structure of propensities and habits which seeks realization and expression in an unfolding activity. (1898: 74)

A feature of this point of view is "the recognition of a selectively self-directing life process in the agent" (Veblen [1900] 1961: 156–157). As noted by Seckler (1975: 53), this constitutes a perfectly humanistic point of view. Human action is teleological; what is always true is "the fact of activity directed to an objective end" (Veblen 1898: 75). This activity works through habits and is not directed by rational case-by-çase calculation, but rationality in all senses is not absent. After all, Veblen ([1909] 1961: 238) argues that "human conduct is distinguished from other natural phenomena by the human faculty for taking thought" and, further, that rationality in pecuniary matters is something that is particularly encouraged by the prevailing institu-tions and customs of business enterprise. It is, therefore, not surpris-ing to find Veblen discussing the gradual modification of certain business practices in the face of new technological circumstances in terms of a process of adaption of habits. What Veblen calls the "New Order" of business he sees as having

arisen out of the endeavours of the business men to profit by the enlarged opportunities which these altered material conditions have offered them. It has been their work to turn the new industrial situation to account for their own gain while working under rules of the game of business that have come down from the old order. . . . It has taken time and experiment as well as the help of legal counsel to discover and work out suitable expedients of business procedure and to get into the habit of them. ([1923] 1954: 229)

This, it should be noted, is a process that is slow and imperfect but that involves both intelligent appraisal and a high degree of creativity in the working out of "suitable expedients." It is a process of rational adaption, through experiment or trial and error, of some standard practice or routine, and within the constraints provided by social and legal norms (rules of the "game of business"), which are taken as given for the purposes at hand. Such processes of adaption play a considerable role in Veblen's system, particularly when he is discussing alterations in habits or practices that do not carry great social or normative significance, or alterations to rules or practices within a given context of more fundamental social and legal norms (Rutherford 1984).

Although Ault and Ekelund (1988) refer to habits as exogenous in Veblen's scheme, their interpretation is undermined by the fact that Veblen repeatedly analyzes alterations in habits, particularly business habits, in terms of a response to altered cost–benefit conditions. As Raines and Leathers (1991: 11) argue, new habits reflect "choices made by businessmen seeking to exploit pecuniary opportunities made possible by the continuously changing material conditions." Of course, this does not imply highly flexible adjustment on a case-by-case basis. Veblen is talking about the more gradual adjustment of habits and routines to shifts in technological and material conditions.

Among those influenced by Veblen, Wesley Mitchell was particularly concerned with the issue of rationality and rational decision making within economics. Many of Mitchell's ideas are an outgrowth of positions taken from Veblen. For example, Mitchell (1944a: 214) refers to "the emphasis of William James and other psychologists upon habits" as a significant part of what has "undermined confidence in the older conception of conduct as guided by calculation." Mitchell's (1910a, 1910b, 1914, [1916] 1950, [1918] 1950) attacks on orthodox notions of rational calculation explicitly include both the hedonistic calculus of Bentham and Jevons and the theory of utility maximization expressed in ordinal terms.

Mitchell's main complaint is that the orthodox assumption of rational calculation *overstates* the rational element in economic life, not that rationality is entirely absent. Indeed, Mitchell (1910b: 199) argues extensively that economics deals with the type of activity in which rational thought is particularly present. Mitchell's claim, it must be understood, is not that rationality, or even economic rationality, is a fundamental part of human nature, but that it is itself a product of the rise of pecuniary institutions. Pecuniary concepts train men in the use of reason, to rationalize economic life, so that the use of money lays the foundation for a rational theory of that life (1910b, 1944b). Economic rationality is thus "an acquired aptitude – not a solid foundation upon which elaborate theoretical constructions may be erected without more ado" (1910b: 201).

Mitchell's institutional notion of rationality differs from the usual orthodox conception in two principal ways. First, Mitchell explicitly rejects the idea that rationality consists of case-by-case calculation. Economics may deal with activities in which rational thought is very often present, but "rational thought" here does not mean thinking everything out anew each time. For Mitchell, people develop habits and establish routines, but the routine itself may often be "rational" in the sense of allowing the agent to be reasonably successful in achieving his or her goals (1910b: 199). Second, Mitchell points out that not all areas of life are equally pervaded by pecuniary and rational standards. The habits and routines established in some areas of life may be much less rational. Mitchell often argues that consumption decisions are not usually analyzable on any assumption of rationality. This is because household consumption decisions are deeply affected by the many other social norms surrounding family life, by a lack of information, and by the absence of a clearly defined relationship between particular purchase decisions and family welfare (1910b: 209–216, [1912] 1950: 3–19). These conditions subvert the processes of rational adaption. At the same time, business habits and routines are better adapted or more rational owing to a well-defined end (profit), the reinforcement given to that end by the prevailing institutional system, and the availability of information. Nevertheless, even within business, the decision maker does not operate as a calculating machine or as "an ideally perfect money maker" (1910b: 212–214; see also Rutherford 1987). Habits and routines, even in business, do involve departures from case-by-case maximization.

Commons, too, rejected the notion of case-by-case maximization. Commons argued that people develop a set of "habitual assumptions" that provide the basis for routine transactions.[4] The key point he makes is that habitual assumptions allow the daily routine to be carried out without constant thought and attention. For example,

when a new worker goes into a factory or on a farm, or when a beginner starts in a profession or a business, everything may be novel and unexpected because not previously met in his experience. Gradually he learns the ways of doing things that are expected from him. They become familiar. He forgets that they were novel when he began. He is unable even to explain them to outsiders. They have become routine, taken for granted. (Commons [1934] 1961: 697–698)

Habits and routines are of great importance. If they were not formed, "as is well known, the mind could not have a free field for dealing with what is unexpected" (Commons [1934] 1961: 698). Commons's notion of habit does not exclude intelligent or rational appraisal but gives it a particular role: "intellectual activity" concerns itself with making "sagacious" choices in the face of new situations or "strategic transactions." If "the factors are continually changing, then the intellect must be lively to control the strategic ones; but if they run along as usual, then habitual assumptions are enough" ([1934] 1961: 306, 698).

Among other old institutionalists, the contribution of J. M. Clark deserves special mention.[5] Like Veblen, Commons, and Mitchell, Clark thought of most human behaviour as habitual and not based on a case-by-case calculation. Clark, however, explicitly mentions information and decision making costs as a reason for habit. Again referring back to William James, Clark talks of the effort involved in decision making. Even within a hedonistic framework, the existence of such costs means that "a good hedonist would stop calculating when it seemed likely to involve more trouble than it was worth" (Clark 1918: 121). Significantly, this does not mean Clark agrees that calculations will be done exactly to the point where the marginal cost equals the marginal benefit. His point is that the existence of information and decision costs create a logical problem in the notion of optimization. The individual cannot "in the nature of the case" tell exactly when the optimal point has been reached. The stopping point is arbitrary, and "no claim to exactness" can be made (Clark 1918: 121).

The individual, then, is not (and cannot be) an exact calculator. Instead, the individual develops habits. Habit is the "static element" in a human nature that is otherwise active and dynamic. It is, however, only through habit that the "marginal utility principle is approximated in real life:"

For only so is it possible to have choosing which is both effortless and intelligent, embodying the results of deliberation or of experience without the accompanying cost of decision which, as we have seen, must prevent the most rational hedonist from attaining hedonistic perfection. For habit is nature's machinery for handing over to the lower brain and nerve centres the carrying on of work done first by the higher apparatus of conscious deliberation. (Clark 1918: 122)

Habits embody previous deliberation, but such deliberations, at best, only approximate optimal solutions. Habits may be reasonably well adapted, but can also embody "past mistakes" or "unconsidered impulses," and they can persist even when no longer appropriate, after the conditions that originally gave rise to them have changed.

Clark's work represents the most sophisticated discussion of habit to be found within the OIE. Clark sees that experience and intelligent deliberation often lie behind the initial formation of the habit, but his discussion of information and decision-making costs allows him to break the orthodox connection between rationality and perfect optimization. Other old institutionalists struggled with this problem, wishing to reject the idea of maximization without totally abandoning the idea of rationality, but none expressed it so clearly as Clark.

From the foregoing it is clear that the major figures within the OIE consistently rejected the notion of case-by-case maximization. Instead they conceived of human behaviour as being very largely a matter of the prevailing social norms and institutions together with the more particular habits and routines that individuals develop out of the regular patterns of their daily life. These various habits and routines can become quite unconscious. As Commons argues, an individual may be unable to explain the rules of his workplace to an outsider. To old institutionalists, such habitual and rule-following behaviour is quite at odds with orthodox notions of rational maximization, and yet rationality is not eliminated.

That habits can have an economizing function is recognized by many old institutionalists. From William James's idea of habits economizing "the expense of nervous and muscular energy" to Commons's discussion of routine, and, most notably, J. M. Clark's understanding of information and decision-making costs, the fact that habit and routine are a necessary part of human functioning is well established in the OIE. Habits and routines are also seen as more or less "rational" or well adapted to circumstances, and this raises the question of whether old institutionalists thought of habits and routines as adapting to new conditions in an optimal fashion. That is, are habits chosen to optimize, subject to informational and cognitive constraints, or (alternatively) do the processes of experiment and selection result in the habits that give the best results being arrived at? J. M. Clark's argument provides a penetrating criticism of any attempt to interpret habits or routines as themselves the result of some maximizing choice or calculation. The case with Veblen and other old institutionalists is less explicit, but the whole tenor of these discussions militates against an optimizing-choice interpretation. In the discussion of the evolution of habits and routines, virtually all old institutionalists do incorporate a process of adaptive learning through trial and error. In some areas this process may work poorly owing to a lack of information or of clear performance criteria, but on the whole habits and routines will tend to be adapted until a satisfactory level of performance is achieved. These adaptive processes work best in the case of business, but even here it is doubtful that old institutionalists can be properly interpreted as thinking of business practices as evolving to produce optimal results. Even in the case of business, the processes of experiment and trial and error take time and may fail to locate the best rule or habit, both because the number of all possible rules may be very large and because the surrounding economic environment may not remain stable for the required period of time.

4.2.2   *Social rules and norms*

Many of the notions concerning the limits to rational appraisal and the development of habits are carried over into the discussion of social norms. Social conventions, customs, and norms are often seen as originally deriving from widely adopted habits. Norms, however, have additional attributes: they are supported by social sanctions and may become internalized by the individual. If an individual follows a norm *entirely* because of external sanctions and the probability of being caught, then that person is not engaging in genuine rule following. However, old institutionalists refer often to ideas of socialization and internalization, concepts that obviously carry with them the notion of genuinely rule-guided behaviour.

In the area of norms, William James again set much of the tone of later work. James links the idea of habit and habit formation to that of the formation and internalization of social norms. People become habituated to the patterns and ways of life they are brought up within and come to regard these patterns as the way things should be. For James, habit is "the enormous fly-wheel of society, its most precious conservative agent." Habit "keeps us all within the bounds of ordinance," and prevents the disintegration of social life. It "saves the children of fortune from the envious uprisings of the poor," it "holds the miner in his darkness, and nails the countryman to his log cabin and his lonely farm through all the months of snow." Its influence is such that "it dooms us all to fight out the battle of life upon the lines of our nurture or our early choice" (1893: 143). However, James does not present these social consequences as the *reason* for individuals to adopt social norms.

All writers in the OIE take the importance of norm-guided behaviour as a given. Norms are thought of as being built up slowly out of the established patterns of life and associated ways of thinking. Thus, Veblen ([1914] 1964: 7) argues that

under the discipline of habituation this logic and apparatus of ways and means falls into conventional lines, acquires the consistency of custom and prescription, and so takes on an institutional character and force. The accustomed ways of doing and thinking not only become a habitual matter of course, easy and obvious, but they come likewise to be sanctioned by social convention and so become right and proper and give rise to principles of conduct.[6]

There is here an explicit recognition of the social sanctions and processes of socialization that differentiate norms from mere habits or routines. For example, Veblen (1899b: 111) speaks of the conventional standards of consumption being maintained by the individual "habitually contemplating it and assimilating the scheme of life in which it belongs," and "by popular insistence on conformity . . . under pain of disesteem and ostracism." Reference to the disesteem of others might provide a rationalist explanation for any single individual adopting a prevailing social norm. As Veblen (1899b: 30) puts it, "only individuals with an aberrant temperament can in the long run retain their self-esteem in the face of the disesteem of others." However, to complete the argument would require a rationalist explanation of why individuals take the trouble to enforce a norm upon non-conformers. Non-conformism may impose costs on others, but although Veblen's discussion of norms is not inconsistent with at least some norms providing economic benefits to the group by solving problems of coordination and cooperation, this is not the explanation he stresses. Rather than emphasize the potentially beneficial role of norms in cases where actions impose externalities on others, he focuses on norms as matters of group identification and social status. Veblen argues that a very common aspect of human nature is the propensity to emulate and make invidious comparisons.[7] Each individual rates himself in relation to others and seeks success in terms of his *relative* standing in his community. Thus, "a social system may contain a hierarchy of status groups, in which members of a group that is neither at the top nor at the bottom attempt to conform to the norms of the next higher group and to maintain the norms of their group in order to keep out those below" (Coleman 1990: 259).

The emphasis on status groups raises some difficult questions. If norms work to exclude or put certain individuals or groups at a disadvantage, it is not clear how such norms can gain widespread legitimacy. As admitted by Coleman (1990: 187–288), "it may be that not all such acceptance can be accounted for by rational choice theory as currently constituted."

The internalization of norms raises additional problems. Once established, accepted, and internalized, norms tend to take on the character of goals in themselves. They "take their place as proximate ends of endeavor . . . they occupy the interest to such an extent as commonly to throw their own ulterior purpose into the background and often let it be lost sight of" (Veblen [1914] 1964: 7–8). The fact that norms become the proximate ends of endeavour has considerable significance in Veblen's discussion of institutional change. Because norms are taken as goals, they are not evaluated in the same way as other rules. Norms, in fact, often provide the criteria against which other rules and practices are judged. This makes norms particularly resistant to change. Veblen, however, was well aware that even norms change over time, particularly as basic, underlying, economic conditions change. As already mentioned, the description of institutional change that Veblen gives is often cast in behaviouristic terms, but this can give rise to misinterpretations.

There is no doubt that, in contrast to his discussion of habits, Veblen wished to emphasize the impersonal forces of cumulative causation and "efficient cause," as opposed to the forces of individual intention and choice ("sufficient reason"). For example, in his discussion of Marx, Veblen ([1907] 1961: 437) argued that the Marxian analysis of institutional change via class struggle was one in which "material exigencies" control the life of society, but only through men "taking thought of material (economic) advantages and disadvantages, and choosing that which will yield the fuller material measure of life." The problem with this was that "under the Darwinian norm . . . this initial principle itself is reduced to the rank of a habit of thought" ([1907] 1961: 437–438). The process, therefore, cannot be thought of in terms of individual or class advantages, or in terms of sufficient reason, but in terms of efficient cause, or of how and to what extent changes in material conditions might reshape "men's habits of thought, *i.e.*, their ideals and aspirations, their sense of the true, the beautiful, and the good" ([1907] 1961: 438). Thus,

there is, for instance, no warrant in the Darwinian scheme of things for asserting *a priori* that the class interest of the working class will bring them to take a stand against the propertied class. It may as well be that their training in subservience to their employers will bring them again to realise the equity and excellence of the established system of subjection and unequal distribution of wealth. ([1907] 1961: 441–442)

Public or class opinion is "as much, or more, a matter of sentiment than logical inference," and the "sentiment which animates men, singly or collectively is as much, or more, an outcome of habit and native propensity as of calculated material interest" ([1907] 1961: 441). Thus, any "revision of the principles of conduct will come in as a drift of habituation rather than a dispassionately reasoned adaptation of conduct" (1923: 19). This, however, does *not* rule out the use of intelligence or reason but defines its area of applicability. In his discussion of the impact of machine discipline on the workman, he argues "it is by virtue of his necessarily taking an intelligent part in what is going forward that the mechanical process has its chief effect upon him" ([1904] 1975: 307–308). The "machine process is a severe and insistent disciplinarian in point of intelligence," it requires "close and unremitting thought, but it is thought which runs in standard terms of quantitative precision" ([1904] 1975: 308). The exercise of intelligence plays a key role in the operation of this disciplining effect. Industrial occupations have cultural significance "somewhat in proportion as they tax the mental faculties of those employed." It is a matter of habits of thought, and therefore it is as "processes of thought, methods of apperception, and sequences of reasoning" that industrial occupations have importance ([1904] 1975: 312). The largest effects are to be found not among mere "mechanical auxiliaries," but among those who "are required to comprehend and guide the process" ([1904] 1975: 312–313). New habits of thought are generated by individuals *reasoning* along new lines, but the lines along which reasoning travels are strongly affected by the nature of those activities undertaken in the pursuit of a living.

Veblen's aim was thus not to entirely eliminate a role for human intelligence and reason but to indicate three things. First, that the intentions of a single individual or small group of individuals cannot change a social norm. Something affecting society as a whole or significant sections of society is required. Second, it is the social norms themselves that provide the proximate ends of human endeavor. Because of this, changes in norms cannot be explained in terms of a process of adjustment or adaption to *given* ends, but only in terms of processes that *alter* the goals, ideology, or way of thinking of individuals. Such changes in preference create substantial difficulties for standard, rational choice approaches (Hargraves Heap 1989: 103–107). Third, that changes in norms are often the result of changes in patterns of life that are more or less forced on groups by significant alterations in their technical and economic environment.

In Veblen's words, it is the "exigencies of life which enforce the adaptation and exercise the selection" ([1899b] 1924: 191).

There is in Veblen, then, a distinction between the more or less "rational" adaption of habits and routines to given ends that occurs *within* an established system of more fundamental norms and institutions, and the processes of change that affect the more fundamental norms and institutions themselves. Such norms specify many of the socially acceptable goals of action. Such goals do change over time and the process is generally not one that totally dispenses with human thought or intelligence. It is, however, often a slow process, one that takes place with resistance, and usually only as the surrounding economic environment changes in ways that make the old ways of life and ways of thinking obsolete or no longer appropriate.

Many of Veblen's ideas can also be found among later writers in the OIE tradition. It is widely accepted that individuals take over many of their habits and "mental tools" from the society that surrounds them, that social norms have a prescriptive authority over individuals, and that individuals internalize norms. Mitchell (1910b: 202–203) speaks of social norms and institutions giving rise to a "standardization of thinking and acting," while Commons talks both of the individual's "institutionalized mind," and the variety of physical, economic, and moral sanctions that lie behind social rules. Mitchell and Ayres present a number of arguments very close to Veblen's. Mitchell's thinking on the links between pecuniary institutions and norms and the spread of rational habits of mind is a case in point. For Mitchell (1944b), as for Veblen, rational appraisal had the status of a habit of mind (or norm) itself and therefore could not act as the basis of an explanation of the adaption of habits of mind. Habits of rational appraisal and pecuniary norms evolved together. Ayres (1962) makes substantial use of the Veblenian notion of institutions being concerned with matters of status and utilizing criteria of "ceremonial" rather than instrumental adequacy.

On the other hand, virtually all old institutionalists since Veblen have adopted an instrumental philosophy that would seem to provide, at least potentially, a much larger role for rational appraisal in the adaption of norms and institutions than Veblen was willing to concede. Instrumentalism implies an ongoing evaluation and adaption of both means and ends. Means are evaluated in the light of their success in achieving goals, but, over time, the goals (or ends in view) are themselves subject to appraisal in the light of the consequences of attempting to achieve them (W. Gordon 1980: 43). This suggests a process of adaptive rationality that might apply to social norms as much as to other types of rule, but exactly when or how such adaptive processes might take effect against the established institutions based on status or other ceremonial criteria is often left very unclear. We are given the rational and non-rational in the form of the instrumental and the ceremonial, but no guidance as to what determines the choice of criteria. In the work of many old institutionalists, the rational appraisal and adaption of social rules is presumed to be something that requires organized investigation and intervention. These processes obviously apply to legal norms, but the adaptive processes that have an impact on customs and social norms are usually not explored to the same extent.

A good example is provided by the work of J. R. Commons. Commons stresses the beneficial function of norms and other social rules in resolving conflicts and producing security and predictability. Customs "begin as adaptations of human behavior to new conditions" (Commons [1934] 1961: 50) and continue to adjust to new conditions as individuals and groups attempt to adapt to threats to their economic interests or to new opportunities (1909). Unfortunately, Commons provides much less detail on the development and change of customs and social norms than he does on the development and alteration of legal norms through political and judicial institutions. It is, however, clear that Commons thought that rationalist explanations had limits. In particular, customs can become outdated and survive even "after the 'reason of them' has disappeared" ([1934] 1961: 50).

Nevertheless, for Commons and, to some extent, Ayres, adaptive processes operate, although slowly and not entirely surely, on social norms. Both writers stress that social norms can be resistant to instrumental prompting, but fundamentally the processes of social change are processes of adaption that are based on an appraisal of consequences. Veblen's discussion is different. He is particularly aware of the difficulties of discussing norms and changes in norms in rationalist terms. Norms often define the criteria of acceptable performance. Norms change as the goals of life themselves change and, for Veblen, the evolution of norms is less a matter of appraisal of consequences than of shifts in the economic environment enforcing new habits of life that, in turn, bring about changes in values and goals.

4.3 Rationality and rule following in the NIE

A somewhat greater disparity of viewpoints concerning rule-following behaviour exists within the NIE. In some areas of the NIE, particularly in agency theory and in some applications of game theory, individuals are presented in traditional case-by-case maximizing terms. Even where habits, routines, or norms are included in the analysis, an effort is often made to interpret such rule following in terms consistent with rational maximizing choice. But there are also those who adopt an evolutionary perspective and explicitly reject a maximizing framework (Heiner 1983; Nelson and Winter 1982). In this literature arguments can be found that are strikingly similar to some of those developed previously in the OIE. Hayek, for example, has argued that man is "as much a rule-following animal as a purpose seeking one" (Hayek 1973: 11).

Where rule following is incorporated into the NIE, it is usually seen as the result of one of four things: (i) information and decision-making costs; (ii) cognitive and information-processing constraints; (iii) the risk of making errors in the attempt to adjust on a case-by-case basis; and (iv) some advantage that flows to the individual by virtue of the fact that his behaviour is rule determined. These four reasons are applied to habits, routines, rules of personal conduct, and also to social rules and norms.

4.3.1   Habits and routines

The most usual criticisms of the idea of case-by-case maximization are based on information and decision costs or on bounded rationality. It is obvious that significant information and decision-making costs can mean that developing a habit or following a rule that economizes on these costs can be advantageous to the individual. The NIE now abounds with arguments that recognize this point. According to Langlois (1990) and Langlois and Csontos (1993), following a rule can be construed as a "reasonable response to particular decision situations" (Langlois 1990: 693), and, more generally, there is nothing in the notion of rule following that is necessarily at odds with the orthodox method of situational analysis. A similar view is expressed by Frank (1987b: 23), whose words might easily have been spoken by an adherent of the OIE:

To gather the information and do the calculation implicit in naive descriptions of the rational choice model would consume more time and energy than anyone has. . . . Anyone who tried to make fully-informed, rational choices would make only a handful of decisions each week, leaving hundreds of important matters unattended. With this difficulty in mind, most of us rely on habits and rules of thumb for routine decisions.

In this view, habits represent departures from case-by-case maximization. The quality of decisions is reduced, but the cost of this quality reduction may be more than offset by the saving in information and decision-making costs. Of course, whether this is the result will depend on the particular rule chosen, the extent to which it economizes on information, and the effect it has on the quality of the decisions made. This raises the question of whether such rules can themselves be thought of in optimizing terms; as balancing the marginal cost of a more refined decision rule or procedure against its marginal benefit, and achieving the "optimally imperfect decision." Ault and Ekelund (1988: 438–439) suggest a positive answer:

The point is that individuals choose habits as a response to a particular cost–benefit situation in order to maximize expected welfare with respect to both production and consumption decisions. . . . Habits are simply ex ante decisions or choices taken on the basis of some particular probabilistic calculus – they are the decision not to have to choose repeatedly.

Presumably, such habits will also adjust (optimally) to changes in the underlying cost–benefit situation.

The major problem with this optimizing point of view is exactly J. M. Clark's argument that no claim to exactness can be made. The decision concerning the adoption of habits or rules, and exactly which habit or rule might be best, is itself a complex decision requiring costly information (Etzioni 1987: 509). For the decision to be optimal, this information, too, should only be collected up to the optimal point, but this simply leads into an infinite regress. As Winter (1964: 262–263) points out, once imperfect and costly information enters the picture, optimization arguments are subject to a *reductio ad absurdum*. Thus,

at some level of analysis, all goal seeking behavior is satisficing behavior. There must be limits to the range of possibilities explored, and those limits must be arbitrary in the sense that the decision maker cannot *know* that they are optimal. (1964: 264)

This brings us to Hayek's discussion of ignorance and uncertainty and Herbert Simon's ideas on bounded rationality and satisficing behaviour. Hayek contends that there are limits to human reason. Standard rationality assumptions, according to Hayek, overstate the "intellectual powers" that people have and understate the tremendous complexity of the social world they operate within (Hayek 1967: 90). Individuals face pervasive uncertainty and ignorance, and rules are devices that are used "because our reason is insufficient to master the full detail of complex reality" (Hayek 1960: 66). Like Hayek, Simon wants to move away from notions of maximizing calculation and optimality. He substitutes the idea of individuals as developers and modifiers of habits, decision rules, and heuristics, but without abandoning all notions of rationality (Simon 1955, 1957, 1959).

Simon's point is not that rationality is absent, but that it is bounded by cognitive constraints. People are not capable of solving complex problems in an optimal manner. What they do instead is to develop decision rules that can be easily grasped and followed and that work reasonably well for the purpose. Individuals may seek better rules, ones that give superior performance, but the process takes time and does not necessarily, or even usually, lead to rules that approximate optimal results. All of this is very reminiscent of much of the OIE.

Bounded rationality arguments are now not uncommon within the NIE. Williamson, for example, refers to bounded rationality as a reason for the lack of comprehensive contracting and for the substitution of forms of hierarchical control that make smaller demands of cognitive competence.[8] Nelson and Winter also make extensive use of the concept in their discussion of the evolutionary selection of a firm's "routines." Commenting on Simon's work, they argue:

> Man's rationality is "bounded": real life decision problems are too complex to comprehend and therefore firms cannot maximize over the set of all conceivable alternatives. Relatively simple decision rules and procedures are used to guide action; because of the bounded rationality problem, these rules and procedures cannot be too complicated and cannot be characterized as "optimal" in the sense that they reflect the results of global calculation taking into account information and decision costs; however, they may be quite satisfactory for the purposes of the firm given the problems the firm faces. (Nelson and Winter 1982: 35)

Although attempts have been made to interpret satisficing as maximizing subject to information-processing costs and cognitive constraints, the same problem arises as before. To maximize subject to these constraints is a complex problem that itself runs into bounded rationality constraints.[9]

A recent extension of the bounded rationality problem has been provided by Ronald Heiner (1983). Heiner's argument is that there is often a gap between an agent's competence at problem solving and the difficulty of the decision problem faced. Given such a "C – D gap," which will tend to exist in complex decision problems, agents will be subject to unpredictable errors and mistakes in selecting the most preferred alternative. The extent of these errors may mean that an agent will do better by following a simple rule rather than by attempting to maximize in each case. The behaviour patterns generated "are *not* an approximation to maximizing so as to always choose most preferred alternatives." Rule-governed behaviour means "that an agent must ignore actions which are actually preferred under certain conditions" (Heiner 1983: 568).

Given that in Heiner's view the individual may gain by following a rule rather than by attempting to maximize on a case-by-case basis, it might be argued that rule following is consistent with a rational choice between alternatives. On one occasion, Vanberg argues that such rule following might be "quite compatible . . . with choice and calculation at the 'constitutional' level:"[10]

We can view an individual's adoption of a behavioral rule as a personal constitutional choice among potential alternative general patterns of behavior. To adopt a rule in this sense is rational if it is perceived as a more advantageous strategy compared to potential alternatives, where attempting to maximize on a case by case basis can be viewed as *one* alternative. (Vanberg 1988: 9)

This might suggest that the problem can be thought of in terms of a rational maximizing choice on a metalevel. As already mentioned, however, such a choice is also complex and may not be compatible with optimizing choice. There may be advantages in rule following, it may make sense for individuals to adopt a rule rather than attempt to maximize, but if maximizing itself is subject to information costs, bounded rationality, or C – D gaps, the choice of rule cannot be seen in optimizing terms. As the old institutionalists also found, there is a need to separate the concept of rationality from the notion of optimization. Thus, Simon distinguishes procedural from substantive rationality (Simon 1976), Heiner (1990: 31) argues that "the traditional link of rationality to optimal decisions is valid only at the limiting extreme where agents have infinite decision reliability," and Vanberg (1993) distinguishes maximizing from adaptive forms of rationality.

Adaptive arguments provide an alternative to notions of rational maximization. It is possible to argue that people will learn from their experience with the rules they adopt, that they will experiment and imitate others who are more successful, and that this process will gradually converge on the rule that performs best (Mueller 1986: 5). Such arguments are somewhat undermined, however, by the weight of empirical evidence that suggests that individuals do not always readily adapt their rules of thumb, even when faced with considerable amounts of contrary evidence (Nisbitt and Ross 1980; Kahneman, Slovic, and Tversky 1982). This problem is compounded by the practical difficulties that people often face in subjecting rules to critical test and the frequently ambiguous, or even misleading, feedback that can be generated by implementing a rule (Einhorn and Hogarth 1978). This is particularly the case where decision makers are operating within an uncertain and changing world. According to Jacquemin (1987: 15), such environments mean that "it cannot be postulated that the producer is able to classify clearly a trial as a success or a failure or that there is a continuous tendency toward increasingly favorable results." Learning and improving on one's rules is not the simple process that it is often assumed to be (Rutherford 1990b).

In addition, it is sometimes argued that an individual may adopt a rule if that rule gains him a *reputation* for a certain type of behaviour that will in turn benefit himself. A baker may give a "baker's dozen" because being known as a man who does so will increase his business. Doubtless such advantages from following certain rules do exist. However, the argument probably applies to no more than a small number of the rules that people follow, and cannot, by itself, explain why an individual would not break his own rule to his advantage if he could get away with it (with out-of-towners for example), or if the cost to his reputation was less than the benefits gained. In other words, the argument does not really provide an additional explanation for genuine rule following. It either presumes the structure of incentives is such as to always make following the rule the preferred alternative, or it must involve some uncertainty or decision unreliability, in which case it is simply a particular example of a bounded-rationality or C – D-gap type of argument.

4.3.2   *Social rules and norms*

As noted in Chapter 4, some adherents of the NIE object to the use of social norms as basic explanatory variables, arguing that norms "should themselves be explained in terms of people's individual objectives and interests" (Harsanyi 1968: 321). Arguments such as these lie behind many of the objections to the OIE made by Seckler (1975) and Ault and Ekelund (1988), among others. There are, however, many weaknesses in the various rational choice explanations of social rules and norms that have so far been advanced. These problems are independent of the methodological problems of reduction discussed in Chapter 3.

Within the NIE one can distinguish arguments that relate purely to the question of why a particular individual may follow or uphold a norm, given that it is already widely accepted, from arguments that relate to the question of why people in general might adopt certain rules and give them normative status. The first is obviously the easier question, but still not without its difficulties. Given that a norm already exists, one might argue that an individual will adopt that norm in order to avoid sanctions. This, however, fails to explain genuine rule following. Sanctions explain compliance only in those cases where the individual's behaviour can be observed by others in a position to impose the sanction; moreover, people often follow norms even in situations where violation of the norm would obviously go unpunished. One might also ask why an individual would bother to impose sanctions on violators, particularly if their own material interests are not at stake.

The fact of compliance in the absence of credible external sanctions implies that individuals internalize norms. They follow the norm because to violate it creates feelings of unease. The difficulty here is that "if people respond to internal, non-material rewards, we seem forced to abandon the purposive rational actor model" (Frank 1992: 150). Attempts have been made to explain internalization of norms in narrow rationalist terms, but they are not particularly satisfactory. James Coleman (1990) argues that parents socialize their children out of self-interested motives, but this can only explain the inculcation of norms that directly benefit other family members, and not those norms that regulate behaviour toward the community at large. According to Frank (1992: 51):

Coleman's explanation of internalization of norms is unsatisfying. . . . In particular, most parents would be puzzled by its implicit assumption that their primary motive for teaching their children honesty was to prevent theft within the family. Indeed, most parents would be mortified to learn that their adult children were stealing from outsiders, even if they could be assured that their children would never be caught and punished.

However, if it is argued that parents instill norms in order that their children be good citizens, it is not clear, on the basis of a rational egoist model, why they should have such social objectives. It might be possible to reconcile rational choice with the internalization of norms by arguing that individuals who have internalized certain norms (such as honesty) can be distinguished from opportunists, so that those who have internalized these norms reap material benefit (Frank 1987a).[11] Even if accepted, however, the argument is difficult to extend to all social norms.

Why individuals impose sanctions on others is also difficult to explain. Akerlof (1976), Axelrod (1986), and Basu, Jones, and Schlicht (1987) all make reference to the metanorm that requires individuals to sanction non-conformers on pain of social disapproval.[12] Unfortunately, this leads into an infinite regress: "People do not usually frown upon others when they fail to sanction people who fail to sanction people who fail to sanction people who fail to sanction a norm violation." Thus "some sanctions must be performed for other motives than the fear of being sanctioned" (Elster 1989b: 105). Such arguments have an even more difficult time in the case of what

Ullmann-Margalit (1977) has called inequality-preserving norms. Such norms may have to do with preserving a position of economic or social status for a particular group. The norm provides a sanction for non-conformity and so can alter the payoffs the individual faces in such a way that conforming is the best choice. A rational individual will thus choose to conform in order to avoid the sanction, but, as already mentioned, the problem here is to explain how such norms can be legitimized so that they are accepted (and enforced) not just by the group that benefits, but even by those who are targets.

A further argument is that norms exist because they promote self-interest, "over and above the avoidance of sanctions" (Elster 1989b: 105). Following an existing norm may be individually useful in a variety of ways. It may act as a signal to others or it may add credibility to a threat or a stated or implied intention to act in a certain way.[13] An individual may have an incentive to adhere to a given norm if conformity to that norm acts as a signal to others that he is a person of a particular type. Following certain norms can establish a reputation that may be of value to the individual. If it is difficult to switch adherence to the appropriate norms on and off as opportunity suggests, the desire to establish a certain reputation may give rise to genuine rule following. Alternatively, if an individual threatens to act in a particular fashion that may not be entirely rational under the circumstances, then the fact that the threatened behaviour is consistent with a norm adds credibility to the threat. If a person believes that another's actions will be genuinely rule guided, then this can bring about beneficial results for the follower of the norm. In the usual examples, however, only *one* party follows the rule or norm; the others behave rationally. If all followed the norm, then the result might not hold. For example, norms of retribution can lead to vendettas that benefit no one. The more general criticism of this class of arguments is simply that it is very easy to think of norms (e.g., Hindu customs of widowhood) that do *not* appear to work in the interests of the individuals who follow them.

On the second question, the standard rational choice explanations are that social rules and norms develop because they solve certain problems of social coordination and cooperation and thereby produce group benefits. Standard game theory treats the emergence of social conventions and norms in this way, but problems do exist. In a simple two-person coordination game concerning, for example, which side of the road to drive on, rationality indicates that each individual will desire a coordinated solution in the form of a social rule, and that a solution, once established, will be in everyone's interest to maintain, but it does not indicate *which* solution to choose. Driving on the left or right are equally good solutions and rationality does not provide a unique answer. The choice may therefore depend on the "salience" of one particular rule (Lewis 1969; Schelling 1960), but choice on the basis of salience is often considered non-rational, not capable of strict justification in terms of the usual economic sense of rationality (Hargraves Heap 1989; Gilbert 1989; Sugden 1991). This is to say that rationality can provide an explanation of why everyone in a given society drives on the same side of the road, but cannot explain or predict which side of the road is chosen. The particular rule arrived at may be a matter of historical accident. In more complex games, this problem of indeterminacy is compounded (Sugden 1991; Binmore 1987, 1988).

Another point to note is that many social rules, particularly norms relating to group membership or social status, do not appear to be of any obvious material benefit to the groups that adopt them, and some even seem to impose costs (Elster 1989a). Admittedly, being a member of a group, particularly if that group in some way feels superior to those outside, can convey positive externalities to each member (Coleman 1990: 258–259). The norm works in this way if conformity to the group norms "is sufficiently difficult that outsiders cannot easily enter the group" (Coleman 1990: 258). However, these positive externalities often relate less to any tangible rewards of membership than to fulfilling "a psychological need to be part of a group" (Axelrod 1986: 1105). Reference to such psychological needs again violates the rational egoist model of the emergence of norms.

In a recent survey of the various attempts to explain norms in rational choice terms, Jon Elster concludes that rational choice models do not provide a full explanation of social norms (Elster 1989a, 1989b). Vanberg (1993: 187), however, argues that an "evolutionary perspective" using the concept of "adaptive rationality" may "help to systematically account for observed behavioral tendencies which appear to defy explanation in standard rationality terms." Vanberg's argument revolves around two main points. The first stems from Hayek's notion that rule following is a response to humankind's imperfect understanding of their environment. Rules are not chosen as a result of a full rational appraisal. In Hayek's words, "what we call understanding is in the last resort [man's] capacity to respond to his environment with a pattern of actions that helps him to persist" (1973: 18).[14] Social rules, like habits or routines, may be best seen as more or less reasonable adaptions to a complex world and not necessarily as optimal in their functioning. The second point is that rules, even if once reasonably well adapted, may become less well adapted if the environment changes. A rule may not adjust to new conditions owing to a perverse structure of individual incentives or the lack of any mechanism to shift society as a whole from one rule or set of rules to another. Thus, adaptive rationality on the part of individuals is not necessarily at odds with the existence of apparently dysfunctional norms, and a study of incentive structures might indicate when adaption will and will not occur. This position does suggest, however, that all social norms were originally more or less well adapted, something that is not entirely obvious. In any case, the extreme persistence of some norms and the highly emotional attachments that people develop for certain principles or ways of life seem to go beyond the degree of conservatism that might be consistent with adaptive models. Elster argues that neither the original emergence nor the persistence of norms is likely to be fully encompassed in rationalist terms. Two issues come to the fore here. Why is it that normative significance is attached to certain rules in the first place, and why does norm-guided behaviour sometimes seem to be undertaken almost in spite of the costs involved?

On the first question, Elster (1989b: 115) suggests only that a "good research strategy" might be to investigate the roles of emotion, envy, honour, and the psychology of conformism in the formation and maintenance of norms. Elster is not alone in his viewpoint. Robert Sugden, in recent work (Sugden 1986, 1989), shows how rules or conventions can evolve spontaneously. He then asks why certain rules become social norms. Why do people come to believe that they themselves and other people should or *ought* to behave in particular ways? In a passage reminiscent of Veblen, he argues:

The mechanism that can transform conventions into norms is the human desire for the approval of others. Although this desire is rarely considered by modern economists, introspection surely tells us that it is at least as fundamental as the desire for most consumption goods. That we desire approval should not be surprising: we are after all, social animals, biologically fitted to live in groups. (Sugden 1989: 95)

The second question involves the sometimes non-consequentialist character of norm-guided behaviour. Rational processes, whether maximizing or adaptive, are oriented toward an outcome. With norms, the only concern is to follow the norm. This is because, as Veblen argues, norms can contain or specify the appropriate goals of action and are not themselves subjected to appraisal to the same extent as other rules. When internalized, norms become a part of the individual's personality and resist evaluation in consequentialist terms. Indeed, as Veblen remarks, norms must often be taken as powerful motivators of action. Reference to norms (particularly norms of equality and justice) is often a necessary part of explaining the adaptions made to *other* social rules. In the words of Douglass North (1981: 58), strictly neoclassical rational choice approaches

would never allow us to explain most secular change ranging from the stubborn struggle of the Jews in antiquity to the passage of the Social Security Act in 1935. Secular economic change has occurred not only because of the changing relative prices stressed in neoclassical models but also because of evolving ideological perspectives that have led individuals and groups to have contrasting views of the fairness of their situation and to act upon those views.

Norms frequently "have a grip on the mind and an emotional appeal that is largely independent of their contribution, if any, to individual or social welfare" (Elster 1989a: 124), and the processes that result in their change are much less well understood. Thus, it seems doubtful that rationality and rule following can be completely reconciled, at least on the basis of any straightforward application of adaptive versions of rational behaviour. Elster himself suggests that rationality, or behaviour that is outcome oriented, and norm-guided behaviour, or non-consequentalist behaviour, might be made part of a more general theory of action. This would remove the dichotomy between rationality and rule following without reducing either one to the other:

Among the alternatives to rational-choice theory, the (as yet undeveloped) theory of social norms holds out most promise. It is radically different from rational choice theory, whereas the other alternatives are largely variations on the same consequentialist theme. They are different species of the same genus, whereas the theory of norms is a different genus altogether. . . . Eventually, the goal of the social sciences must be to construct the family comprising both genera – to understand outcome-oriented motivations and nonconsequentialist ones as elements in a general theory of action. (Elster 1989c: 35)

Similar views can be found elsewhere. Ekkehart Schlicht (1990: 716) has argued that "the crucial features of obedience, routinization, contracting, and so forth, which pose difficulties in an abstract rationality framework, contain so many features which go beyond the rationality/irrationality dichotomization that a rationality view, bounded or not, seems inappropriate unless the concept is conceived as comprising many things not usually considered rational."

4.4   Conclusion

The OIE universally accepts that much human behaviour is of a genuine rule-following type. To the extent that rationality is included within the OIE, it is of an adaptive type, and even adaptive rationality is seen to have its limits. The main criticism to be made of the OIE is that it fails to make clear the exact roles of rationality and rule following, or how the two interact in processes of adaption. Ault and Ekelund (1988: 432–439) complain of the imprecision of Veblen's notions of "expedients, adaption and concessive adjustment" and support the neoclassical view that habits and institutions change in response to alterations in "cost–benefit configurations." This lack of exactness is undoubtedly one reason for the survival of maximizing models, and even more recent work within the OIE has done nothing to improve matters. In the view of Clarence Ayres, all of man's actions involve some combination of tradition and intelligence (Ayres 1962: 102), but exactly how the two are combined or when one will dominate the other is left unspecified. Similarly, Allan Gruchy argues that the conduct of individuals reflects "the use of some reason" but "is nevertheless largely determined by the culture in which the individual is placed" (Gruchy 1987: 3). Mention is sometimes made of Herbert Simon's work on the cognitive limitations that prevent maximization, but Simon's satisficing framework has not been widely adopted within the OIE.[15]

In the NIE, there is a consistent effort to explain rules and norms in rationalist terms. Stemming, perhaps, from Becker's (1976) argument that rational choice models can provide an understanding of "*all* human behavior," new institutionalists, and particularly those of neoclassical persuasion, have attempted to reconcile all types of rule following with rational choice. The attempts to interpret rule following in *maximizing* terms, however, run into logical difficulties as soon as imperfect information or cognitive constraints are allowed to enter the picture. The alternative, adaptive, concept of rationality is gaining ground and is now quite widely applied. It is favored over the sociological norm-guided model. Dennis Mueller, for example, has argued that an adaptive approach "allows us to begin with a unified view of human behavior," and it avoids the "methodological leap" of moving to a sociological model (Mueller 1986). Attempts have recently been made to formalize adaptive models (Heiner 1983; Cohen and Axelrod 1984; Cross 1983). Such adaptive arguments have been applied to habits and routines and to social rules and norms. The more serious problems in the adaptive rationality approach are to be found in the discussion of norms. It is one thing to argue that information costs and cognitive constraints make habits and routines perfectly sensible things for individuals to follow, and that individuals can, even if imperfectly, appraise and adapt these habits and routines over time. It is quite another to argue that the many types of norms that can be thought of are all types of rules that are similarly sensible things for individuals or groups to adopt or that norms change so easily.

In their explanations of habits and routines, both the old and new institutionalists have focused primarily on information costs and psychological constraints on case-by-case maximization. In both traditions, habits and routines are seen as devices that allow the individual to economize on information and information-processing capacity. Habits and routines are also thought to adjust or adapt over time. The OIE, however, clearly rejects a maximizing perspective on habits. Habits may be useful, even necessary, but they cannot be assumed to represent an optimal response to information costs and information-processing costs and constraints. This contrasts with the position taken by some members of the NIE, but is very close to the viewpoints of Hayek, Simon, Nelson and Winter, and Heiner. These writers reject the optimization approach, but like the old institutionalists they do not reject *all* notions of rationality or the idea that habits and routines adapt over time.

The contrast in the case of social norms is in some ways more pronounced. In the OIE, norm-guided behaviour is, for the most part, simply taken as a given, as a type of explanation that to a large extent replaces the rational choice explanation of behaviour. It is recognized that norms do change, and for some members of the OIE adaptive processes are at work here too. Others, particularly Veblen, argue that norms provide the ends of action and change only when new circumstances alter patterns of life. It is this tendency within the OIE to take norm-guided behaviour as a given that has infuriated more orthodox economists who wish to explain norms in terms of individual rational choice. As Elster has argued, however, most of these arguments do not entirely succeed. The broad range of norm-guided behaviour has not, as yet, been successfully explained in individualist and rationalist terms, and severe problems seem to stand in the way of doing so. Indeed, those who continue to argue that *all* human action must be explained in purely rationalist terms are guilty of what Elster has christened "hyperrationality": the failure to recognize the limitations and boundaries on the operation of reason, or "the irrational belief in the omnipotence of reason" (Elster 1989c: 17).

Old and new institutionalists thus face exactly the same problems. Both have recognized that information costs and bounded rationality provide a role for habits and routines. Many in both groups also recognize that once information costs and bounded rationality are allowed to enter the picture, choice can no longer be presented in optimizing terms. The alternatives so far made available (versions of adaptive rationality) maintain an outcome orientation and a looser conception of rationality but lack the simplicity of the rationality-as-maximization approach. Social norms raise even more difficult problems. Much human behaviour does appear to be norm guided, and although processes that adapt goals to altered circumstances undoubtedly play a part in the evolution of norms, these processes are poorly understood. It is only too easy to find examples of norm-guided behaviour that seem to be remarkably persistent and to defy explanation in any type of rationalist terms.

At the beginning of this chapter it was stated that the issue facing both old and new institutionalists is how rational evaluation and rule following might be combined or reconciled. A move has been made to resolve this problem where habits and routines are concerned by employing the adaptive models suggested by Simon and Heiner and others, but the solution seems further off in the case of social norms, despite a growing literature attempting to reconcile aspects of the economic and the sociological approach (Margolis 1982; Opp 1985; Kayaalp 1989; Lindenberg 1990; Schlicht 1990). For the time being it does little good for those in the NIE to attack the treatment of norm-guided behaviour found in the OIE, as an alternative rationalist explanation of norms does not yet exist in complete or acceptable form. This does not mean that models based on rationality should be abandoned. On the contrary, their explanatory reach should be fully explored. Nevertheless, the problems presented by norm-guided behaviour are such that the traditional dichotomy between rationality and rule following is less likely to be solved by a reduction of norm-guided behaviour to some type of rational choice process than by the generation of a broader conception of human motivation that can encompass both those aspects that respond to self-interest as narrowly defined and those that are driven by other ideals or psychological needs.

CHAPTER 5

Evolution and design

Within institutional economics, and within the social sciences in general, reference is often made to the social and economic functions that various institutions perform, either for particular groups or for society as a whole. Fundamentally, institutions are considered necessary to the very existence of an orderly, functioning, social and economic system. Institutions are frequently presented as constraining the operation of self-interest and preventing society from degenerating into a Hobbesian war of all against all. Douglass North (1981: 11) has put it bluntly: a purely "individualistic calculus of costs and benefits would suggest that cheating, shirking, stealing, assault and murder should be everywhere evident." When J. R. Commons (1950: 104, [1924] 1968: 138) writes of institutions as rules that generate a "workable mutuality" out of conflict of interest and create a "security of expectations," he is making essentially the same point. Similarly, Alchian and Demsetz (1973: 16) argue that institutions provide ways of "resolving the social problems associated with resource scarcity" and related conflicts of interest, and that institutions "help a man form those expectations that he can reasonably hold in his dealings with others" (Demsetz 1967: 347).

Similar things are also said in other ways: that institutions provide a basis for action in a world that would otherwise be characterized by pervasive ignorance and uncertainty (Hayek 1973: 11–18; O'Driscoll and Rizzo 1985: 6); that institutions create a degree of standardization and predictability of behaviour (Mitchell 1910b; Heiner 1983); that they solve recurrent coordination problems (Lewis 1969), prisoners' dilemmas (Ullmann-Margalit 1977; Schotter 1981), or other similar types of problem.

Within the neoclassical tradition it is usual to emphasize the function of institutions in reducing transactions costs and improving economic efficiency. Thus, hierarchies will replace markets when they work to reduce transactions costs (Williamson 1975), ideology functions as "an economizing device" (North 1981: 49), the common law represents an attempt to achieve economic efficiency (Posner

81

1977), and a "primary function of property rights" is to internalize externalities (Demsetz 1967: 348).

It is sometimes recognized that institutions may serve only sectional interests and may operate to the detriment of other groups or the social whole. In the NIE, treatments of the state, particularly rent-seeking approaches and work on the impact of pressure groups and distributive coalitions, often have such implications (Mueller 1989; Olson 1982). Old institutionalists, too, have not infrequently seen institutions as serving the interests of some groups at the expense of others or of long-term social benefit. Most obviously, this view is found in Veblen's analysis of the leisure class and the financial elite (Veblen [1899b] 1924, [1904] 1975).

That institutions perform all types of social and economic functions is undeniable. As argued in chapter 3, however, reference to the function of an institution does not, in and of itself, explain either its origin or its persistence. Human beings are intentional actors, and institutions are the intended or unintended outcomes of the intended acts of individuals. Individuals may design or modify institutions (frequently through some type of collective choice) with the intention of performing, or performing better, some function. At the same time, institutions may arise and persist in an undesigned fashion, as the unintended results of intended actions.

That institutions may be deliberately designed and enforced or may evolve in unplanned or "spontaneous" processes is recognized in both the old and new institutionalism. Different writers and groups have, however, placed very different emphasis on the two. Within the OIE, Veblen gives most attention to non-deliberative processes of institutional evolution, whereas Commons emphasizes the opposite processes. Neither excludes the other process from their analysis, but Veblen's discussion of political processes is very brief and is often more implicit than explicit. Much the same can be said of Commons's discussion of the evolution of custom; he concentrates on the actions of legislatures and courts in making and modifying the law in the light of their respective social purposes.

The emphasis on design and evolution also varies significantly within the NIE. The neoclassical literature contains both types of process. Property rights and economic organizations are frequently explained primarily in terms of deliberative efforts at design. The role of design is most obvious in the public choice literature and other discussions of the theory of the state. Evolutionary arguments appear more frequently in the discussion of the emergence of basic social conventions, but even elsewhere evolutionary arguments can be found, often playing a back-up role to explanations based on intentional design. In the more Austrian parts of the NIE, the emphasis is heavily on evolutionary and spontaneous processes of institutional development, this being a central part of Hayek's program and that adopted by other modern Austrians. Indeed, Hayek and those who have followed his lead, have tended to dichotomize explanations into those based on evolution *versus* those based on design. Attitudes such as this lie behind a number of the criticisms of J. R. Commons's emphasis on processes of collective choice (Seckler 1966, 1975: 130; Schotter 1981: 3–4), and have also created tensions between the Hayekian evolutionist viewpoint and the "contractarian constitutionalism" of public choice theorists such as Buchanan (1978).[1]

5.1   Invisible-hand explanations

Before proceeding further it is important to define exactly what processes of institutional development are to be included under the headings of "evolution" and "design," and to clear up a number of other basic issues relating to the distinctions often made between the processes of evolution and design and the institutions that result from them. Austrians, and Hayek in particular, have tended to associate spontaneous processes not only with an absence of intentionality concerning the social outcome, but also with particular institutions such as the common law and markets, with beneficial social results, and with the most important explanatory challenge facing the social sciences. The issue of intentionality has not caused much debate, although matters are not as clear as might be thought, but all the other points are certainly matters in dispute, and not only between the Austrians and the OIE.

5.1.1   Processes of evolution and design

The idea of spontaneous processes producing an unintended social outcome is one that can be traced back at least to the work of the eighteenth-century Scottish thinkers David Hume, Adam Ferguson, and Adam Smith (Hayek 1967: 99–100). Hume ([1739] 1951: 529) envisioned a system "advantageous to the public; tho' it be not intended for that purpose by the inventors." Ferguson ([1767] 1966: 187) states the point in similar terms: "Nations stumble upon establishments which are indeed the result of human action, but not the execution of any human design." Smith ([1776] 1976: 1: 477) used the term "invisible hand" to suggest that individual self-interest leads to unintended social benefits: the individual is "led by an invisible hand to promote an end which was no part of his intention." Ideas such as these obviously lie behind Menger's central question: "How can it be that institutions which serve the common welfare and are extremely significant for its development come into being without a *common will* directed toward establishing them?" ([1883] 1985: 146). Menger also defines his objective as "the theoretical understanding of those social phenomena which are not a product of agreement or of positive legislation, but are the unintended results of historical developments" ([1883] 1985: 139). Hayek (1967: 96) frequently uses a paraphrase of Ferguson's statement, referring to the "results of human action but not of human design," but he also uses arguments that explicitly include an evolutionary natural selection component that is not evident in earlier formulations. Hayek's argument runs in terms of "group selection." He talks of "rules of conduct" that have "not developed as the recognized conditions for the achievement of a known purpose, but have evolved because the groups who practised them were more successful and displaced others" (1973: 18). Again, "the structures formed by traditional human practices are neither natural in the sense of being genetically determined, nor artificial in the sense of being the product of intelligent design, but the result of a process of winnowing or sifting, directed by the differential advantages gained by groups from practices adopted for some unknown and perhaps purely accidental reasons" (1979: 155).

Hayek was by no means the first to think of institutional evolution in terms of biological natural selection. Thorstein Veblen, particularly in his earlier work, also used the analogy, arguing that "the evolution of social structure has been a process of natural selection of institutions" (1899b: 188). However, Veblen's actual discussions of institutional evolution do not appear to be as closely patterned on the variation and selection model as Hayek's.[2]

Formulations such as Hayek's have led commentators to distinguish between a "standard" or aggregative version of the invisible-hand and a "functional/evolutionary" version (Ullmann-Margalit 1978). In the first version, the social rule in question is considered the unintended aggregate result of the actions of many decision makers, each intentionally pursuing only their own private interests. This makes it necessary to explain the pattern of individual behaviour in terms of individual motivations, and to *systematically* link it to an unintended aggregate result in the form of a social convention or generally accepted rule of behaviour. In this way, a social institution may be said to result from individual human actions, although the individual actions at issue were not motivated by the desire to produce the social institution.[3]

Standard invisible-hand explanations concentrate on the process through which some social convention, institution, or rule *emerges* out of individual behaviour.[4] For the institution to survive, the incentives would have to be such that once established all individuals would wish to continue to abide by the convention (the rule is self-policing), or the rule would have to be enforced by becoming established in a social or legal *norm* (Ullmann-Margalit 1977). Within the Austrian tradition, the formation of social norms and the common law are usually included within the ambit of spontaneous processes, but legislative processes are not. As will be seen later in the chapter, that the common law is included in the spontaneous category is far from obvious.

The functional/evolutionary approach is based on an analogy with biological natural selection. The emphasis here is less on the individual behaviours that initially produce the social institution than on the social function performed and its effect on the prosperity or "success" of the social unit. That is, to explain a social institution one must first find its contribution to the survival of the society (or organization) in question:

Once this is successfully established, the phenomenon under study is assumed all but explained, the (implicit) filling in being that by performing its function even its faint beginnings – whatever their origins – are reinforced and selected for; consequently this institution is better capable of helping the social unit "succeed," and this "success" of the social unit, in turn, accounts for the institution's own perpetuation in it. (Ullmann-Margalit 1978: 282)

The initial development of an institution, in this treatment, need not be explained. It could be a matter of chance or accident, or the outcome of an invisible-hand process of the standard sort, or even, for that matter, the result of deliberate design.[5] The key issue here is the non-intentional nature of the selection process, which is supposed to be "non-man-made" and carried out by the environment. Individual or collective intentions or purposes are supposed to play virtually no part. Selection is "visualized as a large scale evolutionary mechanism that as it were scans the inventory of social patterns and institutions at any given period of time and screens through to the next those of them that are best adapted to their (respective) roles" (Ullmann-Margalit 1978: 282).

The difficulties with such functional/evolutionary types of argument are, first, that for reasons discussed in Chapter 3, no argument about the growth of institutions can be fully satisfactory unless it specifies the links between individual actions and the social phenomenon in question. Functional/evolutionary arguments do not generally do this. Where some attempt is made to explain the actions of individuals that result in institutions developing, persisting, spreading, or being changed, the argument usually relies on either intentional or standard invisible-hand processes. This is so because of the second problem: the analogy between natural selection in biology and evolutionary processes in human societies is not that close (Elster 1982: 463; Mirowski 1983). Of course, it is not denied that some institutions or social systems may perform, in some important economic or social respects, less well than others, or that an institution or social system may generate adverse consequences. Poor performance, particularly poor comparative performance in a competitive setting, may induce change, but these changes will come about either through the usual invisible-hand or intentional processes. Individuals may migrate, or adopt the strategies of others who appear to be more successful, or undertake other actions that have unintended social consequences, or those in authority may attempt reforms. At the extreme, a social system may collapse and new institutions gradually emerge from the chaos, but the processes involved will be those of the standard invisible-hand type or the deliberate design and enforcement of rules by some governing authority. Thus, it is difficult to see that references to natural selection provide any viable additional non-intentionalist arguments to the more usual invisible-hand type, or can otherwise successfully avoid reference to deliberate processes of institutional design.[6] For this reason, the rest of this section will focus on the standard invisible-hand process.

In contrast to the invisible-hand process are those involving deliberate design. Menger named designed institutions "pragmatic" as opposed to the "organic" institutions that emerge spontaneously. A pragmatic explanation is the "explanation of the nature and origin of social phenomena from the intentions, opinions, and available instrumentalities of human social unions or their rulers" (Menger 1883: 145). This may involve a single authoritative individual (monarch, dictator, or leader) or a group of individuals (a committee or legislature). The primary examples of pragmatic or designed institutions in the Austrian literature are those that emerge from government in the form of "positive legislation" (Menger [1883] 1985: 233). For Hayek (1960: 110–111), the outcome of government action, even if it involves majority rule, is clearly *not* an example of "spontaneous social growth."Other examples show individuals or groups setting up specific organizations to pursue particular objectives. Thus, Hayek includes in his category of "taxis" or "made order" any institution that has been made deliberately to "*serve a purpose* of the mak r" (Hayek 1973: 38). This includes firms, associations, and "all the public institutions, including government" (Hayek 1973: 46).

5.1.2 Distinguishing evolution and design

Spontaneous, invisible-hand processes are distinguished from design processes primarily by the role of intentionality in the production of the social outcome. Richard Langlois (1986b: 242, n. 19) defines an invisible-hand explanation as "any explanation that casts its explananda as the undesigned results of human action." Borrowing notation from Heath (1992: 34) we can more formally state an invisible-hand explanation of a rule R as consisting of "(a) a set of initial conditions, IC, occurring in social collective C, (b) at least one lawlike statement L, and (c) a derivation of R from L and IC such that R is generated from IC by the summation of some independent actions $[X^1 ... X^n]$ of agents $[A^1 ... A^n]$ of social collective C, and the agents of C, $[A^1 ... A^n]$, do not intend actions $[X^1 ... X^n]$ to generate regularity R from IC."[7] Within the usual invisible-hand explanation the social consequence is not merely unintended but also unrecognized (Ullmann-Margalit 1978: 271). Of course, it may be possible that individual agents realize that certain social consequences may follow from their actions. Langlois (1986b: 242, n. 19) has argued that invisible-hand explanations "would include explanations in which some (or even all) the agents know, suspect, or guess at the overall outcome their decentralized decisions would lead to, so long as the pursuit of that outcome is not the principal motivation for their actions." However, what is or is not their "principal motivation" may, in some cases, be open to interpretation.

Somewhat similarly, intentional processes may also involve a matter of degree. Again following Heath (1992: 38), we can "stipulate that R is a (fully) intended consequence of a set of actions $[X^1 ... X^n]$ if and only if each actor $[A^1 ... A^n]$ intended his action $[X^1 ... X^n]$ to bring about (or help to bring about) R and the set of actions $[X^1 ... X^n]$ do bring about R (in the way each actor intended)." Of course, an outcome R may not be *fully* intended. It may be "that not every actor $[A^1 ... A^n]$ who performs action $[X^1 ... X^n]$ intended to bring about R (or intended to bring about R in exactly the way in which R did come about)." Thus "a judgment as to whether R is intentional is, in most circumstances, a matter of degree" (Heath 1992: 43–44, n. 11).

What this implies is that intentionality is a slippery concept. This is not to say that no distinction can be made between a highly decentralized invisible-hand process that gives rise to a social convention and the processes underlying the intense discussions of a constitutional convention by political leaders, but these are polar cases and not all processes or institutions can be quite so easily classified. This point can be made by thinking about the judicial processes that go to make up the common law and the legislative processes that determine statute law.

Hayek's view of the spontaneous nature of the common law is based on the assumption that judges are constrained by precedent, have to fit their judgements within a "given cosmos of rules" (1973: 101), and in any case do not *make* but *discover* the rules that have evolved spontaneously. The fallacy here is that even if it is agreed that the common law often takes over rules that first evolved as customs, it is not possible to deny that judges do have to make decisions between conflicting rules, and do have to make new rules where gaps exist. In addition, judges are not merely individuals pursuing individual interests, but officials, frequently appointed through political processes and occupying a role with an obvious social function. When making their judgements, judges have their purpose and role as judges and the social nature and functioning of the law explicitly in mind. Writers as diverse as Posner (1977), North (1981), and Commons ([1934] 1961) agree that a judge's own conception of the public good will play a significant role in shaping his or her judgements. It is also true that although most cases are brought by individuals in pursuit of private interests only, some cases are brought by interest groups with obvious social goals in mind. It might be countered that regardless of the motivations of plaintiffs or judges, judicial decisions are made by individual judges not by the collectivity of judges, and that no individual judge can be thought of as intending the overall result that will be obtained as the aggregate result of all judicial decisions. Such a view is very much in the spirit of the attempts by Rubin (1977), Priest (1977), and Goodman (1978) to model the common law as the outcome of an invisible-hand process. As explained later in the chapter, these arguments have problems too, but it can also be pointed out that judges in superior courts do make collective decisions, and do so in the full knowledge that they are establishing a social rule. Of course, the body of common law *taken as a whole* was never designed by any judge or group of judges, but then exactly the same thing could be said of legislators and the body of statute law, and statute law is not usually regarded as a spontaneous development.[8]

Similar points can be made about legislative processes. Traditionally, these processes have been associated with the intentional creation of social rules, presumably because legislators are thought of as having that as their primary purpose and as being able to implement their intentions, but matters are not quite so simple. To begin with, legislators are not unconstrained, but face a body of existing law and social convention that they cannot entirely ignore. Second, even if it is true that all legislators have as their main purpose the making of a law, this does not imply that the law that actually emerges out of the political process is exactly as all (or even any) of the participants intended it to be when undertaking the actions that led to the final outcome. Third, even if all laws are exactly as intended, the entire body of law is built up over generations and is unlikely to be (as a whole) what any individual intended or would intend. And fourth, modern economic approaches to political processes tend to stress the self-interested motivations of politicians, and if all politicians are individually interested primarily in securing their own reelection, is it entirely clear how one should regard the aggregate outcome of their political acts? This is not to argue that government legislation should be regarded as entirely unintended, only that it is, perhaps, less fully intended than is sometimes suggested. It is certainly possible for the rulings of a court to represent a more fully intended social result than the acts of a legislature.

A somewhat different point is that invisible-hand and design processes can often be found interacting and playing some role in the history of a given institution. Austrians frequently cite money and markets as examples of spontaneous developments arising out of invisible-hand processes. While this may account for the earliest origins of these institutions, it is also the case that governments were involved in the development and regulation of both institutions from a very early stage (Polanyi 1944; Hodgson 1992a). As Hutchison (1973: 25–26) has argued, the notion of spontaneous institutional development requires a degree of unselfconsciousness rarely encountered in modern societies: "once this awareness . . . has come into existence, about any kind of social phenomena, decisions will be subject to deliberate, conscious, or 'planned' intervention." The case of markets is particularly illuminating as any developed market is, in fact, a highly complex phenomenon consisting of an array of social conventions and norms, common law rules, statute laws, and enforcement agencies that together define the ways in which individuals acting for themselves or for organizations can conduct economic exchanges. To regard such markets as purely spontaneous developments is a gross oversimplification.

Shifting attention to organizations such as firms, corporations, or the organs of the state raises similar difficulties. Organizations are often presented as designed and "directing individual actions toward

particular ends to comply with the will of the sovereign authority"
(Leathers 1989: 366). However, how an organization actually operates and the results it does achieve will depend on much more than
the components that are deliberately designed. Organizations, too,
develop their own informal rules, traditions, and customs. Corporate
"cultures" can vary widely. The informal rules that make up these
cultures may be extremely important in the functioning of the organization, but were not designed by anyone. It should also be observed
that several writers in the NIE have attempted to present organizational evolution as the outcome of a non-intentional process driven
by competitive selection. Although, again, these arguments are not
without fault, they serve to indicate the variety of viewpoints that are
possible.

5.1.3   Social consequences

The second distinction Austrians make between spontaneously developed institutions and those that are designed is that spontaneous
processes are particularly associated with the development of socially
beneficial institutions. The limitations on the spontaneous generation of social rules and the difficulties involved in defining "social
benefit" are the subject of later parts of this chapter and of Chapter 6,
respectively, but a few general comments at this point are in order.

First, the classical and Austrian focus on *beneficial* unintended
social outcomes stems not from anything inherent in the invisible-
hand process that necessarily gives rise to beneficent results, but
from the problem that these authors are addressing: that of how
social orders that might appear to have been designed (presumably
because of their beneficence), can, in fact, evolve in an unintended
fashion. The invisible-hand mechanism answers this question, but
finding an answer does *not* imply that the invisible hand will always
function to produce needed institutions, or that it will never operate
to generate adverse consequences. Indeed, it is one of the central
tenets of the OIE that institutions (especially conventions and norms)
may be at odds with the social benefit.

The second, related, point is that there are many types of unintended consequences, and the standard discussion of the invisible
hand picks up on only one of these (Boehm 1992). The social or
aggregate consequences of decentralized individual actions may be
undesired. The analysis of phenomena such as the depletion of
common property resources, externalities, business cycles, and even
segregated neighbourhoods (Schelling 1978) can all be carried out
in invisible-hand terms. Unintended consequences may even be

perverse in the sense of actually undermining the interests of those whose actions generated the result. The Marxian analysis of the contradictions of capitalism can be presented in this way, as can much of Veblen's discussion of how institutional systems evolve.

A third point is that reference to evolutionary forces of competition and selection of institutions does not guarantee that those institutions that survive will serve the social benefit.[9] Without organized intervention it may not be possible for a society to shift its social rules in a way that adapts to new conditions. In addition, the results of competition depend on the nature of that competition and the criterion of "success" involved. Competition may create losers as well as winners, meaning that the outcome in terms of "social benefit" may be highly ambiguous. These points are explicitly recognized in the Veblenian discussion of institutional change that includes both the idea of "culture lag" and of the role of institutions in establishing and maintaining systems of status.

It cannot, then, be presumed that the unintentionally evolved institution will necessarily perform well or be preferable to a designed alternative. Of course, the opposite presumption must also be guarded against. In the Ayresian part of the OIE, there is a tendency to see evolved institutions as *entirely* backward looking, resistant to change and with no positive functions. A substantial part of this comes from Ayres's definition of an institution that seems to associate the term with "ceremonial" functions only and to exclude any convention, law, or organizational form that is instrumentally effective (Ayres 1962: 184). Such a definition, contrary to Ayres's claim, hinders rather than advances the analysis of the derivation and functioning of social rules.

5.1.4 Explanatory challenges

The third argument often encountered in the Austrian literature is that invisible-hand processes pose important explanatory challenges that are lacking from design explanations. Menger ([1883] 1985: 146) talks of the invisible-hand explanation of socially beneficial institutions being "perhaps the most noteworthy" problem of the social sciences. Menger, however, did not deny the importance of pragmatic institutions. Although his words imply that he felt that the explanation of such institutions was a less noteworthy problem, his discussion nonetheless provides a place for both, and is relatively balanced in nature (Prisching 1989).

This balance is very largely lost in Hayek's work. Hayek's attacks on the excesses of rational constructivism, most obviously socialism, led him to the view that *the* task of social theory is to explain "those unintended patterns and regularities which we find to exist in human society" (1967: 97). Thus, for Hayek, it is "no exaggeration to say that social theory begins with – and has an object only because of – the discovery that there exist orderly structures which are the product of the action of many men but are not the result of human design" (1973: 37). Hayek's view, that the development of systems of social order, or socially beneficial institutions, in an unintended way is the only real problem in social science, has often been repeated. Schotter (1981: 5) goes so far as to *define* economics as "the study of how individual economic agents pursuing their own selfish ends evolve institutions as a means to satisfy them," a definition that he clearly regards as being at odds with the view that institutions are the outcome of purposeful collective design and enforcement.[10] Langlois (1986b) goes slightly less far, but argues strongly that the invisible-hand type of explanation of institutions should be the central focus of the NIE.

For those who would concentrate attention on evolutionary and invisible-hand processes, it is clearly the unintended development of social conventions and institutions that provides the key explanatory problem for social science. This problem is obviously one of great interest and importance, but unless one accepts Hayek's normative agenda it is not obvious that the design of institutions through collective decision making does not also involve worthwhile and interesting explanatory problems, or that it should be banished from any institutional economics.

Setting normative issues aside, the implication that the deliberate design of institutions is a relatively uninteresting problem seems to be based on the idea of the design of an institution as uncomplicated process whereby an authoritative decision maker simply imposes his or her wishes on society (Schotter 1981: 21, 28). Of course, few institutional design processes are that straightforward. They more often involve negotiation and bargaining between interested parties and the functioning of the formal institutions of government. This is the subject of J. R. Commons's work and of public choice theory. Both assume the state has its origins partly in limitations on the operation of spontaneous processes, and partly in the desire of groups to alter the distribution of income in their favour (Rutherford 1989a: 165–166; Mueller 1989: 12–39). Public choice theory goes on to analyze in detail the effect of voting rules, direct and representative democracy, political parties, rent seeking, bureaucratic behaviour, and so on. This analysis of collective decision making is hardly trivial or uninteresting. In many ways, it is quite similar to that embedded in standard invisible-hand explanations.

When dealing with collective choice processes, particularly of a complex sort involving political parties, vote trading, organized pressure groups, and so on, the outcome is the result of the *interaction* of the intentions and goals of many different individuals and groups. As just mentioned, although the process as a whole aims (to some extent) to produce some deliberately implemented and enforced institutional rule, the exact specification of the design that emerges at the end of the day may not correspond with the original intentions of all (or any) of the parties involved. The final outcome may, in this more limited sense, also be the unintended result of the interaction of intentional actors. In the study of collective choice, it is important to understand how the results of collective decision making emerge out of the intended actions of the various interacting participants in the process. This also provides an interesting and important explanatory challenge.

The same point may be made in a slightly more formal fashion by using part of the classification of types of explanatory argument provided by Elster (1982: 463, 1983: 84). Elster identifies intentional arguments, where an action is explained as the outcome of the individual's goal and his situation, and intentional/causal explanation, in which explanation is a mixture of "*intentional understanding* of the individual actions, and *causal explanation* of their interaction." That is, "First we must 'understand' why – i.e. for the sake of what goal – the actors behave as they do; and then we must 'explain' why, behaving as they do, they bring about what they do." The traditional distinction between design and invisible-hand arguments seems to suggest that the former consists only of intentional explanations while the latter consists of intentional/causal explanations. The point here is that *both* are of the intentional/causal type, and *both* raise similar explanatory problems, problems that relate to social outcomes that are the result of the interactions of individuals.[11] Whether it is (primarily) a social result or (primarily) an individual result that is being intended by these interacting individuals is an important (although sometimes debatable) point of interpretation.

5.2   Evolution and design in the OIE

Within the OIE one tends to find highly integrated discussions of the history of the entire legal/social/economic system, including the evolution of social conventions and norms (customs), laws, and economic organizations. Such integrated treatments allow one to see the exact roles that are being given to invisible-hand, judicial, legislative, and other design processes, but the attempt to deal with the social whole often results in a lack of detail and a complexity of argument that creates difficulties in exposition.

In order to simplify the discussion somewhat, the two major approaches to the development of custom and law will be dealt with in turn: Veblen's discussion of social and legal rules emphasizes customary rules and non-intentional processes; whereas Commons focuses on judicial and legislative processes. Issues pertaining specifically to organizational forms will be dealt with separately.

5.2.1   Veblen on custom and law

As already mentioned, Veblen believed that social customs, conventions, and norms played a large role in shaping the goals, aspirations, and behaviour of individual members of a society. In Veblen's view, such conventions and norms initially grow out of the "habits of life" of the group, patterns of thought and behaviour that are derived primarily from the then prevalent methods of livelihood. Material and technological conditions shape patterns of life and these in turn become conventionalized. Habits of life also include certain ways of thinking that become conventional. These include the community's technological knowledge and commonly held values and beliefs.[12]

Veblen thought of institutions as fundamentally a matter of social conventions that are the result of a kind of consensus reached through the "discipline" or conditioning influence of the methods of livelihood in effect at the time the institutional system first arises. Veblen does not supply much detail on how exactly social conventions are originally formed, but it is clear that he thought of them emerging within groups that share the same pattern of life, and so come to habitually act and think along the same lines. Over time these conventions come to take on normative significance. Most important to Veblen are the basic values or organizing "principles" that are derived in this way. For example, an economic system based on "predation" will be built around the principles of mastery and obedience, while a market or pecuniary economic system will tend to become based on the principle of pecuniary success. Of course, institutional systems do not spring fully formed from the start, and Veblen does discuss a number of processes of internal development. Some of these are deliberative and involve judicial and legislative decision making, but Veblen's emphasis is on the non-deliberative processes through which institutions and institutional systems develop.

Perhaps the most important of these is what Veblen calls the "crossing and grafting" of institutional principles ([1914] 1964: 50–51). Basic principles and conventions are extended by analogy to other lines of activity, even lines remote from material pursuits. As indicated previously, this process may also involve the very considerable elaboration and metaphorical extension of basic principles, and through these processes entire and complex systems of social order, religion and belief can arise.[13] The same set of basic principles and values, extended and elaborated, come to infuse the entire society, its economic, political, legal, and religious institutions. Institutional systems become "pervaded by a certain characteristic logic and perspective, a certain line of habitual conceptions having a degree of congruity among themselves, a 'philosophy', as it would once have been called" (Veblen [1915] 1954: 267). In addition to this, and despite the fact that Veblen does not discuss judicial or political processes in much detail, he makes it clear that institutional systems are stabilized by the formal establishing of social conventions and norms in law and constitutions ([1919] 1964: 17–18).

Veblen's thinking on the internal development of an institutional system is evident in his discussion of the institutional system of business. The business system is based on the principles of individual pecuniary gain. These principles are crossed and grafted onto other areas of life. Thus: "apart from their effect in controlling the terms of livelihood from day to day, these principles are also in great measure decisive in the larger affairs of life, both for the individual in his civil relations and for the community at large in its political concerns" (Veblen [1904] 1975: 268). Pecuniary principles have a "cultural bearing" that is both "wide-reaching and forceful." They have a "peculiar hold upon the affections of the people as something intrinsically right and good" and are "drawn on for guidance and conviction even in concerns that are not conceived to be primarily business concerns" ([1904] 1975: 382).

Veblen's *The Theory of the Leisure Class* ([1899b] 1924) is an extended examination of the impact of the institutionalized criterion of pecuniary success on matters of taste and fashion. He also devotes attention to the effect of pecuniary criteria on literature, government, and education ([1904] 1975: 382–399), and the whole of *The Higher Learning in America* (1918b) is a detailed treatment of how business principles are applied to universities and displace the principles of scholarship. Business profit-seeking also leads to the extension of the use of credit and the development of the methods of corporate finance. Markets in "vendible capital," debentures, preferred stock, and the capitalization of intangible assets are the expression and result of the elaboration and refinement of the businessman's pursuit of profit (Veblen [1904] 1975; Raines and Leathers 1991). Along with this, the conventions and principles of the system of business are reduced to written form, formally installed in law, and thereby given an increased degree of stability (Veblen [1919] 1964: 17–18).

The processes involved in this development of the institutional system are of both an invisible-hand and of a design type. Individuals adopt the prevailing pecuniary criteria, but in adopting them and pursuing their interests thus defined, they generate unintended institutional consequences. The social institution of fashion, for example, did not itself result from the efforts of a designer, but as an unintended result of the actions of individuals seeking to display their wealth through the medium of dress. Similarly, the expansion and development of the various market institutions of capitalism arose largely out of the individual businessman's competitive pursuit of his own profit. The greater recourse to loan credit, to methods of salesmanship, and so on, were undertaken with no intention of producing the overall development of business institutions that actually occurred. At the same time, Veblen depicts the government as quite deliberately acting "with a main view to . . . expedience for business ends" ([1904] 1975: 285): "representative government means, chiefly, representation of business interests" and the "government commonly works in the interest of the business man with a fairly consistent singleness of purpose" ([1904] 1975: 286). Government actions, then, take the form of a deliberate forwarding of the interests of the dominant (business) interest group.

The processes considered so far all relate to Veblen's discussion of the elaboration and refinement of an institutional system derived from a *given* material and ideological basis. Institutional systems, however, also change over time, particularly as the material basis of the system is altered. Such alterations, however, are not presented by Veblen as simply exogenous to the system, but as an integral part of the process of cumulative causation. The key element in this process of change is technology, the pace and direction of technological change itself being a function of the existing institutional system. In Veblen's discussion, prevailing institutions can have a profound effect on technological change. This is because technological activity, like all other activities, is culturally embedded and becomes affected by institutionally determined preconceptions and goals. In Veblen's view, the prevailing institutional preconceptions are "the medium through which experience receives those elements of information and insight on which workmanship is able to draw in contriving ways and means and turning them to account for the uses of life" ([1914] 1964: 50–51).

Note that Veblen is concerned with the process of contriving new ways and means and with the way in which new ways and means are turned to account – in other words, with the processes of both invention and innovation – but some parts of his analysis deal almost entirely with the issue of institutionally determined preconceptions hindering or even preventing technological insight and invention, while other parts deal with the broader question of the role of institutions in determining the goals or aims of action and hence the context within which new technology is developed and introduced.

On the first issue, that of invention, the important points involve the extent to which the crossing and grafting of institutional preconceptions has proceeded in contaminating instrumental knowledge and technological activity, and the nature of the preconceptions themselves. Some preconceptions may be more damaging to technological insight than others. On the issue of innovation the important point is whether the institutionally determined goals of decision makers are compatible with the introduction of new technology. Innovation may proceed through the domestic generation of inventions or through the borrowing of technology from elsewhere (Veblen [1914] 1964: 169–171, [1915] 1954: 64–67; Rutherford 1984: 337–338).

In many cases, Veblen argues that technological insight and invention are more or less adversely affected by institutional preconceptions, but institutions do not always have such a negative effect. In Veblen's interpretation of the business system, the institutional principles of individualism and pecuniary gain do not obstruct technological insight to the same extent as the institutional principles of predatory culture. Indeed, Veblen argues that the habits of mind involved in the growth of the price system had "much to do with the rise of machine technology in modern times" ([1914] 1964: 245). At the same time, the institutions of business result in new technology being introduced and its use determined on the basis of private gain and not on the basis of social advantage. Veblen repeatedly stresses that under business institutions the problem is that new technology will only be introduced if there is a private pecuniary advantage in introducing it. "Inventors, engineers, experts . . . prepare the way for the man of pecuniary affairs," but "the decisive point is business expediency and business pressure." Because of this, the businessman can be seen as working "against, as well as for, a new and more efficient organization. He inhibits as well as furthers the higher organization of industry" ([1904] 1975: 36–39).

Thus, technological innovation is intentional and is undertaken to serve the interests of the innovating group. However, such intentionally introduced technological changes have unintended institutional consequences both short and long term. In the short term the institutional consequences that Veblen discusses are primarily the outcome of alterations in practices undertaken to accommodate the new technology. These shifts are alterations that still respect the more fundamental of the established social conventions and norms. Thus, within the business system, the introduction of new technology results in both organizational changes (discussed below) and a great deal of "shrewd interpretation" and "refinement" of business principles ([1919] 1964: 19, 23) in order to adjust to the new technological means and opportunities.

The principles of conduct which were approved and stabilized in the eighteenth century, under the driving exigencies of that age, have not altogether escaped the complications of changing circumstances. They have at least come in for some shrewd interpretation. . . . There have been refinements of definition, extensions of application, scrutiny and exposition of implications, as new exigencies have arisen and the established canons have been required to cover unforseen circumstances; but it has all been done with the explicit reservation that no material innovation shall be allowed to touch the legacy of modern principles handed down from the eighteenth century. ([1919] 1964: 19)

Changing circumstances result in deliberate adaptions, but the decision making involved may be decentralized, in which case the overall impact may be quite unintended. As an example of this, Veblen talks of the emergence of the "new order" of business as the "upshot of many minor changes which have converged – or are converging – to this effect, by drift of circumstance rather than by reasoned design, perhaps even without any degree of effectual prevision on the part of those who have been the chief actors in the case" ([1923] 1954: 329).

Over the longer term, however, new technology may have quite different consequences, and consequences not only unintended but even *contrary* to the interests of those who introduced or exploited the new technology in the first place. Such consequences may involve a shift in even the most fundamental of institutional principles. This kind of fundamental change can occur, in Veblen's view, where new technology changes the basic patterns of livelihood and habits of life and thought of some significant section of the population. The old ways of doing and thinking fall into disuse and are replaced by others more in line with the new conditions of life:

The new terms of workday knowledge and belief, which do not conform to the ancient canons, go to enforce and stabilise new canons and standards, of a character alien to the traditional point of view. It is, in other words, a case of obsolescence by displacement as well as by habitual disuse. ([1919] 1964: 9)

Veblen sometimes uses the language of natural selection to describe this process, but it is not so much a matter of prior institutional variation followed by selection by an exogenously determined environment, as a matter of the new environmental conditions themselves leading to the development, via habituation, of new, more suitable modes of thought and action that may come to displace previously existing conventions and norms. Once new principles are established, the processes of crossing and grafting, of metaphorical extension, and of establishment in law begin all over again. As before, these processes will involve both invisible-hand and deliberate processes of institutional changes, but with the leading role being given to the former:

And the scope and method of knowledge and belief which is forced on men in their everyday material concerns will unavoidably, by habitual use, extend to other matters as well. . . . It results that, in the further course of changing habituation, those imponderable relations, conventions, claims and perquisites, that make up the time-worn system of law and custom will unavoidably also be brought under review and will be revised and reorganized in the light of the same new principles of validity that are found to be sufficient in dealing with material facts. (Veblen [1919] 1964: 9–10)

These institutional changes, including conventions, norms, and laws, come about initially as the unintended result of the alteration in the patterns of individual behaviour, but will eventually prompt deliberate, primarily governmental, processes of legal revision and reorganization. Veblen recognizes that these processes may be slow and halting, particularly where such institutional reorganization faces "a settled and honourable code of ancient principles and a stubborn array of vested interests" ([1919] 1964: 34), but provides no analysis of how, and under what circumstances the opposition of vested interests will be overcome.

In terms of the business system, Veblen saw the impact of modern machine technology as leading to patterns of life and habits of thought quite at odds with conventional standards and business principles. He presented this as a fundamental conflict between established business or pecuniary criteria and those based on the "industrial" standards and values of efficiency and workmanship (Veblen [1904] 1975). In some places he suggested that industrial values and institutions must win out in the end (Veblen [1919] 1964: 32–33), but on other occasions he did not present that result as inevitable, suggesting instead the possibility of a "retreat" to an earlier technological level, or simply a continuing state of tension and conflict (Rutherford 1984: 341–342).[14] As noted in previous chapters, the main weakness in Veblen's system is the lack of a well-defined link between the changing technology, the changing patterns of life it creates, and the changing goals, ideologies, and criteria of validity that Veblen saw as the result. Doubtless, significant alterations in material and technological conditions can and do bring about far-reaching changes in the way people think about the world they inhabit, and in what they regard as important and valuable. These effects of technology and technological knowledge on matters of social and moral philosophy or ideology are, however, often much more gradual and much more subtle than Veblen seemed to think.

Among those who followed Veblen, Wesley Mitchell can also be found arguing explicitly in terms of the importance of unforeseen and unintended consequences. This is particularly obvious in his discussion of the way that the adoption of pecuniary concepts and criteria resulted in the vast elaboration and refinement of the modern system of business. The developed business system includes monetary and banking systems, large business organizations, the financial policies of governments, the interadjustments of prices, security markets, and more. In this way, "pecuniary concepts" have created "a system which is measurably beyond the control of even society as a whole and which ever and again produces consequences which no man willed" (Mitchell 1910b: 208–209). Furthermore, institutional systems may contain conflicting elements, and these can produce further unforeseen results that react upon the communities involved (1910b: 206).

Clarence Ayres adopted Veblen's institutions/technology dichotomy, but expanded Veblen's concept of technology to include all instrumentally effective knowledge. Institutional change, therefore, becomes a matter of the progress of knowledge, or the advance of the "technological continuum," bringing about changes in institutions (Ayres 1962). Ayres gives little detailed analysis of what might affect the direction of the advance of knowledge, tending to see instrumental advance as cumulative and accelerating, but a matter of a more or less self-contained process. Neither does he examine in much depth the exact nature of institutional resistance to change, or the processes through which new knowledge may eventually lead to institutional adjustment. The only exception to this is found in Ayres's highly optimistic accounts of democratic processes as processes through which whole communities can reach agreement on the basis of the best available scientific knowledge (1961: 282–285). Ayres's system, while adopting Veblenian categories, seems to rely much more on deliberative processes of social or collective choice. Because of this emphasis on democratic decision making, Ayres's work has points of contact with that of John R. Commons. In other respects, however, the systems of thought are very different.

5.2.2   Commons on custom and law

Commons's primary concern is not technological advance or the advance of scientific knowledge in general. Commons ([1924] 1968: 376) focuses on the resolution of conflicts of interests, and he rejects the Veblenian notion of habituation to new material circumstances. Institutions arise out of the problem situation created by the fact of economic scarcity. Scarcity is, of course, the basis of the economist's concern with the efficient use of resources, but Commons ([1934] 1961: 6) argues that scarcity also generates a problem in human relationships. Scarcity creates conflicts of interest, conflicts that in the absence of institutionalized constraints will be resolved by private violence to the detriment of productive efficiency. Without an institutionalized system of rules to create a degree of order and certainty, there could be "little or no present value, present enterprise, present transactions, or present employment" (Commons 1950: 104). In Commons's words, institutional rules "are necessary and their survival in history is contingent on their fitness to hold together in a continuing concern the overweening and unlimited selfishness of individuals pressed on by scarcity of resources" (Commons [1924] 1968: 138).[15] The institutional system serves to "ration" economic benefits and burdens, and, if successful, generates a "workable mutuality," if not a harmony, out of conflict (Commons 1931: 656). This point of view has much in common with the view of the role of institutions in the NIE, but, like Veblen, Commons does not provide any detailed analysis on how an institution may evolve out of individual action.

Within his overall framework, Commons constructed an analysis based on the concepts of the transaction, the going concern or organization (such as firms, unions, churches, political parties, etc.), and working rules. The concept of the working rule includes both social rules (such as social conventions, norms and laws) and the rules that exist only within particular concerns. Our interest here is primarily with the processes involved in the evolution of social custom and law, but to understand that part of Commons's work it is first necessary to comprehend the more general relationship between working rules and transactions.

Commons distinguishes the rationing transaction, the managerial transaction, and the bargaining transaction. Rationing and managerial transactions are transactions between a legal superior and a legal inferior. The rationing transaction involves the "rationing of wealth or purchasing power by a superior authority," for example, legislators agreeing on taxes or protective tariffs or judicial decisions transferring wealth from one party to another. Managerial transactions involve the organization and control of production and consist of the relationship of command and obedience between "manager and managed, master and servant, owner and slave" (Commons [1934] 1961: 67–68). Bargaining transactions involve the transfer of rights of ownership between legal equals, but legal equality is compatible with the exercise of economic power. Economic power is determined by the alternative opportunities and bargaining power (ability to withhold) available to the parties involved. The available alternatives define what Commons calls the "limits of coercion," and where the terms of the bargain will settle within these limits is determined by the bargaining power of the parties to the transaction ([1934] 1961: 59–64, 331–335).

Transactions thus involve the use of legal or economic power, but these powers may have limits placed on their use. Working rules can constrain the use of power by requiring that some alternatives be avoided, or by limiting the use of power to reasonable levels. For example, the working rules may require such things as equal opportunity and fair competition, prevent the unreasonable use of bargaining power or the issuing of unreasonable commands, and ensure due process of law (Commons [1934] 1961: 62–63, 331–348). Also, changes in law or other working rules may shift certain transactions from the rationing to the bargaining type, or may restrict the range of rationing or managerial authority and provide more room for bargaining. The abolition of slavery involved the substitution of bargaining for rationing authority while the establishment of a socialist state would work in the opposite direction (Commons [1934] 1961: 761–763). The types of transactions used and the terms upon which they take place depend, therefore, on a process of negotiation carried out within a context of working rules that determine legal and economic power and the limits on the use of such power. Working rules thus have considerable distributive and allocative implications.

The various levels of working rules outlined above represent different aspects of what Commons saw as collective action in control of individual action. But Commons also saw the set of working rules changing over time in what he called a process of "artificial selection." In the most general of terms, this artificial selection occurs as the outcome of a continuing process of conflict resolution. Working rules and changes to the working rules come from two main sources. First, some rules arise from the power of monarchs or other absolute rules, or from the "conscious determinations of legislatures" (Commons [1924] 1968: 136). Second, some rules arise out of customs, common practices, and the decisions of the courts in resolving disputes. The "great bulk" of working rules come from the latter source (Commons [1924] 1968: 136).

Laws are backed by the sovereign power of the state, while other rules may be enforced by social or economic sanctions. The state, in Commons's view, is the concern that has taken over the power to use physical sanctions. The state "consists in the enforcement, by physical sanctions, of what private parties might otherwise endeavor to enforce by private violence" (Commons [1934] 1961: 751). What is important, however, is the control of the power of the state, and historical struggles over that control resulted in the gradual evolution of the political institutions of representative democracy and political parties. The state itself is "an accumulated series of compromises between social classes, each seeking to secure for itself control over the coercive elements which exist implicitly in society with the institution of private property" (Commons 1899–1900: 45; Chasse 1986: 761).

In representative democracies, political parties have become the concerns "through which the sanctions of physical force are directed towards economic gain or loss" (Commons [1934] 1961: 752). In order to serve the interests they represent or choose to support, political parties aim at "selecting and getting control of the hierarchy of legislative, executive, and judicial personalities whose concerted action determines the legal rights, duties, liberties, and exposures involved in all economic transactions" (Commons [1934] 1961: 751). Parties are subject to lobbying and pressure from other organized groups seeking legislation in their advantage, and Commons argues that the legislature in a representative democracy operates through a process of "log-rolling."

Log-rolling, for Commons, is a pervasive phenomenon and is to be regarded as simply the way in which members of a legislature reach voluntary agreements on the legislative acts that will affect the distribution of economic burdens and benefits. Commons ([1934] 1961: 755) objects to the usual outright "crimination" of log-rolling,[16] but although log-rolling is "as nearly a reasonable reconciliation of all conflicting interests as representative democracy has been able to reach," it still has difficulties. The process is slow and inefficient and, particularly if many differing interests are involved, a legislature may become deadlocked. Also, the decisions may benefit only a few at the expense of others. While there are constraints on the actions of legislatures in the form of the customs, opinions, and beliefs of the populace, and, in the case of nations such as the United States, the ability of the courts to rule legislation unconstitutional, there is a real possibility that minority or less well-represented groups will be ignored, or poorly organized groups maneuvered out of opposition to measures not in their interests.[17]

Private collectives, then, engage in what is now called "rent seeking" by attempting to influence legislation to their advantage. Political processes are a method of reconciling politically important interests and of "maneuvering the populations into a unity of national government and a distribution of economic privileges" (Commons 1939: 35). Statute law is a "kind of organizing and experimenting with the efficiencies, scarcities, customs, and expectations of the people, sometimes expediting them, sometimes inhibiting them" (Commons 1925: 382).

Commons's ideas on the operation of legislatures may be partly responsible for the notion that he conceptualized working rules and changes in those rules as the intended outcome of political processes of decision making. However, Commons himself placed much greater emphasis on the customs and common practices of individuals and concerns and the decisions of the common law courts in deciding disputes. Customs arise out of "similarity of interests and similarity of transactions engaged in" (Commons [1934] 1961: 699). This, of course, is quite consistent with the idea that customs arise and spread spontaneously in an invisible-hand fashion, but Commons was not willing to limit his analysis to such invisible-hand processes or to assume that all rules originally derived in that way would be self-enforcing. He was aware that many, if not most, social situations create conflicts over the rules to be followed. In Commons's work there is no presumption that the invisible hand will result in harmony over the rules to be followed; instead it is the court system that must decide disputes and create order, or a "workable mutuality," out of conflict.

When a dispute over some rule, practice, or custom reaches the court, the court will decide on the existing practices or customs. The court bases its decision on its own criteria of precedent, public purpose, and reasonableness, and approves what it considers to be "good" practices and eliminates what it considers to be "bad" practices. In this fashion, a custom may be given legal sanction, or the practice of some particular concern may be generalized into a social rule: "A local practice becomes common law for the nation" (Commons [1934] 1961: 712). This process in which the courts take over good practices and eliminate bad practices is one that Commons is constantly referring to. Commons talks of the development of labor law out of the conflicts brought about by union activity. For example, the 1842 decision holding that "a combination of workmen designed to benefit themselves . . . was not an unlawful conspiracy" ([1934] 1961: 770). Similarly, with the development and refinement of the concept of intangible property out of business practice, Commons traces the development of the court's distinction between a "reasonable" power to withhold (goodwill) from the unreasonable exercise of that power (privilege). Commons criticizes Veblen's cynical view of business versus industry as due to his "failure to trace out the evolution of business customs under the decisions of the courts" ([1934] 1961: 673). It is through this process of common-law decision making that collective action "takes over . . . the customs of business or labor, and enforces or restrains individual action, wherever it seems to the Court favourable or unfavourable to the public interest and private rights" ([1934] 1961: 5).

The evolution of customs and practices on the part of individuals and concerns is thus of key importance in Commons's work. This process, however, is mediated by the court system, which decides the disputes that arise. The courts consider economic efficiency, but their criterion of reasonableness also includes an ideological element and is conditioned by precedent and by the "habitual assumptions" of judges (Commons 1932: 24–25). The operation of the court system is also linked to the broader set of political processes through the political influences that bear on the initial appointment of judges. The overall process of institutional evolution is one that involves a close interaction between spontaneous processes and those involving efforts at institutional design. The evolution of custom is largely spontaneous; statute law is largely a matter of intentional design. In between are the common law courts, deciding disputes and making law, in large part by deciding which rule or practice should be taken over into law, but according to criteria that include social purposes.[18] Commons's system is one of an interaction between evolution and design or, as he would have put it, between the wills of individuals and the collective will as expressed by governments and courts. Thus, in his discussion of Adam Smith, Commons states that the mutuality of market exchange was not a result only of the invisible hand, but a "historic product of collective action in actually creating mutuality of interests out of conflict of interests." Had Smith taken this view:

Instead of an unseen hand guiding the self-interest of individuals towards general welfare he would have seen the visible hand of the common-law courts, taking over the customs of the time and place, in so far as deemed good, and enforcing these good customs on refractory individuals. . . . Within this institutional history of collective action . . . he would have found the reasons why, in his England of the Eighteenth Century, the human animal had reached the stage where he could say, "This is mine, that is yours; I am willing to give this for that." (Commons [1934] 1961: 162)

5.2.3   *Organizations and organizational change*

Both Veblen and Commons discuss organizations and the forces that prompt changes in organizational forms. As might be expected, each writer provides a view consistent with his thinking about the way in which custom and law develop over time, and both provide some interesting links running from organizational change to changes in more general social rules.

Veblen's work concentrates on the corporation, its size, financial structure and internal organization. Veblen has been accused of seeing the firm entirely as a "device for financial manipulation and control" and not as "an administrative device of managerial organization" (Hill 1967: 279, 282), but this is not a correct reading. Veblen was concerned with both aspects (Rutherford 1980, 1992a).

Veblen's discussion of the evolution of business enterprise focuses on the joint impact of new machine technology and the development of markets and financial institutions. Before the advent of machine processes capable of large scales of production, industrial operations tended to be independent of one another, served relatively narrow markets, and were managed by the owners of the concern:

It was then still true, in great measure, that the undertaker was the owner of the industrial equipment, and that he kept an immediate oversight of the mechanical processes as well as of the pecuniary transactions in which his enterprise was engaged; and it was also true, with relatively infrequent exceptions, that an unsophisticated productive efficiency was the prime element of business success. ([1904] 1975: 23)

With modern machine production came larger output levels, the extension of markets (including stock markets) and, most significantly, a growth in the variety and scope of the "conjunctures of business" ([1904] 1975: 24). This gave rise to vastly increased opportunities for profit (or loss) through pecuniary or financial manipulations or through strategic business maneuvers of various kinds. The pecuniary side of the business came to demand more attention and "the point of chief attention for the business man . . . shifted from the old-fashioned surveillance and regulation of a given industrial process . . . to an alert redistribution of investments from less to more gainful ventures, and to a strategic control of the conjunctures of business through shrewd investments and coalitions with other business men" ([1904] 1975: 24–25).

In describing the money-making activities of businessmen, Veblen used the term "predation" and presented business activity as a competitive strategic game played against other businesspeople (and consumers) in which the sole object is private pecuniary gain. These gains are often related more to questionable advertising techniques, stock market manipulations, and the making (or breaking) of business consolidations than to productive efficiency ([1904] 1975: 161). Much business activity actually involves "obstructing, retarding or dislocating" productive activity. The hallmarks of business are meretricious publicity, obstruction of traffic, and limitation of supply ([1919] 1964: 92–93, 100).

Veblen's view of the firm as a device for the manipulation of markets, does not, however, imply that businessmen are not interested in minimizing the cost of production of the output they do produce, or in the efficient management of the industrial plant. For Veblen, the advent of the new technology, particularly when combined with the growing importance and complexity of the financial side of business, led to a growth of specialization of function within the management of the firm (Veblen [1901] 1971, [1904] 1975: 24). According to Veblen ([1914] 1964: 222), the "modern businessman is necessarily out of effectual touch with the affairs of technology as such and incompetent to exercise an effectual surveillance of the processes of industry."

That the business community is so permeated with incapacity and lack of insight in technological matters is doubtless due proximately to the fact that their attention is habitually directed to the pecuniary issue of industrial enterprise; but more fundamentally and unavoidably it is due to the large volume and intricate complications of the current technological science, which will not permit any man to become a competent specialist in an alien and exacting field of endeavour, such as business enterprise, and still acquire and maintain effectual working acquaintance with the state of the industrial arts. (Veblen [1914] 1964: 224)

Veblen ([1914] 1964: 222) argues that businessmen have come to recognize their own technological incompetence, that "a businessman's management of industrial processes is not good even for the business purpose – the net pecuniary gain." Because of this, they have begun to employ professional "experts" in the form of "efficiency engineers" ([1914] 1964: 222, 345). These efficiency engineers "combine the qualifications of technologist and accountant" and have the duty of minimizing cost, or of taking "invoice of the preventable wastes and inefficiencies due to the business management of industry" ([1914] 1964: 222). They are, however, expected to give their findings in terms of price and of business expediency, as "efficiency in these premises means pecuniary efficiency" ([1914] 1964: 345), and while the "immediate oversight of the plant and its technological processes" is delegated, overall control and managerial discretion is not. As one would expect from material presented above: "initiative and discretion in modern industrial matters vest in the owners of the industrial plant, or in such moneyed concerns as stand in an underwriting relation to the owners of the plant" ([1914] 1964: 351).

The idea of the engineer and his industrial or technological functions is pursued further in Veblen's later work. Veblen speaks of the engineers and industrial experts moving into "more responsible positions in the industrial system," and "growing up and multiplying within the system" (Veblen [1921] 1965: 44). The constant supervision of these technological experts has become "indispensable," and they have come to constitute "the general staff of industry, whose work is to control the strategy of production at large and to keep an oversight of the tactics of production in detail" ([1921] 1965: 53). Veblen also discusses the "technology of physics and chemistry" ([1923] 1954: 251), and argues that new advances in technology have thrown "the technicians more and more into a position of immediate and unremitting responsibility" for the "mechanical organization of work" ([1923] 1954: 254). The technician "has come up and grown great as a factor in productive industry, has grown to be one of the major institutions in modern life." ([1923] 1954: 256–257).

Veblen clearly regards both the financial and managerial developments that occur within the firm as intended adjustments to new pecuniary and technological conditions. Nevertheless, it is these adjustments, particularly the development of specialized technological occupations, that provide the basis for the unintended changes in social conventions and norms, as outlined earlier.

Veblen's ideas on organizations have also been carried over into later work in the OIE. Veblen's work suggests a growing separation between ownership and management, and this theme was developed by Berle and Means ([1932] 1947) and by Galbraith (1971). These writers, however, both develop the idea that managers may operate the corporation with goals other than profit maximization in mind, an argument not to be found in Veblen's own work. Veblen's other concern, that of corporations developing in ways designed to exercise monopoly control over markets, is a staple of the OIE.

As might be expected, J. R. Commons's approach to organizations was somewhat different. One of Commons's major concerns was to bring "collective action" in the sense of collective organizations or "going concerns" such as corporations, unions, political parties, and associations of all kinds more explicitly into economic analysis.[19] For Commons ([1934] 1961: 58), a going concern could be viewed as "a joint expectation of beneficial bargaining, managerial, and rationing transactions, kept together by 'working rules' and by control of the changeable strategic or 'limiting' factors which are expected to control the others."

This conception raises a number of interesting points. First, it is clear that Commons is seeing organizations as *coalitions* that are based on the expectation of joint benefit. The relations between the members that go to make up the collectivity are regulated by the concern's own working rules, and these rules may be just as powerful and binding on individuals as social rules enforced by law. Second, the evolution of an organization will occur either out of the resolution of conflicts of interest between different interest groups within the organization or through the organization having to respond to new economic conditions or challenges that arise out of the processes of economic growth. Commons discusses the history of American unionism in terms of the need for workers to organize and reorganize as the expansion of markets altered and expanded the competitive challenges faced by labor (Commons 1909). Finally, in responding to new challenges or to internal conflicts, organizations develop new practices, and these new practices can become the basis of judicial decisions affecting the common law or government legislation or regulation. In this way, Commons saw the "best" practices developed by private collectives being taken over into law and applied to all similar organizations as a part of the process of artificial selection.

Commons's concepts of bargaining and managerial transactions are obviously well suited to the analysis of the growth of firms and the choice between market or hierarchy that has become a staple of the

NIE (Medema 1992). Commons was obviously aware that more or less may be left to the market or brought within a firm, but he provided only hints and no extended discussion of the evolution of the firm in terms of the changing scope of managerial and bargaining transactions. Unfortunately, neither Commons's work on transactions nor his view of organizations as coalitions of interests were developed by later writers in the OIE. If they had been taken up, many of the issues now discussed in the NIE literature on organizations might have been more fully anticipated.

5.3   Evolution and design in the NIE

Many writers within the NIE have placed special emphasis on evolutionary processes. This is most obvious in the game theoretic literature dealing with the evolution of those most basic rules of social order, but evolutionary arguments have also been applied to the common law and to the organizational forms of business. Arguments based on deliberative institutional adjustment, however, are far from absent. The large literature on the theory of the state is a case in point. In contrast to the OIE, the NIE has developed separate literatures on social conventions, courts, legislatures, and on organizations. With the exception of some work in economic history (North 1990), few attempts have been made to provide an integrated discussion.

5.3.1   *Social conventions and the invisible hand*

There is now a large literature that attempts to model the emergence of certain basic social conventions as the unintended outcome of the repeated interaction between self-interested players.[20] The process is an invisible-hand type in that the games are non-cooperative and no individual or individuals intend or design the social rule.[21] The social rule emerges spontaneously, as the result of each player pursuing his or her own advantage within the given context of the game.[22]

Most of the arguments can be related to repeated-coordination, hawk/dove, or prisoners' dilemma games. The characteristic feature of such games is that either more than one Nash equilibrium exists, so that individual rationality alone is not sufficient to generate the desired coordination of action on a single play, or that some or all of the Nash equilibria represent a collectively inferior result. The payoff matrixes for very simple two-person versions of these games are shown in Figure 1.

Figure 1

(a)
Coordination game

		A	
		Drive on Left	Drive on Right
B	Drive on Left	(2,2)	(0,0)
	Drive on Right	(0,0)	(2,2)

(b)
Hawk/dove

		A	
		Dove	Hawk
B	Dove	(2,2)	(0,10)
	Hawk	(10,0)	(-5,-5)

(c)
Prisoners' dilemma

		A	
		Cooperate	Defect
B	Cooperate	(3,3)	(0,5)
	Defect	(5,0)	(1,1)

In coordination games (Figure 1a), it is easy to see that each individual has an incentive to find and maintain a coordinated solution. In the example given here, both coordinated solutions have the same payoffs, but this need not be the case. As long as some coordinated solution is preferred to non-coordination, the basic structure of the game remains essentially unchanged. Two Nash equilibria exist, either coordinated solution being an equilibrium. In a single play the players may fail to coordinate their action, but if the game is repeated, the incentives to find a coordinated solution are very strong, and one would expect coordination to be achieved sooner or later. Once a particular coordinated solution is achieved, for example, all to drive on the right-hand side of the road, the solution will be self-policing. No individual would want to switch from the rule that everyone else is following. In this manner social conventions can be reached and maintained spontaneously. Of course, it may not be easy to reach a coordinated solution, and these difficulties are compounded as the number of players and number of possible solutions increases. In such cases, the process of coordination may be solved through salience (Schelling 1960; Lewis 1969). That is, one solution appears conspicuous because of some particular feature it possesses. Salience is not a matter of one coordinated solution having higher payoffs than another but something about the nature of the solution is suggestive. Salience indicates the importance of shared cultural context in determining the particular solution found. It also indicates that if payoffs vary across solutions the process may not converge on the one that has the highest payoffs, but the one that is most salient. The outcome will be *a* socially desirable one in that coordination is achieved, but not necessarily the most socially desirable one (Field 1984; Vanberg 1986).

A similar point can be made by replacing the notion of a Nash equilibrium by the slightly stronger idea of an "evolutionary stable strategy" (ESS) (Maynard Smith 1982). All evolutionary stable results must be Nash equilibria, but not all Nash equilibria are evolutionary stable. The argument here is borrowed from the biological notion of animals from a homogeneous population meeting randomly in pairwise interactions. One strategy "may be 'defeated' by another, and therefore eventually driven out in the evolutionary sense, if it yields on average a lower return than the other" (Hirshleifer 1982: 14). In biological models the payoffs are measured in terms of biological fitness, but "if we substitute utility for fitness and learning for natural selection, this approach can be adapted to explain human behavior" (Sugden 1989: 91). The average payoff to adopting a given strategy is a combination of the payoffs and of the proportion of the population playing each strategy. In a coordination game, if the payoffs are the same for either of the coordinated solutions, then the first solution to gain more than 50 percent of the population will drive out the other. If the payoffs vary across coordinated solutions, then the solution with the higher payoffs will require a smaller proportion of the population to initially adhere to it in order for it to defeat the other. If mutual driving on the left paid only 2 to each player, while mutual driving on the right paid 5 to each player, then drive on right will defeat drive on left provided more than 2/7 of the population initially choose to drive on the right. If less than 2/7 of the population initially choose the right-hand side, the ESS would be to drive on the left, despite being Pareto inferior.

Coordination problems of a different, but extremely common, type lie behind games of "chicken" or "hawk/dove" (Figure 1b). Here the problem is not to get everyone to do the same thing, but to get people to behave in *complementary* ways. The Nash equilibria consist of the two off-diagonal elements (A plays hawk, B plays dove; A plays dove, B plays hawk) and a mixed strategy of each player playing hawk a certain proportion of the time (8/13 in the example given). If we were to imagine a homogeneous population meeting randomly in pairwise interactions with the only choice of playing hawk or dove consistently (no mixed strategies), then neither strategy defeats the other. As the proportion of those playing hawk rises, so does the probability of costly hawk/hawk interactions, and the average payoff falls. With the dove strategy, as the proportion playing dove rises, so do the returns from adopting the more aggressive hawk alternative. The evolutionary equilibrium will involve 5/13 of the population playing dove and 8/13 hawk. This equilibrium, however, will be characterized by fairly frequent and undesirable hawk/hawk clashes. The way out of this problem, at least in the absence of some external authority to enforce certain patterns of behaviour, is not particularly easy to see.

It has been argued that if the game is modified to allow for strategies that constitute a more complex behavioural rule, then there is a possibility for an evolution toward equilibria that avoid conflict. Hirshleifer (1982: 21) analyzes the case of hawk, dove, and "Bourgeois," where the Bourgeois follows a rule of "when you are the first comer in possession of the resource, play like a hawk; when the late comer, play like a dove."It is assumed that half the time Bourgeois will be in the ownership situation and half the time in that of the interloper. Under these circumstances the Bourgeois/Bourgeois interaction provides another Nash equilibrium, but it is the *only* one of the three strategies that survives in stable evolutionary equilibrium (Hirshleifer 1982: 22).[23] Similarly, Sugden (1989: 91–92) analyzes the case of interactions between three strategies: (i) the rule if A play hawk, if B play dove; (ii) the rule if A play dove, if B play hawk; and (iii) a mixed strategy of playing hawk 8/13 of the time whether you are A or B. If individuals occupy the roles A and B on a random basis, it can be shown that strategy (iii) is not an ESS whereas the other two are. If all but a small group play (iii) and the deviators all play (i), then against (iii) playing opponents they will do no worse than following any other strategy, but when paired with themselves they will gain higher payoffs. Use of the deviant strategy will thus tend to gain, and as it grows the payoffs from adopting it also increase.

Arguments such as these have been used to explain the spontaneous evolution of certain rules such as the rule "first come first served" or the rule of respect for prior ownership. These rules define the role of the first comer (hawk) and those who come after (dove). As long as each individual has a reasonable opportunity to be first, the rule, once established, will be self-enforcing. For each individual who comes late it is better to defer (and possibly come first next time) rather than engage in a fight (Sugden 1989: 85).

What is important to note here, however, is the special nature of the circumstances required to obtain this spontaneous evolution. Each individual must have a reasonably equal chance of playing the role of hawk. If individuals continually find themselves playing dove, the rule is not likely to remain self-enforcing. The rule "If King play Hawk, if not play Dove" is not self-enforcing and is likely to result in periodic and expensive competitions to be King. Less dramatically, individuals may be able to affect the role they get to play by undertaking some prior action or investment activity. In such cases the competition to play hawk may result in some considerable dissipation of the gains.

Just as important is the prisoners' dilemma (Figure 1c). Here the defect strategy is dominant, and the Nash equilibrium is in the defect/defect cell, a solution that represents a collectively inferior result. The difficulties of gaining the cooperative solution in a prisoners' dilemma are considerable, and even if it is gained, it has a strong tendency to break down. Even if all but one individual is cooperating, it pays that individual to defect. No matter what proportion of players initially cooperate, the defect strategy seems to be the only ESS. As with hawk/dove, however, more complex strategies can, under certain conditions, provide a way out of the dilemma.

A strategy that can lead to mutual cooperation is one of reward and punishment, also called "reciprocity" (Vanberg 1986), "tit for tat" (Axelrod 1984), and "retaliator" (Hirshleifer 1982). To take the simplest two-person case first, a strategy of rewarding cooperation by cooperation and punishing defection by defection can lead to mutual cooperation in the case of repeated interactions between the given pair of players. If both players adopt the strategy and begin with a cooperative response, the cooperative solution will be the one initially established. The incentive for each player not to abandon the strategy and defect is that defection will lead to punishment in the form of the future non-cooperation of the other player. As long as the game is to be played an infinite or indefinite number of times,[24] and rates of time discount are not too high, mutual cooperation will be maintained over time. Similarly, if a player who initially adopted a defect strategy knew or was to discover that the other player was playing the retaliator strategy, then he would have an incentive to also adopt that strategy, leading to mutual cooperation. The stability of mutual cooperation based on retaliatory strategies is, however, very fragile. A single defection by either party leads to an endless sequence of retaliations. Similarly, any *misinterpretation* of a cooperative response as a defect response will lead to a sequence of further retaliations. Thus, "the slightest possibility of misperceptions results in a complete breakdown in the success of tit for tat" (Dixit and Nalebuff 1991: 107–108).

Things are even more problematic in the case of a large population engaging in random pairwise interactions. Here we might imagine some of the population playing retaliator and some playing a pure defect strategy. If retaliators can recognize other retaliators and distinguish them from defectors, then the average return to retaliators will be greater than that for defectors and retaliation is the ESS.[25] The crucial difficulty here is in the problem of recognizing defectors. If prior recognition is not possible, and identification only takes place after the first play between any pair, and is not communicated to others, then retaliation may fail to defeat a pure defect strategy. Under these circumstances retaliators do very badly in all first-time encounters with defectors, while the defectors do well. In future meetings retaliators will defect when paired with a (known) defector. All encounters with other retaliators result in mutual cooperation. Which strategy will defeat the other will depend on the exact structure of the payoffs and the rate of the discount involved (Schofield 1985).[26] Thus,

the mechanism of reciprocity cannot be expected to generate sufficient incentives for cooperative behavior generally, but under certain restrictive conditions only. In general, the chances that the interacting parties may meet again and the chance that a defector can be identified as such have to be large enough that sufficient expected gains and losses from future interaction are at stake to make cooperation the preferable choice. These chances typically decrease, however, with increasing numbers of individuals involved in the relevant setting and with a decreasing length of the time-horizon with which individuals engage in particular groups. (Vanberg 1986: 95–96)

For these reasons, the solution to prisoners' dilemma problems frequently requires small communities with shared norms and reciprocity (Taylor 1982), or institutions deliberately enforced by some organized agency. Spontaneous processes based on individual self-interest cannot be relied on to produce cooperative solutions in all, or even in most, cases. As noted in Chapter 4, beneficial social institutions do not always emerge, and society may remain trapped in a stable but undesirable non-cooperative state.

If a social convention is successfully established out of interactions between individuals in one area, it may then spread by analogy to other areas. In a passage that brings Veblen's idea of "crossing and grafting" to mind, Sugden argues that "the conventions that are best able to spread are those that are susceptible to analogy," and that, therefore, "we should expect to find family relationships among conventions, and not just a chaos of arbitrary and unrelated rules" (Sugden 1989: 93–94).

The game theoretic discussion of the emergence of social conventions is so fascinating because it demonstrates that self-interested behaviour can lead to social co-ordination and socially beneficial outcomes. It also provides a basis for understanding the circumstances under which a spontaneous evolution of a social convention is more or less likely to occur. The analysis does, however, have a number of limitations. First, all of the cases discussed above apply to the emergence of an institution in a situation where none existed to deal with that specific problem previously. In terms of historical processes of institutional change, it is more usual to find situations where a relevant institution is already in existence. In such cases even greater limitations apply to spontaneous processes. Although a certain convention or institutional rule may emerge spontaneously, it may not be possible to change that rule without deliberative institutional reform, even if everyone would be made better off as a result. Shifting from one unit of currency or measurement, or changing the side of the road driven on, requires a change by the whole society that has to be centrally coordinated and enforced.

Second, the social conventions that emerge in this analysis have an epi-phenomenal quality. The social convention is simply a product of self-interest leading all individuals to adopt the same rule; the rule does not otherwise have an impact on the players. Another way of expressing this is to point out that the social rule that is the product of the game is always a convention and never a social norm in the true sense. Indeed, the game theoretic analysis cannot, by its very nature, encompass the emergence of a social norm where one did not exist before, as a norm implies social approval and disapproval, the emergence of which would change the payoffs facing each player. Even the notion of the tit-for-tat strategy in a PD game fails to capture the notion of *social* disapproval. The development of a norm means the development of a new payoff structure. Given that social norms do in fact develop spontaneously, and that social disapproval can act as a powerful sanction, this limitation of game theory serves to understate the power of spontaneous processes. However, it is clear that norms do not always emerge to fill a need and are probably also affected by circumstances such as the size of the social group. Furthermore, social norms carry patterns of sanctions that make the development of new modes of behaviour difficult. Innovators suffer social disapproval, discouraging experimentation. This problem is only compounded by the fact that a given social norm may be part of a system of inter-related rules. Institutional change is frequently a matter that involves, to a greater or lesser extent, the deliberate acts of positive legislation. In some cases, changes in law may aim to bring about changes to the existing social norms. Hayek's references to evolutionary group selection do not provide any satisfactory solution to these problems, a point that is recognized even in the Austrian literature (Vanberg 1986; O'Driscoll and Rizzo 1985).[27]

These various limitations to invisible-hand processes mean that particularly in large societies, the basic rules required for social cooperation may not always arise spontaneously out of individual self-interest, be of a self-enforcing nature, or adjust to new conditions. Their spontaneous development may require a pre-existing disposition to adopt social rules, or they may instead have to be deliberately designed and/or enforced in an organized way. Observation tells us that invisible-hand processes cannot be expected to, and often do not, provide solutions to all of the coordination and conflict resolution problems faced by social groups.

5.3.2 *Legislatures and courts*

Limitations on invisible-hand processes are quite explicitly recognized in many parts of the NIE. Although it is sometimes argued that state intervention may *decrease* the likelihood of achieving voluntary cooperation (Taylor 1976, 1987; Mueller 1989: 15), it is also recognized that large, complex, and impersonal economic systems require the organized enforcement and design of property rights and other legal rules: "without the state, its institutions, and supportive framework of property rights, high transactions costs will paralyse complex production systems, and specific investments involving long term exchange relationships will not be forthcoming" (Eggertsson 1990: 317; see also Mueller 1989: 17). The apparatus of the state includes the system of government that establishes laws by statute, and the judicial system that both enforces law and generates common law. Within the NIE, common law courts are generally seen as tending to adjust the law over time in ways that improve economic efficiency (Posner 1977), while the activities of governments in making and altering statute law are often cast in a much more dubious light. The state may be essential for economic growth but it can also be "the source of man-made decline" (North 1981: 20). In either case, however, "positive theories of the state hold a central role in neoinstitutional economics because the state sets and enforces the fundamental rules that govern exchange" (Eggertsson 1990: 59). The normative issues will be explored more fully in Chapter 6.

The discussion of the rule-setting role of the state has undergone considerable development within the NIE. The early literature on property rights has been described as containing only a "naive theory" (Eggertsson 1990: 249–250). In this approach the formal political, judicial, or decision-making processes are not explicitly modelled at all; it is simply presumed that property rights will adjust on the basis of changes in the set of relative prices facing the individuals making up the community involved. This type of naive theory has been strongly criticized by Field (1981: 185), who points out that it implies that political and economic processes function as if there was some "omniscient social maximizer" who will choose the set of property rights so as to maximize social "output net of overhead costs." In very similar terms Eggertsson states:

The role of Government in the naive theory of property rights is implicit. It is assumed that the state will create a general framework of property rights that permits individuals to maximize the community's net wealth by taking advantage of the division of labor and market exchange. In situations where transactions costs are high, the state maximizes wealth either by assigning property rights directly to individuals, or by redefining the structure of rights in specific ways. (Eggertsson 1990: 271)

Both Field and Eggertsson find examples of the naive view in the early work of Demsetz (1967), North and Thomas (1973), and also in Richard Posner's interpretation of common law (Posner 1977, 1981, 1987).[28]

The problems with the naive approach are both theoretical and empirical. On a theoretical level, two main issues arise. First, the informational requirements for such a maximization process are considerable. One specific issue is that of the difficulty of estimating how enforcement costs may vary with the rule structure (Field 1981: 187), but the problem is more general than enforcement costs alone. The second issue is that if institutions always adjust to relative prices in such a way as to maximize "net wealth," then the specific history and traditions of a given society or culture do not seem to matter. The naive theory is inconsistent with giving any kind of real importance to history and with notions of path dependence (Field 1991). The empirical difficulties are that legal rules do appear to differ across countries even where technologies and endowments are pretty much the same (Field 1991), and that, as Eggertsson points out at length, it is quite easy "to find cases from all parts of the world that contradict the naive theory." Thus, "a rudimentary knowledge of economic history or modern economic systems rules out the naive model as a general theory" (Eggertsson 1990: 271, 275).

At the other extreme to the naive theory is the interest group or rent-seeking theory of the state, an approach that has been applied quite broadly to the explanation of changing property right structures in economic history (Ekelund and Tollison 1982; Libecap 1986). This approach focuses on the *redistributive* effects of changes in property rights. A group may invest resources in lobbying and in making political contributions, in an attempt to gain a particular change in property rights in its members' favour. This may occur despite the fact that the property right arrangements favoured adversely affect the total level of national income. Thus, to understand "the observed pattern of property rights" one must analyze the "likely winners and losers of economic and institutional change and their interaction in the political arena in specific settings" (Libecap 1986: 228). It is generally argued, following Olson (1971), that redistribution will occur from "broadly defined interests to narrowly defined ones, from unconcentrated industries to concentrated industries, from the disorganized to the organized," but exactly "which groups are sufficiently organized to win redistribution gains" may vary from place to place and from time to time (Mueller 1989: 449).

A pure interest group theory, however, also has a number of difficulties. Although a good deal of government legislative action can be seen as redistributive and corresponding to the interests of small interest groups, not all government legislation, even redistributive legislation, can be explained in this way (Mueller 1989: 457). Norms of fairness and social justice seem to play a role both in which redistributive programs are adopted and which are not. The explanation is also often stretched past breaking point, as when Landes and Posner (1975: 893) argue that First Amendment rights in the United States were "extracted by an interest group consisting of publishers, journalists, pamphleteers and others who derive pecuniary and non pecuniary income from publication and advocacy of various sorts." As Mueller (1989: 244) dryly observes, "by such fruit has the dismal science earned its reputation." A final, and important line of criticism, is that the interest group theory seems to imply that those in control of the state apparatus have no interests (other than the social interest) of their own. Thus, "in much of the rent-seeking writings there seems to be a presumption that the state will somehow supply output-maximizing property rights, if only special interest groups can be contained" (Eggertsson 1990: 279).

More complex models of the state attempt to combine both the public good–providing and redistributive or exploitative view of the state. One particular example of this is found in the economic history of Douglass North (1981, 1990). North's analysis begins with the state in the control of a ruler. The state is "an organization with comparative advantage in violence, extending over a geographic area whose boundaries are determined by its power to tax constituents" (North 1990: 21) and is thought of as "trading" certain public goods, notably protection and justice, for tax and other revenues. The ruler attempts to maximize his net revenues, but this maximization is constrained by the possibility of the ruler being deposed by other powerful individuals or groups, and by the available means for gathering revenue. The state establishes and enforces a set of property rights, but the set of property rights that maximize the ruler's income (subject to his constraints), will generally depart from the set that would maximize wealth for the nation as a whole. This is because, first, the ruler needs to "avoid offending powerful constituents," and, second, because an "inefficient" property right (e.g., a monopoly) may lead to higher net revenues for the ruler. In the first case, the ruler is responding to the bargaining power of important individuals and groups who may be able to challenge him and take over control of the state; in the second case, he is responding to the high transactions costs of measuring and collecting taxes on income as compared with other sources of revenue. Even in the absence of powerful interest groups, the state would still not necessarily provide wealth-maximizing property rights (North 1981: 28).

To the extent that the set of property rights established does allow growth to occur, the growth process itself will lead to changing relative prices and changing bargaining power among groups. As a result, property rights will be altered to reflect the new set of relative prices and new alignment of pressure groups. A change in relative prices that "improves the bargaining power of a group of constituents" may force the ruler "to give up some of his rule making power" (North 1981: 29–30). Historically, such processes have resulted in the development of a polity that includes "a representative body reflecting the interests of constituent groups" and capable of "bargaining with the ruler," and, ultimately, to modern representative democracy with multiple interest groups (North 1990: 49). There is, in this, many similarities with J. R. Commons's view of the historical evolution of the state.

The public choice literature has also produced models that combine many of the elements outlined above with an application of the economic model to the behaviour of politicians. Politicians are assumed to be interested in their own reelection, and they therefore attempt to maximize the votes that they receive (Downs 1957). This has led to a large literature on the strategies and policies adopted by individual politicians and political parties to achieve and retain office, and to forward the legislation they wish to see passed. This includes the analysis of median voter theorems, log rolling and vote trading, and control of committee agendas. Complete models also incorporate interest groups. A politician may support an interest group in order to obtain funding for his or her advertising and campaigning. The policies of interest groups may or may not be compatible with the interests of voters, but voters, due to "rational ignorance,"[29] may not be well informed concerning a politician's activities. Political processes are thus conceptualized as a competition between politicians "in which politicians provide policies or legislation to win votes, and voters and interest groups provide campaign funding as well as votes." The legislation provided will consist of "either public goods with characteristics that appeal to given groups of voters or income transfers from one sector of the population to another" (Mueller 1989: 229). The outcome of these political processes is not easy to predict, although within the public choice literature it is argued that the forces acting on politicians will frequently result in property rights that have adverse economic consequences:

If political transactions costs are low and the political actors have accurate models to guide them, then efficient property rights will result. But the high transactions costs of political markets and subjective perceptions of the actors more often have resulted in property rights that do not induce economic growth. (North 1990: 52)

The judicial system and the evolution of common law has also been the subject of much debate in the NIE. Posner's argument is that the common law tends to yield economically efficient solutions, but he provides no analysis of why this might occur, other than the argument that judges give weight to economic efficiency in their decisions. Since then the literature has divided into (i) works that seek to find an alternative foundation for Posner's argument, one based on an invisible-hand process; (ii) works that emphasize the significance of precedence in the common law in constraining the decisions of judges; and (iii) works that see the decisions of judges as the outcome of several factors, including precedence and their own (ideological) convictions of the public good.

Rubin (1977) and Priest (1977) have both attempted to explain the (supposedly) efficient nature of the common law in invisible-hand terms. The preferences of judges are suppressed by assuming their decisions to be of a random nature. Individuals, pursuing their own interests, bring cases to court. The upshot is that the greater the incentives individuals have to challenge a given rule, the more it will be challenged, and the more likely that it will be overturned. The final, and critical, part of the argument is that individuals will tend to challenge inefficient rules more frequently than efficient rules as the potential gains from litigation will be greater (versus out of court settlements) in such cases. This argument has been modified by Goodman (1978); in his view, litigants who benefit from an efficient rule will be able and willing to invest more in the litigation than those who favour an inefficient rule, and this increases the probability that the judge's decision will favour the efficient outcome. These arguments do have the characteristics of an invisible-hand process. Individual litigants bring cases to court on the basis of their own private interests, and the overall impact on the character of the common law is an unintended consequence. The argument has its problems, however, both with regard to its efficiency implications (as explained in Chapter 6) and the associated characterization of the processes by which judges make decisions. Rather than being random or a function of the expenditures of each side, the decisions of judges are strongly affected by precedent and their own conception of the public good.

The best examples of the work emphasizing the importance of legal precedence and other rules is that of Hayek and Heiner (1986). Hayek's views were outlined earlier. Heiner's pertain to rule following more generally, as discussed in Chapter 4. Given the complex decisions facing judges and the unreliability of their individual judgement, attempts to provide "optimal" solutions on a case-by-case basis could produce "growing conflicts and misaligned incentives" (1986: 243). Precedent constrains judicial decision making, but such constraints may result in actual performance superior to the result if case-by-case maximization were attempted.

Finally, some writers stress the judge's own idea of the "public good." An example of this line of argument is found in North (1981). North claims that many key legal decisions have, in fact, run counter both to the interests of important and well-organized interest groups and also to long legal precedent. He argues that although the initial appointment of judges may reflect pressure group influence, their "subsequent decisions over a wide range of policies reflect their own convictions of the 'public good'" (1981: 57). With regard to the recent history of court decisions in the United States, North argues:

> The Miranda decision, and indeed many of the Warren Court decisions, were not only reversals of legal developments over a long precedent but ran counter to the major interest groups. The Court's support of school busing and the decision of Judge Boldt on Indian rights over the fishing in

Washington State are still other instances; indeed such judicial decisions are so common that observations reflecting a judge's view of the public good are everyday occurrences. A positive theory of ideology is essential to an analysis of the role of the independent judiciary in affecting resource allocation. (North 1981: 57)

Again, this position has substantial similarities with that of J. R. Commons.

5.3.3   Organizations and organizational change

A large literature in the NIE deals with the evolution of particular organizational forms (particularly firms). This literature generally takes the surrounding legal/institutional environment as a given and focuses on the cost-reducing properties of certain organizational forms and organizational innovations (Coase 1937; Williamson 1975, 1985). The approach to the firm found in the NIE is based on the concept of a firm as a set of long-term contracts between the owners of various different resources. These long-term contracts substitute for market relations between individual resource owners. The firm is thus a coalition that, to continue, must supply some benefits to those who make up the coalition over a purely market relationship.

One claimed benefit is in the larger joint output that can be produced by a team as compared to the same individuals working apart from each other and with only market relationships existing between them (Alchian and Demsetz 1972). Team production, on the other hand, generates problems of shirking, and this in turn leads to members of the team selecting or employing an agent to monitor the performance of team members. The performance of the agent can be ensured by granting the agent a claim on the firm's residual income.

In contrast, Williamson and others emphasize the problems created by purely market interactions for the owners of highly specialized assets. For Williamson, the major function of organizations is to economize on the transactions costs that would be borne in the attempt to utilize the market by writing contingent claims contracts. Given bounded rationality, opportunism, and asset specificity (sunk costs), complex contingent claims contracts are difficult and "costly to write, execute, and enforce." Thus:

Faced with such difficulties, and considering the risks that simple (or incomplete) contingent claims contracts pose, the firm may decide to bypass the market and resort to hierarchical modes of organization. Transactions that might otherwise be handled in the market are thus performed internally governed by administrative processes instead. (Williamson 1975: 9)

The structure of firms can thus be seen as the outcome of the problems of agency and the existence of transactions costs, and should respond to these costs. Williamson (1985) explains the development of the M-form firm, vertical integration, the financial decisions of the firm, and many other phenomena in terms of their ability to reduce transactions costs. Although this is a persuasive argument in many respects, it has been criticized for overlooking the fact that the organization of firms has other functions and responds to other factors than simply the problems of agency and the reduction of transactions costs. In particular, the structure of firms may have to do with the requirements of technology, or with certain power relations and conflicts within the firm, or with establishing a position of market control (Chandler 1977; Dugger 1983; Perrow 1986; Marris 1988), exactly the issues raised in the OIE. Furthermore, neither agency theorists nor transactions cost theorists are very explicit about exactly how the evolution of organizational forms comes about (Dow 1987).

Some agency theory adopts a strong version of functionalism and presumes that every organizational device has a function and that the function explains its presence. Williamson shows a greater concern with the processes involved and seems to suggest that organizational innovations stem from the successful organizational experiment occasionally carried out by some particularly insightful manager. Given this success, other firms will attempt to imitate and the innovation will spread. This explanation relies on the intentions of those who control the firm and their desire to reduce costs or increase profits. As long as the process is thought of in terms of adaptive rationality, it is not, as claimed by Dow (1987), inconsistent with the notion of bounded rationality used elsewhere in Williamson's work. Williamson also sometimes makes reference to competitive pressures of selection and to evolutionary explanations of the organization of firms.

A number of analysts have attempted to apply evolutionary ideas to the firm (Alchian 1950; Enke 1951; Friedman 1953; Nelson and Winter 1982). Those who emphasize evolutionary selection in explaining the nature of the firm believe that certain behaviours, decision rules, or organizations are selected regardless of the intentions of the actors involved. They argue that even if the managers of firms do not intend to minimize cost or maximize profits, competitive selection favours the survival of those firms that are behaving (or are organized) in ways that do generate optimal results. In fact, as already mentioned, it is extremely difficult to avoid giving intentions a key role. First, competition, to be competition, requires some condition of viability such as positive profits. It is hard to imagine managers of firms in capitalist markets not realizing this. Second, there have to be processes that generate new routines or decision rules. Again, it is hard to believe that such processes are comparable to random variation in biology. Moreover, there must be some method by which "successful" routines or rules are generally discovered or spread to the population at large. Given these problems, it is not surprising to find "evolutionary" models frequently referring to processes consisting of a deliberate search for profitable routines by potential entrants and by those firms already in the market making low or negative profits (Nelson and Winter 1982), and to processes of imitation, whereby firms attempt to copy routines that are successful elsewhere (Nelson and Winter 1982; Alchian 1950). Such models may avoid maximizing assumptions but are usually still intentionalist in nature (see also Jacquemin 1987: 13–17).

A final issue concerns the link between organizations and more general social rules, which has not received much attention in the NIE thus far, although this is beginning to change. Obviously, it is recognized that organizations attempt to change legal rules in their favour, or maintain already favourable ones, through involvement in political processes such as lobbying or making campaign contributions, or by engaging in court challenges. North points out that economic organizations may "devote resources to changing political rules directly to increase their profitability" (1990: 79), and that "the institutional framework is being continuously but incrementally modified by the purposive activities of organizations bringing cases before the courts" (1990: 97). In addition, organizations, in pursuit of their own objectives, may behave in ways that gradually alter the informal rules, customs, and traditions that constrain their activity (1990: 86–87).

North also looks at how organizations may bring about institutional change more indirectly, through their effects on the nature and size of the stock of knowledge available to a society. In any given society, entrepreneurs will seek economic advantage along lines that are in a large part determined by the existing institutional structure. In pursuing their objectives, they will create a demand for certain types of knowledge; therefore, the stock of knowledge accumulated will be deeply affected by the nature of the goals that entrepreneurs pursue. The knowledge accumulated may relate to "piracy" or to productive industry (North 1990: 78). The nature of this knowledge, in turn, will affect the long-run economic growth performance of the society in question. Economic growth will bring about changes in relative prices, in relative bargaining power, and also in the beliefs and subjective perceptions of decision makers. The extent and direction of institutional change is thus affected in unintended ways by the entrepreneur's pursuit of his or her own objectives (North 1990: 84).

5.4   Conclusion

The foregoing discussion has highlighted a number of similarities and differences within and between the OIE and the NIE. Within the OIE, there is a key difference between Veblen's view that institutional changes are largely the result of unintended consequences and habituation to new circumstances rather than purpose, and Commons's position that such changes can be attributed to the purposes of individuals and collectives and their interaction through conflict and conflict resolution. Of course, this difference becomes less marked once it is understood that Veblen is talking about the unintended impact of intended technological change on the fundamental patterns of life and ways of thinking of individuals. Indeed, although there are obvious and important differences in emphasis, and in the processes each concentrates upon, both writers find a role for the deliberate design and enforcement of institutional rules, as well as unintended processes of institutional evolution.

Similarly within the NIE, the Austrian component wishes to concentrate almost exclusively on invisible-hand processes, and there is a stronger tendency to try to produce arguments that do not rely on intentionality. Nevertheless, a close analysis of invisible-hand processes in the game theoretic literature does not, despite occasional claims to the contrary, give reason to believe that such processes are sufficient to generate and maintain social order, particularly in the case of large, complex societies. The attempts to apply invisible-hand or evolutionary arguments to the common law and to organizational change are also suspect. In most of the NIE, and obviously in the more general discussions of economic history, both evolutionary and design processes are included.

There are obvious differences between the old and the new. Within the OIE, the arguments are presented in the context of a broad discussion of historical change and frequently lack analytical detail. With the notable exception of the work by North and other economic historians, most of the NIE literature is narrower and more ahistorical, but contains much more analytical detail. The NIE also tends to stress individual rationality, changes in cost–benefit conditions, and economizing to an extent not found in the OIE, but there are also many areas of complementarity and even of agreement.

Examples of complementarity can be found in discussions of the invisible-hand and public choice theory. The game theoretic literature in the NIE dealing with invisible-hand processes is explicitly formal and ahistorical. Even given its limitations, it provides a more penetrating insight into the exact strengths and weaknesses of invisible-hand processes than the more historically oriented discussions of Veblen or Commons. The work in the OIE should, however, serve to remind game theorists that not all unintentional processes of relevance to institutions, particularly to institutional change, generate beneficial consequences or can be captured in given payoff matrixes. The public choice literature, with its detailed examination of a wide variety of models of collective choice, should also be of substantial interest to any member of the OIE. As John Adams (1990: 850) recently tried to tell his fellow old institutionalists, "public choice theory has raised fascinating and valid points about voting procedures and electoral conventions and these deserve inspection." The other side of this is that Commons's insights into political and judicial processes should be found equally relevant by any new institutionalist. Complementarities also exist in the literature on organizations. There is, after all, nothing in Veblen's emphasis on market power and technology, or Commons's emphasis on economic challenges and conflict resolution, that is necessarily at odds with also giving significance to problems of moral hazard and transactions costs.

There are a number of strong similarities in other areas as well. They are perhaps most obvious in the case of Commons and the NIE. Commons's emphasis on pressure groups and political parties, the significance of the common law, the motivations of judges, types of transactions, and collective organizations is in many ways similar to the main concerns of the NIE. North's discussion of judges, his interest in the interaction between organizations and general institutional rules, Williamson's emphasis on transactions and on hierarchy replacing market (managerial transactions replacing bargaining transactions) are areas of particularly close contact.[30]

The connection between Veblen and the NIE is much less close, but this is probably because the NIE has so far placed much less emphasis on new technological means as a driving force of institutional change. Nevertheless, Veblen's discussions of how institutions affect the pace and direction of technological change and the accumulation of knowledge and of how these bring about unintended institutional consequences has links to North's discussion of "the ongoing interaction between organized economic activity, the stock of knowledge, and the institutional framework" (1990: 78). North's distinction between institutions that encourage "piracy" and those that encourage productive activity has much more than a passing resemblance to Veblen's distinction between cultures based on "predation" and those that encourage industry.

Overall, both traditions are strikingly similar in their theoretical subject matter: both discuss how social conventions emerge and spread and are changed, how court systems operate to generate the evolution of common law, the various incentives that act upon politicians and parties and that go to shape the actions of governments, and the forces that lead to organizational change.

CHAPTER 6

Efficiency and reform

This chapter turns to the explicit evaluative and normative issues that have been raised in judging institutions and institutional change and the way they have been dealt with by both old and new institutionalists. The first and most fundamental of these issues is how "efficiency" or "social good" is to be defined. Within the context of changing institutional rules these terms become extremely difficult to delineate in any unambiguous way. Another issue concerns the extent to which evolutionary, market, and non-political processes generally are better guarantors of efficiency or social benefit (however defined) than processes of deliberative governmental intervention and design. The third question of concern here is what is the most desirable type of institutional reform, assuming, of course, that some "failure" in existing institutions has been found to exist. The answers given to these questions vary both within and between the old and the new institutionalism. It useful to begin the discussion with some of the principal approaches and areas of debate.

6.1   Approaches to appraisal

The various approaches to normative issues found within the OIE and NIE can be categorized in a variety of ways. In some categories, the approaches of the old and the new tend to finish up on opposite sides, although with varying degrees of difference and with less distance between the more moderate representatives of each group than is sometimes thought. With other categories, however, no such clear division between the old and new appears. These categories reveal some interesting areas of contact between writers more usually thought to be in opposition.

The most obvious divisions between the old and the new relate to the latter's adoption of a generally favourable attitude to markets combined with a value system that is based on individualistic premises. By contrast, old institutionalists have tended to be critical of markets, have often advocated a greater amount of regulation or direct intervention by government, and for the most part have re-

jected the notion of the ethical ultimacy of existing individual preferences in favour of some other basis for valuation.

Old institutionalists criticize the performance of markets for the
inequities they create in the distribution of income, wealth, and
economic opportunity; the exercise of monopoly and other types of
economic power; financial manipulation and productive inefficiencies; macroeconomic instability and unemployment; the blocking of
technological and instrumental advance; and various forms of "waste"
such as competitive salesmanship (Veblen [1904] 1975; Tugwell,
Munro, and Stryker 1930; Commons [1934] 1961; Mitchell [1935]
1950; Ayres 1962). More fundamentally, the notion of the sovereign
consumer with given tastes and preferences is replaced by a view of
individuals as subject to the pressures of advertising and salesmanship and to the prescriptive power of existing social norms (Veblen
1899b; Galbraith 1971). The old institutionalists' ideas concerning
the power of institutions to mould individual aims and ideals, and the
evolution of such institutions over time, have been the major reasons
for their rejection of orthodox individualism. In place of this, old
institutionalists have adopted a social perspective that incorporates
explicit value judgements. In some cases they have taken to a cultural
relativism (Neale 1990), but in most cases an attempt has been made
to define criteria of judgement that can be seen as independent of
particular cultural norms, and relate instead to the most basic and
universal characteristics of human social "success." This is most
apparent in the work of Clarence Ayres and those who have followed
him, but the majority of writers in the OIE make some attempt to find
a locus of social values that is apart from any particular set of
institutionalized preconceptions.[1] This is, obviously, an undertaking
fraught with difficulty,[2] and a variety of positions can be found in the
OIE, positions that are not consistent with each other in all respects
(Ramstad 1989).

In marked contrast, the new institutionalist tends to look favourably
on markets and voluntary forms of contract, and to be much more
critical of the failures of government. Of course, it is recognized that
markets fail, particularly in the face of public good and externality
problems, and that certain public goods need to be provided by the
government. Nevertheless, it is obvious that governments are *not*
seen as necessarily pursuing the social interest, and for some, particularly those in the contractarian and liberal traditions, the major
problem is how to constitutionally *limit* the powers of government.
The values that lie behind these positions are individualist in nature
and often involve a reluctance to make interpersonal comparisons.

The best examples are the value judgements associated with Paretian welfare economics (that each person is the best judge of his or her own welfare; that social welfare depends only on the welfare of individuals; and the "Pareto postulate" that if at least one person's welfare is higher in social state x than in social state y, and no one's welfare is lower, social state x is preferred to social state y), or those associated with positions adopted by contractarians or by liberal believers in individual rights and individual freedom from coercion. As in the OIE, there is a debate over the compatibility of these major alternative positions (Sen 1970; Rowley and Peacock 1975; Sugden and Weale 1979; Sugden 1985; Pressler 1987).

Despite these differences between the OIE and NIE, which are both deep and real, the problem of institutional evaluation has other dimensions that cut across the lines of division. Perhaps the most obvious of these is the distinction that is often made between the evaluation of particular outcomes or end states and the evaluation of the processes that produce the outcomes. Examples of both types of evaluation can be found in the old and the new institutionalism. Within the OIE, criticisms of market performance sometimes utilize end-state criteria, be they based on criteria of social justice or on other measures of adequate economic performance. However, these appraisals are often linked to, or combined with, an evaluation of the process that produced the particular outcomes. Such process orientations stem naturally from the old institutionalists' evolutionary perspective and the influence of American pragmatist philosophers such as John Dewey (Petr 1984; Liebhafsky 1986; Tilman 1990). Here the evaluation concerns the processes involved in social choice or in arriving at social values; the acceptability of the process being judged on the basis of such values as democracy and participation in decision making, the representation of all interests, or the use of instrumental or scientific (as opposed to "ceremonial") *methods* of appraisal (Tool 1977; Hickerson 1987).

Somewhat similarly, the NIE contains both end-state and process approaches. The most obvious examples of end-state criteria are the conditions for a Pareto optimum or those embodied in a social welfare function, but other criteria such as productive efficiency or economic growth can also be found, although not always carefully distinguished from efficiency in a Pareto (welfare) sense (Saraydar 1989). It is noteworthy that many criticisms of the use of Pareto criteria, particularly when applied to changes in institutional rules, can now be found within the NIE (Demsetz 1969; De Alessi 1983; Eggertsson 1990), and approaches that are based on the evaluation

of the process that guides institutional choice or evolution are becoming more common. Two examples can be found in the work of
Buchanan and Tullock (1965) and Hayek (1967, 1973). Buchanan
and Tullock use a standard based on voluntary agreement, applied to
constitutions rather than the particular outcomes of constitutions,
while Hayek stresses individual freedom and the virtues of spontaneous evolutionary processes.

Further distinctions that cut across the old and the new can be
found both in Hayek's categories of rationalist and anti-rationalist
and in what might be called evolutionary optimism and pessimism.
For Hayek, "rationalism" means that people can, through the exercise of rationality and the use of scientific methods and knowledge,
come to understand the operation of the social system enough to
successfully redesign or modify the institutional system to better
serve the social benefit. With the notable exception of Veblen, who
made almost no proposals for active intervention in the institutional
system, virtually all old institutionalists are out-and-out rationalists.
However, so are virtually all neoclassicals. Even contractarians such
as Buchanan – who, on the basis of their own rational appraisal of
the system, propose the adoption of a modified constitution – fall
into the rationalist category. Rationalists also reject the Hayekian
(and more generally Austrian) view that spontaneous processes will
somehow work to select the best institutions. The rejection of this
optimistic view of spontaneous processes is obvious in Veblen and
elsewhere in the OIE, and is becoming more common in the NIE
(Buchanan 1975, 1978; Basu, Jones, and Schlicht 1987; Binger and
Hoffman 1989; North 1990). Writers in both the old and new institutionalism argue that institutions that are efficient or serve the common good may fail to emerge, while inefficient institutions may
persist (Veblen 1923; North 1990). At the same time, some old
institutionalists, especially Ayres, have produced highly optimistic
accounts of how political processes may work to guide institutional
change.

6.2   Efficiency and reform in the OIE

In the evaluation of institutions, the OIE can again be divided in a
Veblen–Ayres and a Commons wing. Both Ayres and Commons were
deeply influenced by John Dewey, but Ayres applied these ideas to a
Veblenian foundation, whereas Commons developed a somewhat
different interpretation related to his own system of thought. A great
deal of the more recent discussion of normative issues within the OIE
has been devoted to building upon the Ayresian position (Tool 1979,

1986), although more recently still the OIE has developed a "radical" wing that looks back to Veblen for inspiration and finds Ayres's approach not radical enough (Dugger 1989b). Commons was working toward progressive reform, and certainly not radicalism.

6.2.1   Veblen, scientific values, and instincts

Veblen's comments on the normative appraisal of institutions are not easy to interpret. He bases his argument in modern science and technology, but he also notes that his values are not absolutes, but derive from a particular material circumstance. In addition, he sometimes adopts a more humanistic stance, and certainly seems to give the basic instinctive nature of mankind a normative role (Coats 1954; Leathers 1990).

For Veblen ([1904] 1975: 310), modern science and technology brought with them certain habits of thought and "norms of validity." In the case of modern science and technology, these norms consist of a "scepticism of what is only conventionally valid," a thinking in terms of "impersonal cause and effect" and tangible performance, and a "matter-of-fact" conception of things ([1904] 1975: 310, 373; [1919] 1964: 12). These notions obviously lie behind a great deal of Veblen's criticism of business institutions and other cultural systems built on norms derived from earlier modes of thought:

The constituent principles of the established system of law and custom . . . have been conceived and formulated in terms of a different order from those that are convincing to the twentieth-century scientists and engineers. . . . The modern point of view in matters of law and custom appears to be somewhat in arrears, as measured by the later advance in science and technology. ([1919] 1964: 12)

Modern science and technology and their associated values frequently provide the benchmark for Veblen's evaluations. Science and technology are a "matter of tangible performance directed to work that is designed to be of material use to man"; the technician's world is one of material realities, and his "responsibilities are the responsibilities of workmanship only" (Veblen [1923] 1954: 107). Underlying virtually all of Veblen's extensive discussions of business (including his discussions of consumption behaviour and universities) and other "predatory" systems are the materialistic assumptions of modern science. Veblen ([1919] 1964: 22) adopts the role of the impersonal, sceptical, scientist probing the "vexation and misery" caused by outmoded, non-scientific, institutional principles.

Veblen suggests that the institutional system that will eventually emerge through habituation to the new material and technical conditions, and therefore embody the modern scientific point of view, is a scientific version of socialism. The "discipline of machine technology" is peculiarly designed to inculcate such "iconoclastic habits of thought as come to a head in the socialistic bias" (Veblen [1904] 1975: 351). The classes so affected look to an institutional system "run on lines of industrial coherence and mechanical constraint, not on lines given by pecuniary conjunctures and conventional principles of economic right and wrong" ([1904] 1975: 337). To the extent that Veblen provides any details of this system, it consists of an organization for economic planning, with engineers or technicians operating and coordinating the industrial system on the basis of technological criteria and in a way that "consistently and effectually" takes care of the material welfare of the underlying population ([1921] 1965: 166).[3]

All of this gives the impression that Veblen treated the values he associated with modern science and technology as ultimates or, at least, as the "best" set of values yet to arise in the course of human history. This, however, is far from being obviously the case. Veblen often appears to adopt more humanistic values and, as argued by Ross (1991: 213), "the hard-boiled mechanist in Veblen never fully dominated the humanistic idealist." Furthermore, Veblen not infrequently denied that science represented an ultimate or best set of values. In the preface to *The Instinct of Workmanship* ([1914] 1964: xi), he states, "The analysis proceeds on the materialistic assumptions of modern science, but without prejudice to the underlying question as to the ulterior competency of this materialistic conception considered as a metaphysical tenet." Even more clearly, he argues that "modern culture" has *not* "an all-round superiority, but a superiority within a closely limited range of intellectual activities, while outside this range many other civilizations surpass that of the modern occidental peoples" ([1906] 1961: 1). He does say that the particular strengths of matter-of-fact and scientific insight give modern civilization a clear advantage in competition with other cultures, but this is not to be taken to mean that modern civilization is best in all respects. In creative art, deft workmanship, mythmaking, metaphysical insight, religious devotion, political finesse, and "warlike malevolence and abandon," other cultures have surpassed the modern ([1906] 1961: 2–3). Such things as these "have all in their time been felt to justify themselves as an end of endeavor." They have since come to "dwindle in men's esteem . . . while the achievements of science are held higher" ([1906] 1961: 3), but this

latterday faith in matter-of-fact knowledge may be well grounded or it may not. It has come about that men assign it this high place, perhaps idolatrously, perhaps to the detriment of the best and most intimate interests of the race. There is room for much more than a vague doubt that this cult of science is not altogether a wholesome growth – that the unmitigated quest of knowledge, of this matter-of-fact kind, makes for race-deterioration and discomfort on the whole, both in its immediate effects upon the spiritual life of mankind, and in the material consequences that follow from a great advance in matter-of-fact knowledge. ([1906] 1961: 4)

Scientific values, then, only appear superior once a scientific view has been adopted. The circular and self-referential nature of this position is explicitly recognized by Veblen ([1908b] 1961: 32; Samuels 1990). Nevertheless, there are indications in Veblen's writings that he sought another basis for values, one that was independent of the preconceptions embodied in particular cultural schemes and founded on his view of the basic instinctual nature of mankind.

Veblen ([1914] 1964: 13) defines instincts as "hereditary traits." Instincts do not "automatically determine response" in the human case, but they "all and several, more or less imperatively, propose an objective end of endeavour" ([1914] 1964: 3). These ends may be quite general in nature and leave a "wide and facile margin of experimentation, habituation, invention and accommodation" ([1914] 1964: 14). Despite this, "these native proclivities alone make anything worth while, and out of their working emerge not only the purpose and efficiency of life, but its substantial pleasures and pains as well" ([1914] 1964: 1).

Veblen identifies two instincts in particular with the "material well-being of the race," its "biological success," and "continued life-interests" ([1914] 1964: 25). These instincts are the parental bent, defined as a concern with the "life and comfort of the community at large, and particularly for the community's future welfare," and the instinct of workmanship, defined as a concern with "serviceability for the ends of life," or "efficient use of the means at hand and adequate management of the resources available for the purposes of life," and an interest in "practical expedients, ways and means, devices and contrivances of efficiency and economy, proficiency, creative work and technological mastery of facts" ([1914] 1964: 31, 33). Veblen attaches considerable importance to these instincts. Although he sees workmanship as quite capable of being sublimated to other more urgent concerns, or "contaminated" or distorted by other instincts, proclivities, or institutionalized principles, he also argues that it is workmanship with its emphasis on efficiency and technological proficiency that has "brought the life of mankind from the brute to the human plane" ([1914] 1964: 37). Veblen also clearly associates workmanship and parental bent with those values that prevail "generally throughout both the highest and lowest cultures" ([1914] 1964: 14, 26–27). It is this idea of instinctively based values that enabled Veblen to resist charges of subjectivism,[4] maintain his stance of scientific objectivity, and yet adopt a more broadly humanistic position than would be suggested by the values of modern science and technology alone. There are, of course, links between workmanship and technological advance, and between what Veblen called the instinct of "idle curiosity" and the development of science, yet what is important to understand is that modern science and technology are simply *particular*, and historically relative, manifestations of these instincts. The instincts themselves are broader, capable of more varied expression, and more fundamentally connected with the human spirit and basic human values. In this way, for example, Veblen can give generous treatment to the system of handicraft, owing to its workmanlike characteristics, despite its heavy admixture of pre-scientific teleological and animistic habits of thought ([1914] 1964: 231–298). What consistently draws Veblen's criticism are "predatory" cultures based on principles of mastery and obedience and invidious distinction, at odds with workmanship and parental concern.

Note that although Veblen associated workmanship and parental bent with human welfare and progress, he did *not* think that such instincts were always present in sufficient force to bring about socially desirable institutions or progressive change, or even to avert disaster. In a famous passage Veblen writes:

In the course of cultural growth most of those civilizations or peoples that have had a long history have from time to time been brought up against an imperative call to revise their scheme of institutions in the light of their native instincts, on pain of collapse or decay; and they have chosen variously, and for the most part blindly, to live or not to live, according as their instinctive bias has driven them. In the cases where it has happened that those instincts which make directly for the material welfare of the community, such as the parental bent and the sense of workmanship, have been present in such potent force, or where the institutional elements at variance with the continued life-interests of the community or the civilization in question have been in a sufficiently infirm state, there the bonds of custom, prescription, principles, precedent, have been broken. . . . But history records more frequent and more spectacular instances of the triumph of imbecile institutions over life and culture than of peoples who have by force of instinctive insight saved themselves alive out of a desperately precarious institutional situation, such as now faces the peoples of Christendom. ([1914] 1964: 24–25)

This clearly suggests that while the community's material welfare (even survival) is bound up with the expression of the instincts of workmanship and parental bent (as opposed, for example, to the "self-regarding" impulses),[5] there is no guarantee that the processes of cumulative institutional change will actually work out to allow such an expression. Evolution is not necessarily a matter of improvement or of greater efficiency. Institutionally embedded patterns of thought and action can fail to adjust, or adjust too slowly, and lead societies to disaster.

Despite this viewpoint, Veblen was not someone who advocated active social engineering or held that scientific knowledge was primarily instrumental in purpose. Perhaps influenced by C. S. Peirce's view of science (Dyer 1986; Rutherford 1990c), Veblen saw science as an expression of idle curiosity. Science "creates nothing but theories," it is knowledge "without ulterior purpose," knowledge of "what takes place" rather than of "what had best be done" ([1906] 1961: 18). Thus, while being highly critical of existing institutions, Veblen was not an active reformer and only occasionally involved himself with practical suggestions or with organized attempts to bring about institutional change.[6] This attitude provides a clear contrast with many of his more reform-minded contemporaries, and also with later institutionalists such as Mitchell, Commons, and Ayres who were all heavily influenced by the instrumental philosophy of John Dewey (Tilman 1984). In the words of Dorothy Ross (1991: 213): "Veblen wanted science to provide critical insight into the course of evolution, not become a tool to control it. Although in the end he could not keep fully to that proscription himself, it separated him sharply from his liberal colleagues' conception of their task."

In recent years some institutionalists have become critical of the reformist stance that dominates the OIE, and have looked back to Veblen for a foundation for a more radical approach (McFarland 1985; Dugger 1989b). To date, this attempt to define a "radical institutionalism" has not successfully surmounted the twin difficulties created by Veblen's rejection of activism and the more reformist position implied in the instrumentalist philosophy that has since become a distinguishing mark of the OIE (Rutherford 1993).

6.2.2 Ayres and instrumentalism

No other member of the OIE adopted quite the same positions as those put forward by Veblen. Later institutionalists were strongly influenced by John Dewey's instrumental view of science and took a far more activist view of their role in generating, through enlightened government intervention, institutional and economic reform. Wesley Mitchell's discussions of institutional reform and social values show the first step in the combination of the Veblenian critique of business institutions with an explicitly reformist position and instrumental view of science.

Mitchell's response to social problems (and particularly the problem of business cycles) was to suggest that "intelligent guidance" be injected into the processes of economic evolution. Specifically, Mitchell suggested that an advisory national planning board be established, but the board would not impose its own social values. Mitchell thought that the goals pursued by this board should be those democratically arrived at through political processes: "in a democratic country national planners would have to serve as an agency for accomplishing what the majority desired." Nevertheless, the board could act as "an agency for focusing the intelligence of the nation upon certain issues, in the hope of formulating plans that would command sufficient confidence among their fellow citizens to be given trials." It could devise objective indices of standards of living and implement policy in an "experimental fashion," judging and revising plans on the basis of actual experience (Mitchell [1935] 1950: 101–102).

Mitchell's interest in planning, however, reflects another viewpoint – one that more fully links his work to the instrumental value theory of John Dewey and Clarence Ayres. Following Dewey, Mitchell made no sharp distinction between means and ends. Social values are not independent of the attempt to implement them. Mitchell argues that social values themselves evolve as a result of the processes involved in the attempt to apply knowledge to the solution of social problems. National planners

by throwing light upon the consequences that different lines of action would produce could contribute much toward making social valuations more rational. Perhaps in the long run the chief gain from trying to plan national policies in the light of their probable consequences would be the attainment of a more valid scale of social values than now prevails among us. (Mitchell [1936] 1950: 135)

This, then, shifts the emphasis from specific problems, specific instruments, or the social values that exist at a particular point in time to the *processes* of problem solving and democratic discourse as the source (or locus) of social values and their evolution over time. It was this point of view that was much extended by Clarence Ayres. Ayres combined many elements taken from Veblen, including the emphasis on workmanship and its contribution to the long-term progress of mankind, with a highly optimistic account of the potential of scientific knowledge and democratic processes to resolve problems and define social values.[7]

Ayres reinterpreted Veblen's instincts as "culturally significant patterns of behavior," and included both idle curiosity and parental bent as aspects of "the master pattern" that Veblen called workmanship (Ayres 1958: 289).[8] Ayres took over Veblen's concept of workmanship and elaborated it into his own notion of the "technological continuum," defined as the cumulative growth of tools, skills, and technological and scientific knowledge. This technological continuum is inherently progressive and is the force that both drives and provides continuity to the "life process" of mankind:

All that man has done and thought and felt has been achieved by the use of tools. The continuity of civilization is the continuity of tools. All the arts, all the sciences, and the whole elaboration of organized activity . . . together owe their existence and derive their substance from the continuity which links the surrealist's pigments to the clays with which the Aurignacian caves were daubed, and in terms of which the cyclotron is but a continuation of Neanderthal experiments in chipping flint. (Ayres 1962: 222)

In this fashion, Ayres (1962: 111) takes Veblen's point that technology prompts institutional change and turns it into "a master principle of economic analysis," with technology seen as "peculiarly dynamic" and "itself inherently progressive and the agent of social change."

Again building from Veblen, Ayres opposes this "inherently progressive" technological continuum to the static and backward-looking system of established institutions. Such institutions embody what Ayres calls "ceremonialism," including myths, mores, arbitrary distinctions of status and rank, and conventionalities of all kinds. For Ayres the problem of value is to distinguish those values that are a part of the progressive movement along the technological continuum, part of what enhances the "life process," from those that are merely ceremonial, with no progressive instrumental role or function.

Ayres applies these arguments to every community, and on that basis he claims to have found in the technological continuum a criterion of value that is transcultural, the "same for all ages, all peoples, and all cultures" (Ayres 1957: 125). What Ayres calls "true" values are not a matter of individual taste or institutional conditioning but a matter of demonstrable efficiency in the maintenance and promotion of the technical continuum and the life process. In terms of economics, Ayres argues:

Throughout the ages every community has owed its existence to its heritage of tools and apparatus. . . . It is by carrying on this instrumentally organized activity that every community – and each separate individual – "makes a living." Whatever contributes to carrying on this activity is economically valuable, and whatever arrests or even hinders this activity is therefore economically deleterious. (1962: 222–23)

He goes on to maintain that every economic choice "involves a judgment as to which of the alternatives presented will in fact contribute most to the continued efficient working of the technological system upon which all life depends" (1962: 223). His concern is long term, with "our continued – perhaps indefinitely continued operation," and not with "immediate, and perhaps temporary, operational success" (1952: 310).

Ayres presents such judgements in terms that make no distinction between positive and normative judgements. Value judgements are similar to scientific judgements, and the making of correct judgements itself depends on the growth of knowledge. In this manner Ayres argues that in determining "whether anything is good or bad, or whether any act is right or wrong," what is being sought is "clear and certain knowledge of its causal bearing on the life process of mankind" (1961: 122). Questions of value are not essentially different from "the mechanic's choice of the right tool" (1962: 219), and, as everyone "knows what *better* and *worse* mean with reference to tools" (1961: 8), values can be established in an objective manner provided the requisite scientific knowledge is available. Ayres is not always easy to interpret on this point, but his position appears to be that human life and history consist of a developmental sequence that rests upon the cumulative growth of ability and technique. Value can properly be found only within and through this instrumental process, and hence the technological continuum becomes both the criterion and locus of value. Ayres has sometimes been accused of placing machines above people, but he went to considerable lengths to combat such views, arguing that technology is "not something to be considered *instead of* the values of human life and personality," and that the technological continuum "does in fact contain and embody the judgment of all mankind and of all ages as to what is most valuable in life and what makes life worth while" (1945: 939).[9]

In his book *Toward a Reasonable Society* (1961), Ayres argues that the values of freedom, equality, security, abundance, excellence, and democracy are all true values, both promoted by and necessary for continued instrumental advance. These values are not desirable in and of themselves, but because they stem from instrumental *processes* of valuing. Thus, freedom is a true value not because of the ethical ultimacy of the individual, but because it is an outcome of the expansion of opportunities and alternatives created by industrial and technological advance and is necessary for the continuation of the progress of scientific and technical knowledge: "freedom is the condition *sine qua non* of intellectual, scientific and technological development" (1961: 182–184).

Ayres produces similar types of arguments concerning the other values he endorses. Equality is "the absence of artificial and arbitrary barriers"; inequality is the result of the power of tradition, superstition, and myth. Technological advance occurs in conjunction with the growth of scientific knowledge and instrumental reasoning and is in opposition to notions of "mythical group differences." Technical progress also requires that decisions be made on instrumental and not ceremonial grounds (Ayres 1961: 183–184). Similarly, for Ayres, real security is based on the use of tools, efficient organization, and the growth of knowledge. Security is a requirement for achieving freedom and equality. Maintaining security in the form of high and stable levels of consumption is also required by the high levels of output produced by modern industry. Ayres also discusses security from the effects of war. He does not deny that mankind may destroy itself with the weapons developed by modern science, but he disputes that modern wars have created more devastation in the areas affected than those of earlier times (1961: 214). He also argues that the growth of scientific rationalism leads to a decline in the nationalism that underlies much international conflict (1961: 213–219), and he maintains that new knowledge is progressive even if it is sometimes used for the purpose of war. Knowledge of atomic fusion is a good thing despite its use in war just as the invention of the "stone axe was a good thing notwithstanding its use also as a weapon" (1966: 88). On the issue of abundance, Ayres argues that modern technology is capable of producing abundance, in the sense of a "substantial degree of comfort," for the entire community. He also thought that high rates of economic growth depended on high levels of consumption (1961: 229–239). Excellence is linked to the advance of knowledge and technique. The value of excellence promotes advances in ability and technique and is itself promoted by the mass communication and education that "constitutes a powerful stimulus to the highest achievement" (1961: 247–256).

Ayres's comments on democracy deserve special attention. Democracy is an "operational concept" that stands for "the procedure by which alone all the other values can be achieved" (1961: 282). Democracy is not "merely" majority rule; its "essence" is the "process by which majorities are formed." This process involves "industrial-scientific culture," freeing individuals from prejudice and ignorance. Democratic self-government is "a possibility only because it is possible for large numbers of people – in effect, whole communities – to arrive at common conclusions" (1961: 282–283). Ayres does allow that confusion may exist as conditions change, and it is temporarily unclear "in what direction operational efficiency lies" (1961: 284–285), but "in all such cases the democratic process is a process of learning the truth and operating accordingly, and the unanimity towards which the process aims is that of the universality of science and technology" (1961: 285). If democracy were not an effective instrument, it would be a false rather than a true value (1961: 8–9, 171, 225–227; 1943: 480).

Ayres's attempt to demonstrate the indissoluble nature of the links between freedom, equality, security, abundance, excellence, democracy, and the technological process is prefaced and concluded with an exposition of what he calls the "unity of value." All true values increase together; there are no genuine conflicts between values:

Freedom is a necessary condition to the attainment of abundance, and abundance is a necessary condition to the attainment of freedom. Freedom is possible only among equals, and equality is possible only when men are free from arbitrary social distinctions. These values are attainable only when men have achieved a measure of security; and real security is possible only when men have achieved a measure of abundance. . . . But it is also possible only for those who enjoy freedom among equals; for any other condition implies a threat of insecurity. . . . Only free men can know excellence, and only affluent societies can afford to indulge in such pursuits. But only through excellence can societies become affluent. Such is the industrial way of life. It is a way of life to which modern man has dedicated himself because it is the epitome of the real values that take their meaning from the life process of mankind. (1961: 293–294)

Ayres's value theory pervades all his work. Those who suggest that his value theory is disjointed and incoherent (e.g., Walker 1979: 533) overlook the instrumentalist premise that is applied throughout. Ayres's theory focuses on the instrumental process and the values that are a part of and emerge from that process. Nevertheless, Ayres's approach is open to a number of criticisms, particularly with respect to his downplaying of the possible adverse consequences of instrumental advance, his rejection of the possibility of conflicts between true values, and his highly scientistic view of how values are defined and consensus achieved.

On the first issue, Ayres seems to simply dismiss the idea that rapid advances in knowledge and in technology can create problems in the maintenance of social cohesion and stability. It is also the case that although the growth of knowledge and technique has brought man from living in caves to modern industrial society, the long-term sustainability of the industrial way of life is far from obvious. Ayres does admit that, in a given cultural context, technical change may be a mixed blessing (1961: 169, 227), and that no amount of historical illustration can guarantee that man will not destroy himself with the tools he has developed (1961: 214), but against this he argues that the advance of the technological continuum brings with it the growth of a more rational approach to human affairs and expanded problem-solving abilities. Ayres does not seem to take too seriously problems created by errors in foresight combined with irreversibilities. He is optimistic that modern science will be able to detect problems as they arise and to successfully solve them. All that is required is to substitute instrumental for conventional modes of thought.

Ayres's argument that true values do not conflict with each other is also difficult to accept. In fact, Ayres avoids the possibility of conflicts by making all the specific values he endorses entirely subservient to his single master value of continued instrumental advance. Neither democracy nor freedom nor any other of Ayres's specific values are taken as valuable in themselves; they have value only because they arise from and push forward the technological continuum. It is surely the case, however, that individuals might rationally choose a system of democracy and individual freedom even if such values involved slower rates of instrumental advance.

Finally, Ayres downplays the problem of creating a consensus around particular values by arguing that true values are in some sense "objective." Ayres's position is similar to Dewey's: to say that something is desirable means that it has been so judged after an "impartial review of the relevant facts" (Rachels 1977: 158). However, Ayres seems to go beyond the Deweyian stance. Dewey argues simply that value judgements should be informed, a quite unobjectionable position. Ayres, in contrast, emphasizes the *unanimity* imposed by science; true values are good because they have demonstrable functional significance in terms of the life process, and to endorse other values is to fall into ceremonialism. Ayres's treatment of democracy as a process of generating unanimity on the basis of a rational assessment, the absence of any treatment of conflicts either between or over true values, and his lengthy analogy between value judgements and the mechanic's choice of a tool are all based on the idea that science can determine the nature of the life process and provide "clear and certain knowledge" of the instrumentally best set of actions or principles. In this there is "no room" for differences in taste (1962: 212–19, 1961: 122).

Although it should not be assumed that differences of opinion are not amenable to rational discussion and investigation, Ayres does not demonstrate that differences in outlook are necessarily due only to prejudice, dogma, or a lack of rationality or information. To sustain the Ayresian position, one would have to argue that science can always be conclusive in matters of value judgement. While emotionalism and dogma most certainly do colour debates about desirability, it is not clear that calm rationality and scientific appraisal would lead to agreement unless a consensus had already been reached on what weight or interpretation to give certain facts – in other words, on values.

Despite these difficulties, Ayresian value theory is very common in the OIE. Something of the same optimistic scientism can, for example, be found in Wendell Gordon's (1980) statement that

> the value theory of institutional economics . . . views value determination as a process involving continuously testing a technique (used in an effort to implement values) against the consequences of the use of that technique. It involves evaluating the technology against the results obtained when one uses that particular technology in an effort to implement a value. But, at the same time that the quality or the value of the technique is being tested, the value itself is subject to reappraisal in light of the consequences of the effort to implement it. Thus values themselves are reappraised against the consequences of trying to give them effect. . . . The value theory, then, is that values are created and identified (instrumentally determined) in a process involving self-correcting (or self-adjusting) value judgments. (Gordon 1980: 43–45)

Others, such as Marc Tool, have attempted to add more specific content to the Ayresian approach, but by doing so have edged away from Ayres's own process orientation and tendency to relate everything of value to the technological continuum. Tool talks of the criterion of social value consisting of "the continuity and instrumental effectiveness of recreating community non-invidiously" (Tool 1977: 841). Here, the "non-invidious recreation of the community" is the clearly stated end. Tool repeatedly stresses the "ultimate worth" of every individual and of the desirability of the fullest development of the human potential of all individuals. As pointed out by Mark Lutz "everything can now be seen as instrumental to self-realizing growth of insight and capacity" (Lutz 1985: 164), a humanistic position that contrasts with Ayres's own.

6.2.3 Commons and reasonable value

J. R. Commons's approach to institutional reform and to questions of social value was also influenced by John Dewey and by instrumentalist ideas more generally. Among old institutionalists, Commons's record of involvement with the actual processes of developing and implementing legal and institutional reform has no equal. However, Commons neither adopted the Veblen–Ayres dichotomy between technology and institutions (or the instrumental and the ceremonial) nor did he interpret instrumentalism in the highly scientific fashion of Ayres. For these reasons, Commons's approach has been seen as an *alternative* to that proposed by Ayres (Ramstad 1989).

Commons, like Ayres, stresses process and the continuity of human life and culture, but for Commons these were expressed not in terms of the technological continuum but in the maintenance of the "workability" of the economic and social system through the ongoing process of conflict resolution. Here there are no true and false values, no dichotomization of the instrumental from the ceremonial, but the continuing need to overcome conflicts as they arise in a way that creates a "reasonable" mutuality. As noted previously, Commons's notion of reasonableness included efficiency concerns but was not limited to efficiency. Reasonableness implies workability and a reconciliation of conflicts, and this may diverge from what is implied by efficiency criteria alone.

Commons's conception of reasonable value rests on several assumptions. The first is that the precise content of the concept of reasonableness is not something that can be defined outside of the particular historical context involved. Reasonable value "is the evolutionary collective determination of what is reasonable in view of all the changing political, moral, and economic circumstances" (Commons [1934] 1961: 683–684). The second point is that Commons believed the best *existing* practices provide a practical and achievable end-in-view. Commons explicitly rejected ends of the utopian variety – "heaven, communism, anarchism, universal brotherly love, universal virtue, universal happiness" ([1934] 1961: 741–742). But his emphasis on the best existing practices is quite consistent with continual progress. This is because "there are always individuals and concerns above the average, and the problem of social idealism through collective action consists in bringing the 'average' and those below the 'average' up to the level of those above the average." Third, Commons attached importance to the bargaining and negotiation between the affected parties themselves in determining a reasonable solution to conflicts of interest. Commons was deeply suspicious of the tendency of "experts," including economists, to claim to know best, when not, in fact, aware of all the issues and complexities involved. Commons certainly felt that experts could help in the process of negotiation, but they should not attempt to impose solutions, but provide information and examples of models that might be adopted. In achieving reasonable outcomes, Commons attached huge importance to the representation of all affected parties, and many of his suggested reforms were made with this goal in mind. Although Commons certainly possessed end-state ends in view, he was probably more concerned with establishing *processes* through which interested parties could negotiate solutions to their own conflicts of interest as they arose.

One final point to note is the highly pragmatic nature of Commons's approach. He rejected attempts to return to "any of the individualistic devices of our founding fathers" (Commons 1950: 294). He wished to preserve and increase liberties while recognizing the existence of collective organizations and unequal political, legal, and economic power. What was important to Commons was to ensure that the power of one individual or collective was not used to control the behaviour of others in an unreasonable fashion, and in practice that could be done only by creating new forms of collective action and working rules designed to equalize power, provide representation of interests, and liberate those currently operating under coercion, duress, or unfair competition. Commons's philosophical pragmatism is clearly displayed in the following quotation:

In modern economics the fears are mainly the fear of collective action, whether by governments, by corporations, or by labor unions. All collective action is looked upon with fear as leading straight to some form of dictatorship. But actually, in the cases as they arise, all kinds of collective action can be investigated to see whether, at the time and place, they are conducive to more real and equal freedom for individuals than the type of collective action which they displace. (1950: 237)

6.2.4   Markets and governments

Each of these various value systems has a different approach to the question of the respective roles to be played by markets and by governments. All in the OIE, however, agree that existing institutions are failing to generate the maximum social benefit. That institutional change is required is not in dispute; it is the type of change required and the role of central government intervention.

Veblen's strongest criticism is directed at business and market institutions. In Veblen's presentation, pecuniary and emulative standards of conduct lead to conspicuous consumption and waste ([1899b] 1924). Pecuniary standards lead to financial speculation at the cost of industrial efficiency, and, more generally, to making money at the expense of making goods. The competitive nature of business leads to competitive salesmanship, which is wasteful of resources. The competitive recourse to credit combined with modern methods of capitalization lead to business cycles. Under business conditions, the development of new technology leads to chronic excess capacity and eventually to monopoly consolidation designed to restrict output and control the level of new investment (Veblen [1904] 1975). Business is a matter of pecuniary gain or loss and "gain and loss is a question of accounting, and the accounts are kept in terms of the

money unit, not in terms of livelihood, nor in terms of the serviceability of the goods, nor in terms of the mechanical efficiency of the
industrial or commercial plant" ([1904] 1975: 84–85). Thus markets
are a matter of chicane, manipulation, and exploitation:

[T]he arts of business are arts of bargaining, effrontery, salesmanship,
make-believe, and are directed to the gain of the business man at the cost of
the community, at large and in detail. Neither tangible performance nor
the common good is a business proposition. Any material use which his
traffic may serve is quite beside the business man's purpose, except indirectly, in so far as it may serve to influence his clientele to his advantage.
(Veblen [1923] 1954: 107)

None of this criticism, however, led Veblen to propose government intervention or other action. Veblen saw governments as part
of the established institutional system, generally acting to further
powerful vested interests and not the social welfare. He often suggested that no real change was possible without a fundamental shift
in institutional base, something that could only arise as a result of
habituation to new machine technology and the development of a
new, more socialistic, ideology. He attacked reforms such as those
proposed by J. A. Hobson and others for failing to strike at the heart
of the matter, namely, the fundamental nature of business institutions (Veblen [1904] 1975: 255–260, [1899b] 1924: 344–345).

Veblen provided few details of the type of institutional reconstruction he had in mind. He did briefly outline a system of industrial
planning staffed by technical experts, but he did not indicate what
role, if any, markets might play in this system, nor the form that
political institutions might take. He occasionally made comments to
the effect that he equated "socialism" with radical democracy ([1904]
1924: 355), but how such a radically democratic system was to be
reconciled with his more centralized "soviet of technicians" ([1921]
1965) he never made clear.

Later institutionalists in the Veblenian tradition adopted many of
Veblen's criticisms of markets and of business, but looked to less
radical changes such as government legislation, regulation, and
planning as solutions. A general area of concern for later institutionalists was the problem of business cycles and depressions. Wesley
Mitchell (1927, [1935] 1950: 91) took business cycles as evidence
that "the automatic functioning of our business system is defective,"
and as providing the major justification for his proposed national
planning board. Since Mitchell's work, advocacy of some type of
national planning has entered the mainstream of the OIE. As well as
Mitchell, Rexford Tugwell and others involved in the New Deal were
strong supporters of planning (Tugwell 1932, 1935). J. M. Clark also

suggested a movement toward long-range planning (J. M. Clark [1935] 1965), and, more recently, Allan Gruchy (1939a, 1939b, 1947, 1972, 1987) persistently argued for a planning system along the lines of those in use in Scandinavian countries. Those in the OIE usually treat planning as the only way of overcoming macroeconomic instability.

Another major concern of old institutionalists has been with the inequality of the distribution of income. Members of the OIE have generally endorsed income support programs, Clarence Ayres being particularly associated with guaranteed income schemes (Ayres 1967). In Ayres's view, this proposal was also linked to the problem of depressions caused by underconsumption. For Ayres, "the citizens of industrial society must consume more abundantly . . . because if they do not industrial society will collapse" (1943: 480).

The OIE has also criticized markets for their problems of monopoly and imperfect competition, corporate power, failure to conserve natural resources, and, generally, tendency to promote "modes of living that fail to satisfy our emotional needs and our creative impulses" (Mitchell [1935] 1950: 89, [1936] 1950: 113; Tugwell, Munro, and Stryker 1930; Galbraith 1971). Criticisms such as these often seem to overshadow any appreciation of the things markets do well. Certainly, the idea that markets can be effective instruments for achieving a relatively efficient allocation of resources, and are extremely difficult to substitute for, seems to be insufficiently appreciated. It is often as if the old institutionalist simply refuses to ascribe any important functionality to markets at all. In virtually all cases, the preferred solution to the problems created by markets is seen as direct government intervention in the economy and in the gradual growth of non-pecuniary and non-invidious standards and principles. Despite the emphasis placed on government, there is almost no analysis of the way in which the government works. Moreover, the OIE fails to recognize that governments may fail. Many of its adherents seem to have a naive belief in the "self-corrective" nature of instrumental reasoning as expressed through democratic institutions (Gordon 1980; Rutherford 1990c).

Commons provides a slightly different view of the best type of intervention in the economy. Commons was less disposed toward planning, although he still thought of government as having a substantial role in establishing working rules and in setting up regulatory agencies and commissions. These agencies and commissions, however, should be independent bodies with their own staffs. Examples of Commons's approach are provided by the three major

Wisconsin reform programs with which he was involved. Commons drafted the Public Utility Law of 1907 to regulate public utilities. The law introduced permits without fixed terms and "a modern-type administrative commission with ample power to regulate the companies under its jurisdiction" (Harter 1962: 99). Commons was also a leading member of the American Association for Labor Legislation, which campaigned for the reform of labor law (Chasse 1991). He was instrumental in the formation of the Wisconsin Industrial Commission, which administered programs of industrial safety and workmen's compensation. The commission had considerable authority to adjust regulations to changing circumstances. Finally, Commons helped introduce the first state unemployment compensation program in 1932. It is significant that Commons thought of this program not merely as a way of providing some relief to the unemployed but as one that should provide incentives to employers to keep employment levels stable.

Commons extended his view of the potential role of commissions into a proposal to create a "fourth branch" of government that would investigate and administer working rules. This branch would consist of administrative agencies that would have the authority to experimentally institute rules of behaviour. The legislature's function would be to set only the general working rules and terms of reference of the agencies, and the courts would hear any disputes arising out of the actions of the agencies. Within these limits, the agencies would be free to undertake investigations and make rules to prevent possible disputes, provide for mutual advantage, and gain the cooperation of the parties concerned. They would differ from courts in that courts decide disputes only after the event (Commons 1939: 38–41, 1950: 277–283). In these proposals, Commons was attempting to ensure that all firms would not be forced to adopt the practices of the least scrupulous competitor. He was aware of the problem of agency capture, but seemed to apply it only to previous efforts at public regulation and not to his own proposed administrative agencies (1950: 290).

Unlike most old institutionalists, Commons rejected any further extension of direct government economic planning and even argued that the power of political parties should be reduced ([1934] 1961: 891). This could be done, according to Commons, by encouraging the formation of voluntary collectives to represent all interest groups. It was in the collective bargaining of these groups that Commons found the only refuge from totalitarianism. He even claimed that such collectives could form an economic or "occupational parliament of the American people, more truly representative than the Congress elected by territorial divisions," and that the "preservation of the American economic system against a totalitarian world, and against its own internal disruption, consists mainly in the collective bargaining between organized capital and organized labor, as against government by the traditional political parties" (1950: 33, 262).[10]

In these ways Commons hoped to reduce the role of rationing by legislatures and courts and to substitute a process of collective bargaining, cooperation, and experimental rule making (regulation) conducted in the light of the best available information. Such a process represents "pragmatic social philosophy" that "brings together again, this time by methods of scientific investigation, the separated fields of economics, ethics, and jurisprudence" (1939: 33).[11] Scientific investigation had an important role in Commons's work, particularly in helping to overcome "habitual assumptions" that had become obsolete or inappropriate. However, even with the best available knowledge, conflicts could only be resolved with the aid of all the skills of investigation, understanding, and persuasion, which Commons summed up in his "negotiational psychology" (Biddle 1990b). Although Commons had considerable faith in the functioning of democratic governments and common law courts, nowhere does he suggest that such processes of conflict resolution, even if augmented as he proposed, would necessarily succeed or be smoothly "self-corrective."

J. M. Clark shared a number of Commons's views. Clark (1957) was concerned with the problems created by monopoly, business cycles, what he called "diffused gains and costs" (externalities), and the impact of mechanization on the quality of life. Clark also expressed concern about the rapid pace of economic change and the difficulties of making the required adjustments. He explicitly rejected the idea of the adequacy of the "invisible hand" (1957: 183), and of purely individualistic ideas said that "there has always been more control than the theory of pure individualism calls for, for the practice has never followed the theory" (1929: 75; see also [1926] 1969).

Clark sought a middle road between individualism and socialism. In line with this view, he developed his idea of "workable competition," which relied heavily on maintaining conditions of free entry so that firms inhabiting a given market, even if only a few, are still subject to the discipline provided by potential entry (1940, 1961). More generally, Clark desired a system of social control of business exercised through democratic planning, regulation, and the development of new working rules. Although more disposed toward planning than Commons, Clark also stressed the potentially positive role of the bargaining between large private interest groups. Provided a balance of power existed between such groups, Clark ([1926] 1969) saw their competition and collaboration resulting in a system of "voluntary pluralism" operating through democratic government in a way that would avoid the extremes of socialism and pure individualism (see also Hickman 1975).

This Commons–Clark idea that the bargaining between organized pressure groups could provide a reasonable and workable compromise between conflicting interests is, however, one that has been subject to some telling criticism, particularly from Mancur Olson (1971). The key problem is that the groups that most readily form will be those that promise reasonably concentrated benefits to small numbers of people. Under such circumstances, individuals will have an incentive to voluntarily join and support the group. By contrast, where the group is large and benefits to each individual small, the group may fail to form, despite the large and significant overall social and economic interest. Small special interest groups may thus maintain "disproportionate power" (Olson 1971: 114–131).

6.3   Efficiency and reform in the NIE

Normative issues in the NIE are discussed in terms different from those found in the OIE. The discussion is framed in individualistic terms, usually avoiding interpersonal comparisons, and focuses on the "efficiency" of particular institutional arrangements. This is sometimes presented as the "identification of optimal or efficient arrangements under ideal conditions" (De Alessi 1990: 14), but such idealized approaches have been subject to considerable criticism, and a comparative institutional approach is often substituted. Nevertheless, whether the discussion concerns optimal arrangements or only those practical alternatives that are thought to represent efficiency improvements, numerous difficulties arise. As De Alessi (1990: 14) has pointed out, "Regardless of approach, the description of one contractual or institutional arrangement as more efficient than another typically involves alternatives with different (implicit) distributions of welfare," and "such comparisons raise difficulties at both theoretical and empirical levels."

A separate, but related, issue concerns the extent to which market, or competitive or spontaneous processes more generally, will operate to generate and select the more efficient rule or institutional arrangement. This issue raises the obvious question of whether non-governmental processes have the ability to guide social evolution in suitable directions, or how much deliberate government intervention may be required to produce efficient institutions and/or replace those that are inefficient, outmoded, or otherwise operating to the social disadvantage.

6.3.1   *Pareto efficiency and social welfare functions*

The criterion most widely used for judging welfare in neoclassical economics is Pareto efficiency. A Pareto-efficient position or optimum is defined via a set of marginal conditions requiring that all mutually advantageous trades have been made, that society is operating on its production possibility frontier, and that the marginal rates of product transformation are equal to consumers' marginal rates of substitution. If any of these conditions is not met, it is possible to achieve a Pareto improvement by reallocating inputs or outputs in such a way as to make at least one person better off (in their own estimation) without making anyone else worse off. Once the optimum has been achieved, no such Pareto improvements are available and to increase one person's welfare it will be necessary to reduce that of another. This, of course, assumes given factor endowments, given technology, and given tastes and preferences.

It is argued, further, that an economy in general competitive equilibrium will achieve the conditions for a Pareto optimum. This, however, requires that a set of additional conditions be met – namely, that information and transactions costs are zero, that all resources are fully allocated and privately held, and that all firms maximize profits and all individuals maximize utility. Departures from this idealized perfectly competitive state (due, for example, to transaction costs, externalities, public goods, or imperfect competition) have traditionally been seen as reasons for some kind of government intervention, including public good provision, public utility regulation, anti-trust laws, and imposition of optimal taxes or subsidies to correct externalities.

Within the NIE there has been much criticism of Pareto optimality as a basis for justifying intervention in the economy. Some of this is based on the comparative institutional approach discussed later in the chapter, but some is theoretical in nature. Demsetz, for example, argues that many of the supposed "inefficiencies" that are sometimes used to justify intervention are not inefficiencies at all, but only the results of risk aversion on the part of individuals, or of such things as uncertainty, indivisibility, or moral hazard, all of which are costly to reduce. For Demsetz, the traditional definitions of efficiency ignore the real scarcities and costs of information, and tend to presume people should behave differently than they do. Thus, "a relevant notion of efficiency must refer to scarcity and people as they are, not as they could be" (Demsetz 1969: 9).

Somewhat similar points have been made by others. De Alessi (1983) argues that many supposed inefficiencies are due to the presence of information and transactions costs. In the case of monopoly, if transactions costs were zero the monopoly would discriminate perfectly and the optimal output would result. The "inefficiency" of monopoly thus presumes the existence of transactions costs, but given these costs it can not reasonably be claimed that the monopoly is producing a sub-optimal output. The supposed "loss of efficiency is relative to an environment of zero transactions costs" and "is analogous to the welfare loss associated with the positive price of any resource" (De Alessi 1983: 68).

This point of view implies that "efficiency may be defined as constrained optimization, where the efficiency conditions describe the properties of an equilibrium solution determined by the conjunction of the theory and the initial observations, including the constraints, associated with the particular state of the world under consideration" (De Alessi 1990: 14). The constraints include the system of institutions and property rights that, in turn, affect transactions costs and the equilibrium position achieved. A shift in property rights will shift the equilibrium position that results, but each equilibrium will be efficient given those constraints. Comparison across different institutional regimes therefore requires more than a reference to the conditions for efficiency. What is needed is some "set of value judgements to provide a frame of reference, why one system is better than the other" (De Alessi 1990:15).

The problem raised by De Alessi is closely related to the long recognized difficulties created by changes in the distribution of income. Pareto efficiency is consistent with many different distributions and there is no guarantee that even an ideally competitive system will result in ethically acceptable distributions. Furthermore, most policy interventions, and particularly changes in property rights, are likely to have distributional consequences. Pareto efficiency alone gives no basis for judging between positions with different distributions of welfare.

The literature on social welfare functions can be seen as an attempt to provide criteria for social choice in cases where the notion of a Pareto optimum is an insufficient basis of judgement. The various approaches to social welfare functions share the basic Paretian norms: that each person is the best judge of his or her own welfare, that social welfare depends on the welfare of individuals, and the "Pareto postulate" that if at least one individual is made better off in social state x than in social state y and no one is made worse off, social state x is preferred to social state y.

The Bergson-Samuelson approach is to define a real valued social welfare function with the utility indexes of all individuals contained as arguments in the function. The social choice is defined as that which maximizes social welfare. If the function has an appropriate functional form (for example additive or multiplicative), it satisfies all of the Pareto value judgements, including the Pareto postulate. Unfortunately, it can be shown that for the social welfare function to give consistent results, the utility indexes must be cardinal, and interpersonal comparisons of utility must be possible (Mueller 1989: 373–378). Thus "cardinal, interpersonally comparable arguments are required to select a single best point from among the infinity of Pareto Optima" (Mueller 1989: 379).

Kenneth Arrow has pioneered an alternative method of constructing a welfare function. Arrow's work has been subject to a variety of interpretations, but the most interesting in the present context is to interpret the various axioms as defining a set of basic values that are to be incorporated in, or achieved by, the system of social choice. The question then is whether a process of social choice can be found that satisfies all the axioms.

The basic axioms or postulates consist of the Pareto postulate, the postulate of non-dictatorship, the postulate of transitivity, the postulate of range or unrestricted domain, and the postulate of the independence of irrelevant alternatives.[12] Arrow's impossibility theorem demonstrates that no social choice process (including majority rule) satisfies all the axioms. This is despite their being very moderate and "far weaker than one would wish to impose at the constitutional stage to satisfy reasonable notions of distributional equity" (Mueller 1989: 387). Again, the problem is one of choices over Pareto-preferred alternatives. Either interpersonal comparisons must be made explicitly, or extra value premises added that amount to the same thing. Although there is now some discussion concerning how interpersonal comparisons might be made (Elster and Roemer 1991), most orthodox economists have shied away from making interpersonal comparisons, and little agreement appears to exist concerning what additional value premises might be added.

Further problems are created if certain liberal values are introduced into the picture. Paretian value premises have traditionally been seen as consistent with an individualist or liberal position, but A. K. Sen (1970) shows that acceptance of personal liberty, defined as giving each individual the right to decide over one pair of social alternatives, can, under certain circumstances, give rise to conflicts between individual liberty and the Pareto principle. Conflicts arise where individuals have "meddlesome" preferences in which the consumption choices of others enter into their preference functions. Under these conditions, Pareto-preferred alternatives may be inconsistent with liberal values. If, however, the liberal values are themselves part of the individuals' preference functions, and work to modify or constrain their meddlesome nature, the conflict will not arise (Mueller 1989: 401–402).

The various approaches to social welfare functions demonstrate the impossibility of constructing such functions in a way that will satisfy basic normative principles without involving interpersonal comparisons of utility. Given these problems, most practical welfare analysis in the NIE makes little reference to social welfare functions. Apart from Pareto efficiency, the approaches that can be found are comparative institutional approaches, often based on productive or "dynamic" efficiency concepts, and those based on the contractarian approach to normatively acceptable principles or processes of social choice.

6.3.2 Liberal values and contractarianism

Many writers within the NIE, and most notably, those of Austrian persuasion, adopt liberal values that attach particular importance to individual freedom and the absence of coercion by the state. Attitudes such as this are responsible for much of the Austrian emphasis on the virtues of market organization. Markets are seen as allowing for *voluntary* exchange and as minimizing the need for governmental direction of economic activity. Indeed, it is worth noting the very substantial normative component in Hayek's work. As Scott Gordon (1981: 474) has argued, "In order to comprehend Hayek's philosophy it is necessary to recognize that his distinction between spontaneous order and order by design, between markets and governments, is a normative distinction not an instrumental one; freedom is the only moral value, and it is a property only of spontaneous order."

There are a number of problems with such extreme liberal positions. Even spontaneous orders involve coercion both in the form of legal rules enforced by a state apparatus and social norms enforced by social approval and disapproval. Indeed, given that social norms can be every bit as coercive and restricting to individuals as legal norms, it is not obvious that spontaneous orders (such as traditional societies) will always involve greater amounts of personal freedom than orders with greater amounts of governmental involvement. Even market orders are not able to entirely dispense with government, both for the provision of public goods, and for the specification and enforcement of property rights and other rules necessary for the market to function at all. Most important, individuals may have values other than freedom, and may, indeed, be willing to trade some degree of freedom in order to ensure that certain other values are achieved. If individuals do actually have such values, it is difficult to see how a consistent liberal could ignore the fact or dismiss their importance. The real problem, then, is not to minimize the role of government but to find a method of determining the appropriate role for government, given the valuations of individuals.

The contractarian approach promises to provide both a rational foundation for a modified liberalism and an escape from the apparent "nihilism" of social welfare function impossibility theorems. It does this by replacing the idea of an individual or government making interpersonal utility comparisons and reallocating resources and income in order to maximize social welfare with the much more palatable idea "that individuals from behind a veil of ignorance might make interpersonal utility comparisons by mentally assuming the utility functions of others, and might use these interpersonal comparisons to derive a set of political or constitutional rules that would govern society" (Mueller 1989: 439–440). For this escape to work, however, "it must be possible to reach consensus at the constitutional stage" (Mueller 1989: 440). The liberal nature of contractarian approaches and their normative appeal are apparent in the central importance given to the voluntary agreement among individuals on the rules to be followed. Contractarianism, however, does allow individuals to have values other than freedom, and does not necessarily imply an ultra-minimal state.

Much of the contractarian literature stems from Rawls (1971). Rawls attempts to derive a set of "principles of justice" by considering individuals reaching agreement behind a particularly opaque "veil of ignorance." Because of this veil, he argues, individual rationality alone will lead each individual to reach the same conclusion concerning the rules it is in his or her own interest for all to follow. This does not require bargaining or compromise, but it does require that the veil of ignorance screens out knowledge of the individual's own natural abilities, psychological features, social status, conception of the good, and particular life plans (Rawls 1971: 137–139).

Rawls argues that these conditions exclude probabilistic calculations, and he therefore claims that the maximin strategy is the rational approach. From this maximin strategy he derives his famous "difference principle," which involves maximizing the welfare of the worst off. Unfortunately, it does not seem that Rawls's attempt to show that rationality alone can lead to agreement over principles of justice succeeds. First, under conditions of uncertainty, the definition of rationality is ambiguous. Rawls wishes to break with utility theory and denies the possibility of probability calculations, but there is "the danger of circular reasoning," in that "an experimenter may devise his choice strategy to suit his preferred conclusions rather than derive his conclusions from independently established principles of rational choice" (Sugden and Weale 1979: 113; Mueller 1989: 415–419). Even if this problem could be overcome, Rawls's approach is still subject to many other criticisms. The original position behind the veil of ignorance excludes so much information about the nature of society as to concentrate attention only on end-state and not process conceptions of justice (Nozick 1974). Furthermore, unanimity is generated and the problem of justice "solved" only by eliminating it, that is "by postulating a world in which there is no conflict either of interests or values" (Gordon 1976: 577). Experimental evidence and the amount of discussion engendered by Rawls's difference principle also suggest that rationality alone cannot dictate a single principle of social choice.[13]

As far as the NIE is concerned, the approach of J. M. Buchanan is more important. Buchanan's work owes a considerable amount to Rawls's, but differs in a number of key respects. Buchanan's main concern is with the development of constitutional rules (particularly voting rules) and the effect of the rules chosen on the size and operation of the public sector. Buchanan also imagines individuals agreeing to a constitutional contract behind a veil of ignorance, but one that is a good deal less opaque than that supposed by Rawls. In Buchanan's case, individuals are presumed to face uncertainty about their future roles and economic positions but to understand their own preferences, the structure of external and decision making costs, and the likely behaviour of politicians and bureaucrats. Under these circumstances, Buchanan argues that unanimity over general constitutional rules may well be possible. In any case, agreement among all individuals in the group forms the basic criterion of ethical acceptability (Romer 1988).

Under these circumstances, individuals may agree to allocate the provision of certain activities to the public sector, define the voting rules to be used for various classes of decision, determine general principles and rules governing taxation and expenditures, and agree on distributional norms. It should be noted that the emphasis here is on the selection of rules, not on the attainment of particular end states. Inclusive decision rules (i.e., unanimity) have the advantage of preventing the imposition of externalities or the exploitation of minorities by majorities, but impose high decision costs. Moving away from unanimity reduces the decision costs but raises the external costs. The total of these "interdependence costs" sum up to a U-shaped function of the number of persons required to make a decision. On this basis, Buchanan and Tullock (1965) argue that "it is almost completely meaningless to discuss seriously the appropriateness or inappropriateness of shifting any particular activity from private to public organization without specifying the rules for decision that are to be adopted if the shift is to be made" (Buchanan and Tullock 1965: 207–208). Whether it is "rational" or "irrational" for an individual to approve of a shift will depend on the decision rules that are to apply to that activity. It is rational to shift an activity to the public sector only if the interdependence costs are less with public organization than with market organization. With only a small number of people required to make a decision, the externality costs involved in public organization will be very high. As the inclusiveness of the decision rule increases, externality costs fall, but decision-making costs rise and eventually push up the interdependence cost of public organization.

This raises the question of how to judge the decision-making rules themselves. Buchanan and Tullock argue that traditional Pareto criteria are not appropriate. According to Pareto criteria, for example, a particular voting rule may result in "overinvestment" in the public sector. What is important, however, is not whether the rule results in "overinvestment," but whether it was the result of an "appropriate constitutional decision" (Buchanan and Tullock 1965: 202–205), one that included consideration of both the externality and decision-making costs involved.

Similarly, on redistribution, Buchanan argues that the constitutional level is where arguments concerning redistribution should take place. The constitution may therefore contain generally agreed upon principles of justice or equity. Although Buchanan is aware of the difficulties of confining redistributional issues to the constitutional level, he argues that the alternative is to have "the day-to-day operation of government become a struggle over redistribution, with more and more instances of majorities exploiting minorities" (Romer 1988: 175). This, in turn, erodes the constructive and cooperative attitude "that underlies the prospects for mutuality of gain for all citizens" (Buchanan 1976: 29).

Buchanan's attempt to focus attention on the constitutional level, on the process that gave rise to the rules, rather than on specific outcomes is useful in a number of respects. The idea of agreement over the general constitutional rules to be followed provides a non-arbitrary alternative to the Pareto standard. It is, however, an alternative that, although based on a procedural approach, does not fully accept the notion of politics as a procedure, in the sense of a *continuing* process of dealing with complex and sometimes unresolvable problems and conflicts. Buchanan does talk of the possibility of constitutional "renegotiation" and realizes that a contract cannot be set for all time, but it is still the case that the contractarian approach tends to search "for discrete and final answers" (Gordon 1976: 588).[14] As Sandmo (1990: 63) argues, "in current debates about policy we are clearly not in a situation that resembles the constitutional stage, and the political process must inevitably face the problem of evaluating increases in the utility or standard of living of some individuals against declines on the part of other individuals."

6.3.3 Comparative institutional approaches

A substantial amount of the NIE literature utilizes the "comparative institutional" approach, which frequently compares alternative institutional arrangements on the basis of their productive or dynamic efficiency. The impetus toward this approach came from a dissatisfaction with Pareto criteria, particularly because they seemed to justify government intervention not on the basis of the actual alternatives but on the implicit assumption that the government would act simply to remove inefficiencies. Given the extent of real-world departures from the conditions sufficient to achieve a Pareto optimum, the amount of government intervention that could be justified by reference to such departures is extremely large. This point often seems lost on old institutionalist critics of orthodox welfare economics, but it has certainly not been lost on those within the NIE. Following Stigler's work on agency capture, Coase's criticism of the Pigovian approach to externality problems, and the public choice literature, much of the NIE has turned against the use of the Pareto optimum as a reference point.

It is argued that judging the real world against an ideal instead of the practical institutional alternatives has made economists far too ready to turn to direct governmental intervention. The actual behaviour of politicians and bureaucrats tends to suggest that government is far from a "benevolent despot" acting simply to correct inefficiencies, and this in turn implies a more cautious approach to government intervention. In the well-known words of Harold Demsetz:

> The view that now pervades much public policy economics implicitly presents the relevant choice as between an ideal norm and an existing "imperfect" institutional arrangement. This *nirvana* approach differs considerably from a *comparative institution* approach in which the relevant choice is between alternative real institutional arrangements. (Demsetz 1969:1)

This approach by no means rules out government involvement, particularly in the provision of public goods, but it does lead to a more sceptical view, and a tendency to move governmental policy away from direct regulation or control to efforts to improve the efficiency of markets by reducing transactions costs or creating negotiable property rights. Writers such as Stigler, Coase, and many in the public choice tradition, make particular use of the argument that the machinery of the state can be fairly easily used to further the interests of *particular* interest groups, rather than that of society as a whole, as a reason for preferring the market over the public sector. Demsetz talks of the historical attacks on government-granted monopoly as an attempt to substitute an institutional arrangement (the market) that "was both real and fairly well understood." The critics of government policies "were confident of the beneficial results and of the practicality of allowing market enterprise to allocate resources" (1969: 19). This is all very well, but the lack of an explicit welfare criterion is a rather obvious problem, and one that exists in much of the "comparative institutional" analysis found in the NIE.

To the extent that criteria of judgement can be found in the comparative institutional approach, they tend to consist of productive or dynamic efficiency. Many references to improved "economic efficiency" in this literature refer to reductions in production or transactions costs, increases in economic growth, or increased institutional flexibility. How these are related to welfare is, however, often left very vague. It is symptomatic that one can find arguments in favour of the liberalization of anti-trust laws that dismiss counter-arguments based on economic and social goals other than "economic efficiency" on the grounds that to introduce secondary goals would "confuse matters" and complicate the "scientific formation of policy," while at the same time admitting that the standard economic approach based on the competitive model is "over-simplified," that the term efficiency is "open to a variety of interpretations," and that the NIE lacks a well defined standard of "group welfare" (Furubotn and Richter 1991: 3–4).

Another example might be taken from the economic history of Douglass North. Although his primary focus is positive not normative, North consistently discusses the relative "efficiency" of institutions in terms of their contribution to productive activity and economic growth. For North, an "efficient system" of property rights is one that "maximizes social output" (1981: 24), or reduces transactions costs and "encourages economic growth" (1981: 25). Lack of economic growth is attributed to "inefficient property rights" that arise out of the attempts of those who control the apparatus of the state to generate rents together with problems of measurement and transactions costs. Of course, "efficient" institutional changes that reduce transactions costs or increase productivity or economic growth may do so only at the expense of certain individuals or groups. Not only may the distribution of income and welfare be affected, but the additional productivity may be gained at the expense of other non-material values. As argued by Saraydar (1989: 56–57):

Productivity – output per unit of physical input employed – in itself has no normative implications. In neoclassical economics state A is ranked higher in the social ordering (is more efficient) than state B, if and only if state A is ranked higher than state B by one person, and all other persons rank A at least as high as B. Therefore, even from the perspective of a *potential* Pareto improvement, it is illegitimate to conclude that A is more efficient than B on the grounds that productivity in A is higher than productivity in B – for that productivity gain may be bought at a utility loss.

A final example is provided by the notion of "dynamic efficiency," which can be traced back to Joseph Schumpeter's emphasis on innovation and his view that the perfectly competitive conditions required for static efficiency were not necessarily the most conducive to innovation and economic progress over time. Furubotn and Richer (1991: 4) argue that once "dynamic competition takes center stage" the "emphasis must be on the need to create conditions that support innovation and economic growth." This position has obvious links to the emphasis on technological and instrumental advance found in the OIE, and has somewhat similar difficulties. Furubotn and Richter, for example, note "the absence of a well defined and generally accepted standard of dynamic efficiency" (1991: 4). Despite this difficulty, others have also adopted notions of dynamic efficiency. Demsetz (1969: 20) has argued forcefully that the "basic problem facing public and private policy" is the design of institutional arrangements that provide incentives to encourage experimentation (including the development of new products, new knowledge, new reputations, and new ways of organizing activities) without overly insulating these experiments from the ultimate test of survival. . . . These institutional arrangements must strive to balance three objectives. A wide variety of experimentation should be encouraged, investment should be channelled into promising varieties of experimentation and away from unpromising varieties, and the new knowledge that is acquired should be employed extensively. No known institutional arrangement can simultaneously maximize the degree to which each of these objectives is achieved. A difficult-to-achieve balance is sought. . . . The concepts of perfect competition and Pareto optimality simply are unable at present to give much help in achieving this balance.

6.3.4   Markets and governments

As already indicated, one of the most significant dividing lines between the OIE and the NIE is the latter's more positive view of markets, and of non-governmental processes more generally, and its more negative view of government. Not only are economic markets usually seen as giving rise to efficient outcomes, but this idea of competition leading to efficient results is also frequently extended to social institutions, conventions, and norms. Thus, in his 1981 book Douglass North argued that "competition in the face of ubiquitous scarcity dictates that the more efficient institution, policy, or individual action will survive and the inefficient ones perish" (1981: 7). North's choice of language clearly suggests that competition can be thought of in terms of a biological "survival of the fittest" analogy, and such biological analogies have a widespread use within the NIE as a means of supporting the notion of competitive processes leading to efficient results. This can be seen in work on market competition between firms, in the type of invisible-hand arguments outlined in the previous chapter, and in Hayek's notions of "group selection." Interestingly, although the market analogy is quite freely used in the NIE to cover a variety of non-market processes, it is not usually extended to political competition. Nevertheless, it is true to say that a greater variety of opinion can be found within the NIE than is often supposed, and it would be a mistake to think that all writers in the NIE adopt the simple equation between non-political markets and efficient outcomes.

The usual criticisms of political processes relate to the nature of political competition (for a majority of votes in a particular constituency), the poorly informed nature of the electorate, and the role of pressure groups and rent-seeking behavior. Many of these arguments are based on Pareto criteria, but contractarian and comparative institutional approaches give rise to broadly similar conclusions. The first point concerns the fact that politicians represent the interests of their districts. Benefits that flow to other constituencies do a politician little good, and hence each politician presses for projects or policies that benefit his or her own constituency, and the result is "too many pork barrel projects" (Wittman 1989: 1409). A slightly different argument is based on median voter models. Here, political competition for votes drives political platforms to reflect the preferences of the median voter. The amount of public good provision, for example, that corresponds to the median voter's preferred position need not represent the Pareto-efficient point, and will usually result in overinvestment in the public sector.

Perhaps more serious are the many arguments that suggest that pressure groups can affect the actions of governments and government agencies in ways that can benefit the particular group involved and at the expense of society at large. As noted above, the usual argument is that those small groups who can gain concentrated benefits have advantages over larger groups facing more diffused benefits or costs. The ability of pressure groups to manipulate policy is thought to be significantly helped by the rational ignorance of most voters.

The public choice literature on the expansionist nature of government bureaucracy and the self-interested behaviour of legislators has also prompted contractarians to argue that individuals who understand the tendency of governments to expand and act in a revenue-maximizing fashion will want to introduce constitutional rules to "limit the power of public sector agents" (Sandmo 1990: 61) – hence, Buchanan's arguments in favour of earmarked taxes and constitutional rules requiring balanced budgets (Romer 1988: 177).

Governments, then, are usually presented within the NIE as tending to misallocate resources and produce laws, property rights, and regulations that are costly to society. There is a strong bias toward *limiting* the activities of the government rather than expanding them; a position that is at odds with that found in the OIE. Against this, it might be argued that political competition should, over time, lead to more socially desirable outcomes. Wittman (1989), for example, claims that the negative picture of government gives rise to a case of "schizophrenia" in which "(conservative) economists tend to view markets as working well (on the efficiency dimension) and political markets as being inefficient because of monopoly, rent seeking, and poorly informed voters" (Wittman 1989: 1395). Wittman's argument is that political competition is closely analogous to market competition and should give similar results in terms of efficiency.[15]

A different point of view is expressed by North (1990: 7) in charting the evolution of his own thinking away from the efficiency view of government.

In *Structure and Change in Economic History* (North, 1981) I abandoned the efficiency view of institutions. Rulers devised property rights in their own interests and transaction costs resulted in typically inefficient property rights prevailing. . . . In that study I raised the question posed by Alchian's evolutionary argument, but had no answer. It was possible to explain the existence of inefficient institutions, but why wouldn't competitive pressures lead to their elimination? Wouldn't the political entrepreneurs in stagnant economies quickly emulate the policies of more successful ones? How can we explain the radically differential performance of economies over long periods of time?

Of course, "emulation" may not be so easy. Individuals and organizations may have interests that oppose such a restructuring, changing institutions may undermine legitimacy and increase enforcement costs, and many institutions work only as part of a larger cultural whole and cannot be easily taken over into different cultural contexts. This does not exclude the possibility of "political entrepreneurs" attempting institutional changes to improve economic conditions and overcome inefficiencies, but it does indicate that there are factors that tend to resist adjustment through political means.

If political processes may fail to generate efficient institutions, will markets or other non-political processes necessarily fare any better? As indicated previously, Austrian school writers have placed particularly great emphasis on the ability of spontaneous or invisible-hand processes to create and maintain socially beneficial institutions. Although Hayek sometimes indicates that spontaneous evolution does not necessarily result in beneficial outcomes, "his writings are not completely free" from arguments stressing that spontaneous forces alone will automatically generate appropriate rules (Vanberg 1986: 97). Thus:

If by "social processes" we mean the gradual evolution which produces better solutions than deliberate design, the imposition of the will of the majority can hardly be regarded as such. The latter differs radically from that free growth from which custom and institutions emerge, because its coercive, monopolistic, and exclusive character destroys the self-correcting forces which bring it about in a free society that mistaken efforts will be abandoned and the successful ones prevail. (Hayek 1960: 110)

What is interesting here is that Hayek adopts the same optimistic "self-corrective" idea that one can find in parts of the OIE, but applies it to customs rather than to the acts of governments. However, in view of the fact that social customs can be extremely resistant to change, it is difficult to see how a tendency to self-correction could reasonably be attributed to them. Hayek's optimistic account of spontaneous, non-governmental processes is also rejected by Buchanan, who puts Hayek in the "Panglossian category" (Buchanan 1979: 275), and develops a critique of the idea that invisible-hand processes necessarily give rise to beneficial results (Buchanan 1978: 29–33; Vanberg 1983). Also, as demonstrated previously, the game theoretic analysis of invisible-hand processes does *not* indicate that they will always operate to generate efficient results. Needed institutions may fail to develop altogether, or those that do may be sub-optimal in nature. What is socially most beneficial may not be a stable solution from a game theoretic or evolutionary perspective. Thus, Binger and Hoffman (1989: 70–71) argue that the theory of repeated games

raises the possibility that efficient institutions might develop. . . . However it also should caution us that institutions need not be efficient to persist. In both finitely-repeated and infinitely-repeated games inefficient supergame equilibria do exist. Moreover, in games with many possible strategies there are likely to be many possible inefficient equilibria, some of which are more or less efficient than others. Thus, just because we observe that an institution endures and seems to "do better" than some other institutions does not mean that it is necessarily efficient.

Indeed, it is becoming increasingly common for writers within the NIE to comment on the apparent inefficiency of certain evolved ethical conceptions (Rubin 1982) and social norms and conventions more generally (Basu, Jones, and Schlicht 1987; Elster 1989a). One key element in such arguments is that social norms often have self-sustaining patterns of social sanctions that strongly discourage violation even under circumstances in which everyone could be made better off by violating the norm. Even where a norm or convention was once efficient, the structure of sanctions may sustain the norm or convention when circumstances have changed. Thus, the extension of the market analogy to such phenomena is highly questionable:

Individuals choose in the marketplace, in shops, in labor markets. They do not choose between institutions, customs, and social norms. These evolve in response to a multitude of individual decisions spread over different domains and large stretches of time. Standard neoclassical economics deals with choice in the marketplace and shows that, given certain conditions, individual rational decisions lead to optimality. That, too, is a very special kind of optimality, namely, a situation where it is not possible to make anybody better off without making someone else worse off. To claim the optimality of social institutions by citing the above argument from neoclassical economic theory, which applies to the limited domain of market exchange, entails a trespass which needs much greater justification than is provided by the protagonists of the NIE. (Basu, Jones, and Schlicht 1987: 9)

It is often argued that, apart from social conventions and norms, the common law tends to consist of efficient rules. As indicated previously, Posner (1977: 1981) attributes this to judges explicitly including efficiency considerations in their judgements, but for Hayek the common law is an example of a system of "grown" rules that embodies much accumulated experience. Hayek, however, provides little by way of any specific mechanisms that could generate efficient rules, and the attempts of Rubin (1977), Priest (1977), Goodman (1978), and others to provide an evolutionary or invisible-hand explanation that does not depend on the preference functions of judges have not been successful. The difficulty with these arguments is clearly that the individual's interest in which rulings to challenge and in how much to invest in the litigation will not always correspond to the social interest. Individual and social costs and benefits can easily diverge. The argument by Goodman simply presumes that individual interests do mirror social benefits (Goodman, 1978: 395). Rubin, however, recognizes that problems are created by free ridership and the difficulties of mobilizing large groups (Rubin 1977: 60–61). This point has been emphasized and extended by Hirshleifer (1982: 50), who argues that "each side has the problem of mobilizing its strength" so that the outcome of the conflict depends not simply on efficiency considerations but also on "comparative effectiveness at mobilization." Furthermore, once the outcome is "seen to depend on ability to mobilize we would expect to see a kind of arms race between the contenders," a competitive investment in mobilization that would be wasteful of resources. This, ironically, makes the argument one that is exactly equivalent to the interest group models of the determination of statute law, with similar, and adverse, consequences for efficiency.

It is also worth noting Menger's attitude to the common law. Vanberg (1986), Prisching (1989), and Boettke (1989) have all quoted from the following passage from Menger that refers to the belief in the "higher wisdom" of common law:

This assertion is, however, erroneous in every conceivable respect. For common law has also proved harmful to the common good often enough, and on the contrary, legislation has just as often changed common law in a way benefiting the common good. . . . The theory of the "higher wisdom" of common law thus not only contradicts experience but is at the same time rooted in a vague feeling, in a misunderstanding. It is an exaggeration carried to the point of distortion, of the true statement that positive legislation has upon occasion not comprehended the unintended wisdom in common law, and, in trying to change the latter in the sense of the common good, has not infrequently produced the opposite result. . . . If the rules and institutions of common law not infrequently prove to be highly suitable in respect to the common good, it was the task of science to make us understand this advantage. . . . But never, and this is the essential point in the matter under review, may science dispense with testing for their suitability those institutions which have come about "organically." It must, when careful investigation so requires, change and better them according to the measure of scientific insight and the practical experience at hand. No era may renounce this "calling." (Menger [1883] 1985: 233–234)

Turning to the narrower issue of market competition as opposed to the regulation of firms, the NIE is very much disposed toward the market. Relying on the market is seen as removing the possibility of regulated firms capturing the regulatory agency or otherwise influencing the regulations to their own advantage, and markets (even imperfectly competitive markets) are thought to provide strong incentives to productive efficiency and innovation. The first of these arguments has been challenged by Victor Goldberg (1974). Goldberg's point is that resort to the market does not necessarily prevent special-interest groups from attempting to change property rights in their favour. In his response, Coase (1974) admits that "since property rights can be changed in such a way as to raise as well as lower the costs of transactions," one cannot say that "a move from regulation to a private property rights system, the use of the market, will necessarily represent an improvement" (1974: 493), but then proceeds to make the empirical claim that "there have been many studies of regulated industries which make it abundantly clear that producers are able to secure restrictive arrangements with government regulation that they were not able to secure through the delimitation of property rights" (1974: 495). Coase's claim may be just, but Goldberg's point should be taken as a caution against assuming that shifts from regulation to markets will *necessarily* work to improve economic efficiency.

The favourable attitude toward markets in the NIE also shows up in the more forgiving view of vertical and horizontal integration than that embedded in anti-trust laws. The transactions cost analysis of Williamson (1975: 258) has provided the basis of arguments that many phenomena previously regarded as monopolistic could be given an efficiency explanation, and that anti-trust enforcement should proceed "more selectively." Williamson himself takes "a relatively conservative position with respect to the role of transactions costs in justifying greater organizational freedom for firms," but there is little doubt that "transaction cost theory served to buttress arguments favoring antitrust liberalization" (Furubotn and Richter 1991: 1–2). Of course, there is debate over how far justifications based on transaction costs can be taken, and exactly which phenomena they cover. Horizontal mergers, high market concentration, and barriers to entry are particular points of contention (Kauper 1980).

The argument in favour of markets – particularly where markets are conceived of not in terms of static, perfectly competitive conditions, but in terms of dynamic process – often revolves around a notion of competitive selection leading to efficient results (Alchian 1950; Enke 1951; Friedman 1953). The competitive selection argument, however, is rarely specified in detail, and when considered more closely does not provide strong reasons for believing that only the most efficient firms will survive. First, even if all agents are fully informed optimizers, transactions costs, adjustment costs, or increasing returns can create problems. These include, in addition to standard externality and public good problems, a type of market failure that arises as a result of a "lock-in" to a particular technology or practice. The cases of QWERTY and Betamax video systems are now too well known to require further comment (Kindleberger 1983; David 1985; Arthur 1989; Hodgson 1991a). Second, if agents are non-optimizing, but are attempting to adapt under competitive pressure, the adaptive processes will only give optimal results under special circumstances. These include the discovery of an organization or procedure that gives optimal results, some mechanism that spreads that organizational form or procedure, and no entry of agents using forms or procedures giving non-optimal results. In many cases these conditions will be violated. The economic environment may be too changeable, adaption may lead only to a local optimum, and imitation may be difficult. It is also true that, even in the case of market competition, efficient forms or procedures that produce diffuse benefits may be rejected in favour of those that produce smaller total but more concentrated returns (Hodgson 1991a; Dow 1993). It has also been argued (in a rather Veblenian fashion) that a firm with market power may be able to survive better by deviating from profit-maximizing behaviour, if by doing so it inflicts damage on its rivals (Schaffer 1989).

Nelson and Winter's evolutionary approach and attitude to markets and private enterprise is particularly worthy of close examination. They argue that the preference many economists have for competitive decentralized markets over government is based less on static efficiency arguments than on arguments such as those provided by Hayek concerning the informational requirements of planning. Thus "economists tend to argue *for* free enterprise and *against* central planning much more strongly than could possibly be justified by the theorems of welfare economics" (Nelson and Winter 1982: 359). Although sympathetic to free enterprise, Nelson and Winter also argue that "the advocates of free enterprise have been too facile in arguing the merits of the stylized [competitive] system in a stylized dynamic environment" and have not properly recognized the extent to which "fundamental problems of economic organization" are "either dispatched by assumption in those stylized arguments or are subsumed in a 'minimal' list of government functions" (1982: 362). They note the lack of theoretical justification for the argument that competitive markets can adapt to or track "a moving equilibrium" better than any other, and that similar problems exist with the claim that competition will generate greater levels of innovation. They also express concern over the usual neoclassical treatment of property rights, with externalities being seen as "merely" problems in "the definition and enforcement of property rights" (1982: 363), and observe that the "private enterprise" solution to organizational problems is often not a decentralized or market solution but one that "involves large elements of centralized planning and direction within the boundaries of large private corporations," corporations that also draw on government support (1982: 364).

The conclusion Nelson and Winter draw from these considerations is highly pragmatic:

These considerations do not imply any particular judgment on the merits of the private enterprise solution as against any specific realistic alternative, nor do they render Hayek's insights irrelevant. They do, however, caution against the ascription of general systemic virtues and faults to particular real organizational arrangements. The "private enterprise" of agriculture is vastly different from the "private enterprise" of aircraft manufacturing. And both of these sectors are substantially and differently shaped by public programs. The unique organizational characteristics of a particular sector ought to come to the fore in the analysis of policy toward that sector. (1982: 364)

Thus, although there is much in the NIE that conveys a Panglossian view of non-political processes, such as those embodied in the invisible hand, in common law, and in market competition, there is also a substantial amount of literature that suggests a different view, in which both governmental and non-governmental processes may or may not, depending on specific circumstances, operate to produce desirable results. It is also clear that the mere existence of competition does not ensure that only the efficient institution, policy, or

organization will survive. The effect of competition depends critically on the exact nature and circumstances that surround the competition itself. War is competition of a sort, so are arms races,
competitive rent seeking, and competitive advertising. Competition
may express itself in lower costs, new products, useful innovations, or
in competitive investment in redistributional efforts of a socially
wasteful or even destructive kind. As Hirshleifer (1982: 47) has
observed, "to refute the idea that strife and contention lead to
efficiency in any all-encompassing sense we need only look about us":

> The harmonistic or Panglossian argument, which economists are perhaps
> predisposed to favor, is that wherever mutual advantage is present we can
> expect continual progress toward its achievement. Refuting that contention
> has been the main concern of this paper. At every point in time, each
> decision-making agent will be weighing the relative attractiveness of co-
> operation and conflict strategies – of seeking *mutual* advantage on the one
> hand, or on the other hand *unilateral* advantage even at the expense of
> others. (1982: 53–54)

6.4   Conclusion

Both old and new institutionalists have addressed the questions of
appropriate welfare criteria for judging institutional change and the
appropriate role of governmental intervention in the allocation of
resources and in the system of institutions. The major differences
between the old and the new are clearly to be found in the normative
significance given to individual preferences and to voluntary exchange, the use of interpersonal comparisons, and of the necessary
role of government. These differences are not trivial, and it would be
a mistake to pretend they do not exist. Clearly, Veblen's normative
position is a long distance from that contained in orthodox neoclassical economics. Nevertheless, there are some points of contact, and
once more, it is possible to find some middle ground.

With regard to welfare criteria, old institutionalists have developed their ideas at least partly in response to their evolutionary
framework and the attention that approach focuses on issues of long-
run social development and growth rather than on issues of static
efficiency. This has led them to adopt welfare criteria that explicitly
endorse particular social values or particular processes through which
social values are to be generated. The new institutionalism has
moved somewhat, but not entirely, away from static efficiency notions but has maintained an individualistic approach. Its supporters
are therefore somewhat reluctant to make interpersonal comparisons or to adopt particular sets of social values, but this is combined

with a significant amount of criticism of Pareto criteria and of much work that refers instead to process criteria such as voluntary agreement or to dynamic efficiency notions involving economic and technological innovation. What is interesting here is that, despite considerable variation in the particulars involved, both old and new institutionalists can be found emphasizing those procedures that pertain to democratic decision making and the generation of agreement and consensus. In their different ways Ayres, Commons, and Buchanan all share this ideal. In addition, the emphasis on dynamic efficiency and the importance attached to innovation and adaptability by writers such as Demsetz, Furubotn and Richter, and Nelson and Winter, express something of the same notions as are contained in Veblen's and Ayres's view of the importance of technological and instrumental advance. Similar difficulties also arise. It is not always obvious how or why a consensus over social values should be reached, and neither tradition provides much guidance in those cases where conflict and disagreement persist despite the best efforts of scientists and politicians. It is also often unclear exactly what is and what is not in the long run interest of a society. One might argue that what is required is institutional flexibility and openness to innovation, but the possibility that what seems like progress and appropriate adaption will generate unforeseen, adverse, and irreversible social and environmental consequences cannot be ignored.

It is interesting that there are those in both the OIE and the NIE who attempt to circumvent these problems by postulating one master value to which all others are related, and by arguing that self-corrective forces exist. Ayres relates all values to instrumental advance and finds democracy to be self-corrective. Hayek relates all values to individual freedom and finds spontaneous orders to be self-corrective. These solutions are equally simplistic and over-optimistic. The problem of social value is in large part a problem of difficult conflicts and trade-offs between things that are valued, and neither government (however democratic) nor markets nor common law courts can guarantee a timely or adequate corrective to emerging social problems.

Although far from all writers adopt either of the extreme positions taken by Ayres and Hayek, it is nevertheless true that a great deal of dogmatism exists concerning the proper role of governmental or political processes as opposed to non-political market or spontaneous processes. Many old institutionalists are deeply suspicious of market processes and think the government, provided it is democratic and all interests are represented, is capable of leading to enlightened intervention in the public interest. It is surely one of the great failings of the OIE that the instrumentality of markets is insufficiently recognized. Furthermore, and despite the emphasis on government, it has produced (with the notable exception of Commons) little by way of any analysis of how political decisions are made. Similarly, many writers within the NIE have argued for the efficiency of market and spontaneous processes very broadly, utilizing only weak arguments by analogy. A closer analysis of invisible-hand, common law, and even competitive market processes reveals that there are no guarantees that the inefficient will be eliminated in favour of the efficient or socially beneficial. This may occur, but whether or not it does will depend on the specifics of the case.

In conclusion, it seems that a genuine pragmatism is the only viable approach to policy matters, that is, an approach that does not start with any particular bias toward the instruments that may function best in any particular situation. In contrast, both the NIE and the OIE tend to be too dogmatic. Certainly, the NIE provides a useful corrective to the over-optimistic view of political processes contained within the OIE, but the opposite also holds true. The OIE criticism of markets is a useful counterweight to the over-optimistic view of economic competition in the NIE. The fact is that the decision made in each particular case will depend on the details of that case, the best available information and knowledge, and a healthy concern with the costs of making errors. As Menger was aware, we should be "cautious about constructivist attitudes of self-overestimation as well as about defeatist perspectives emphasizing drawback necessities" (Prisching 1989: 49).

Conflicts and complementarities

The preceding chapters have dealt in detail with those standard dichotomies that have been an integral part of the official rhetoric of both the OIE and the NIE. That such a sharp division between the two traditions should be so ingrained is not surprising. The OIE has frequently expressed outright opposition to more orthodox programs, anything less being seen as an undesirable lack of "paradigm discipline" (Stanfield 1989). Similarly, the NIE is associated with such negative views of the old that it would be impossible for anyone to admit to a serious interest in the old without casting doubt on their own theoretical credentials.

In many ways, this extreme distancing of the two traditions is not helpful. Each faces a common set of problems, and each can learn from the other. This is *not* to suggest that the old and the new institutionalisms are the same or can simply be stuck together in a single program. Indeed, the old and the new both contain more than one identifiable research program. Nevertheless, these various programs attempt to deal with many of the same issues and contain points of contact and areas of complementarity. Furthermore, an appraisal of the strengths and weaknesses of these programs leads to an understanding of the underlying difficulties that *any* attempt to develop an institutional economics must face, and points to those directions that might be taken in the pursuit of a more satisfactory program of research than either the old or the new currently provides.

7.1 Conflicts

As argued in Chapter 1, the old and the new institutionalisms can each be divided into two main streams. The new has a neoclassical and an Austrian branch, although not everyone can be easily classified. The more strictly neoclassical analysts attempt to explain institutions in terms of the maximizing behaviour of individual economic agents. The Austrians focus more narrowly on the "spontaneous" development of institutions out of individual action. This is not, in itself, inconsistent with neoclassicism, but Austrians tend to interpret rationality in adaptive rather than in maximizing terms. The old institutionalism has a Veblen–Ayres and a Commons wing, although again these two groups are not all-inclusive. The former is built around the distinction between technology and institutions (or the instrumental and the ceremonial) with technology as the dynamic element, the latter around the notion of institutions evolving out of the resolution of conflicting interests. The old and the new differ in many respects, but many of these same differences also appear (although in a less severe form) within each tradition. The dispute centers on five main issues:

i.   The role of formal theoretical modelling as opposed to less formal methods, including historical and "literary" approaches.

ii.   The emphasis to be placed on individual behaviour leading to social institutions as opposed to the effect of social institutions in moulding individual behaviour.

iii. The validity of rationalist explanations as opposed to those that place limits on the applicability of rationalist conceptions.

iv.   The extent to which institutions are the result of spontaneous or invisible-hand processes as opposed to deliberate design.

v.   The basis on which normative judgements can be made, and the appropriate role of government intervention in the economy.

A superficial reading of the old and new institutionalist literature would suggest that the two line up on opposite sides of each of these issues: the new emphasizing formalist techniques, individuals creating institutions, rational action, spontaneous processes, and individualistic normative criteria and a limited role for the government; and the old emphasizing non-formal techniques, institutions moulding individuals, habits and social norms, collective choice, and social normative criteria and a larger role for the government. Closer examination, however, reveals a more complex picture.

Within the OIE there is a widespread rejection of formal methods of analysis. This negative view of formal methods goes back to Veblen's critique of the static and "taxonomic" nature of orthodox theory and his desire to look at historical processes of cumulative change, but the anti-formalism of the OIE has taken many forms, including not only Veblen's and Ayres's literary and historical approach, but also Mitchell's quantitative empiricism and Commons's complex blending of conceptual development, case studies, and practical action. All of these approaches contrast markedly with the formal methods found in the NIE, particularly those of the more neoclassical and game-theoretic types of analysis. At the same time, there is a growing division between the formalistic and the literary approach within the NIE, the latter advocated by writers such as Coase, Demsetz, Williamson, and North (De Alessi 1990: 12). In terms of approach, but *not* in terms of the particular ideas being promoted, the literary blending of history and theory found in much of the OIE is not so different from that found in some of North's more recent work (North 1990). Furthermore, certain new formalisms, such as those involved in modelling dynamic evolutionary systems, can now be found in both the OIE and NIE (Anderson, Arrow, and Pines 1988; Baumol and Benhabib 1989; Dopfer 1991; Radzicki 1990).

The OIE has been directly associated with "holistic" approaches in the sense of concentrating on the issue of how established institutions condition and mould individual behaviour, not merely by providing constraints but by affecting the goals and values adopted by individuals. This contrasts with the perspective of those in the NIE who argue that institutions are either given constraints (and do not affect individuals' goals or preferences), or arise purely out of the self-interested action of individuals. Although some within the OIE, particularly Commons, have attempted to deal both with the individual as a socialized being and with the way in which individuals and groups act to bring about institutional change, such balance is rare. Most obviously, Ayres pays almost no attention to specifying the ways in which individual actions give rise to institutions. Conversely, very few members of the NIE take seriously the notion that institutions mould individual preferences, although the point does receive explicit recognition in North's discussion of the importance of "ideology" (North 1981), and in the rejection of reductionist versions of individualism by writers such as Langlois (1986b).

As for the question of rational choice, the OIE has always taken the view that orthodox economics overstated the rational element in economic life. This is not to say that rationality is excluded altogether, but that the existence of decision making costs and psychological constraints limits the role of rational appraisal and gives rise to habits and rules of thumb. Rationality, here, becomes a matter of gradual adaption over time rather than a matter of instantaneous optimization. In addition, social norms are seen as constraining individual action and shaping preferences and goals. Although some members of the OIE indicate that norms, too, might be subject to adaption on the basis of rational appraisal, others such as Veblen deal with the evolution of social norms in largely non-rationalist terms. Within the NIE, rule following of various types has become increasingly recognized, but it is still the case that many of those in the NIE strongly prefer those explanations of habits, rules of thumb, and even of social norms, that run in purely rationalist terms. Others, however, recognize limits to rationalist explanations, particularly in the case of social norms.

In terms of the issue of spontaneous versus design processes, the Austrian wing of the NIE clearly places most emphasis on the former.

The more neoclassical group, on the other hand, has tended to a more moderate position with government legislation usually being credited with a substantial role in the development of property rights. A variety of views can also be found within the OIE. Veblen's emphasis is on the unintended institutional consequences of technological development, and while governments may give legal backing to institutions, they are not the major agents of change. In contrast, Commons places much greater emphasis on governments and courts, although by no means excluding those spontaneous processes that generate social customs and norms.

On normative issues, an even wider disparity of views is evident. Old institutionalists uniformly reject individualistic approaches, but substitute no single alternative. Veblen refers back to instincts for normative guidance, Ayres to his notions of instrumental reasoning and the technological continuum, and Commons to the reasonable reconciliation of conflicting interests. There is, however, an emphasis on *process* (instrumental processes of valuation and democratic processes of conflict resolution), and on the need for ongoing evaluation and re-evaluation in the light of new conditions and the best available information. Within the NIE, many doubts have been expressed concerning the adequacy of the traditional Pareto criteria, but again no single alternative has attracted universal acceptance. Welfare functions require explicit value judgements, and interpersonal comparisons make many economists uncomfortable. Perhaps the most appealing approach, in that it retains an explicitly individualistic foundation, is the contractarianism of Buchanan and others. Nevertheless, difficulties exist in the idea that unanimity can be generated and maintained over time. Other alternatives, such as comparative and dynamic approaches, fail to clearly define welfare criteria. With regard to the proper role of government, it is clear that the OIE is more favourably disposed toward governmental intervention and the NIE is more favourably disposed toward markets. The extremes are represented by Tugwell and Gruchy on the side of government planning, and by Hayek on the side of market organization, but more moderate positions, recognizing the possibility of both government and market failures, can be found in both camps.

7.2   Complementarities

It has been a large part of the argument presented in this book that the divisions between the OIE and the NIE represent varying responses to the same set of underlying methodological and analytical problems, responses that, taken individually, are frequently one-sided and incomplete. Often, a more adequate solution to the problem in question will require elements from both the OIE and NIE to be combined, but in ways that would generate a research program significantly different from either the OIE or the NIE as currently constituted.

This point can be easily illustrated by the different approaches to formal theoretical model building in the two traditions. The anti-formalism of the OIE originally gave rise to a degree of investigative freedom that resulted not only in a great deal of empirical work, but also in many profound theoretical insights – for example, in Veblen's ideas on the significance of social norms, the impact of new technology on institutions, and the internal organization and financing of corporations; Commons's work on transactions, the common law, and the behaviour of legislatures; and J. M. Clark's many significant contributions concerning decision-making costs, overhead costs, externalities, the accelerator, and workable competition. These insights were all developed in the context of a sensitivity to institutions and to the historical particularities that affect the course of institutional change. What is noticeable about the OIE, however, is that this level of creativity was not maintained, and that many of the insights generated by earlier writers were not developed in any sustained way by those who came later. There are undoubtedly many reasons for this, but one contributory factor must be the distaste for formal theorizing that made theoretical elaboration beyond the stage of conceptual development extremely difficult, and that tended to direct subsequent efforts toward investigation of an analytic–descriptive type, policy analysis, and matters of normative evaluation. Ayres's almost total concentration on normative issues set the tone for a great deal of the post-1945 OIE literature, and one searches in vain for important theoretical developments. The significant developments in the theories of transactions costs, the internal organization of firms, corporate finance, business cycles, environmental externalities, public goods, common property problems, common law, public choice, and even social conventions and norms have *not* come from the more recent generations of old institutionalists, a failure of such magnitude as to surely raise serious questions in the minds of even the most ardent supporter of the tradition.

These failures, however, should not lead one to the opposite, but equally serious mistake, of relying entirely on formal models. Of course, important insights are often arrived at using formal methods. Formal models can build upon conceptual insights and provide much guidance into the analysis of the sources and functioning of real-world economic and social institutions, but they are abstract, frequently static, and not in themselves capable of fully encompassing the course of institutional history. Formal techniques also tend to focus attention on those particular problems to which the technique is suited, but to concentrate on them is to ignore other issues. As De Alessi argues, both approaches have contributed and will continue to contribute to the area (De Alessi 1990).

There is nothing about the nature of institutional economics that would lead one to conclude that either formal or non-formal techniques should be excluded on methodological grounds. In fact, exactly the opposite holds true. The problems inherent in the investigation of a complex, evolving, and path-dependent system, and the limits to all available methods, would seem to indicate that a catholic approach is needed. The point here is that both the formal and the non-formal are required, not that they must always be combined or that some in-between approach must be adopted for all investigations.

In the case of holism and individualism, the complementarity is somewhat different. The emphasis of the OIE is on the conditioning influence of institutions, and the way in which institutions emerge out of the actions of individuals is not always accorded the same degree of attention. In contrast, in the NIE the emphasis is on how individuals (with psychologically given preferences) act to create the institutions that surround them. In addition, the OIE tends, on occasion, to imply the existence of some holistic, supra-individual, actor, while the NIE tends to prefer a reductionist version of individualism. Both of these tendencies create methodological difficulties, but as long as the only alternatives are holism and individualism as conventionally defined, no obvious solution exists. A way out of these problems is provided by Agassi's "institutional individualism." Agassi explains institutions in terms of individual actions, but also rejects reductionism.

Both old and new institutionalists would have to make some significant adjustments if they were to adopt Agassi's approach. The NIE would have to take into account the influence of existing institutions on the goals and actions of individuals, while the OIE would have to consider how *individuals* act within their social setting. This would bring together the two sides of the whole, two sides that have often been pursued separately and without recognition that the other side has any importance or even any real existence. Of course, the methodology of institutional individualism does not imply that all institutionalists should adopt the same theories of institutions. The methodological approach is consistent with a wide variety of views concerning the development and functioning of economic and social institutions.

The complementarities that exist in the case of rationality and rule following are, perhaps, a little harder to see. A significant part of the NIE is focused on explaining institutions in terms of the rational maximizing behaviour of individual agents (Eggertsson 1990: 7), and it is precisely this conception that has always been strongly rejected by those working within the OIE. Despite this apparent opposition, the OIE has never rejected the idea of rationality in any wholesale way. Old institutionalists have instead sought to define the limits and constraints that face the decision maker: information and decision-making costs, psychological constraints, and existing social norms. In many matters the individual is seen as rational in an adaptive sense. Given his goals, he will attempt to establish habits and routines that operate in a satisfactory fashion and will adapt his behaviour if conditions change or superior alternatives become apparent. More problematic is the question of how far social norms can be accommodated within a similar framework, particularly as norms specify many of the goals of action. The NIE is based largely on the postulate of the rational maximizing egoist, but it is becoming increasingly clear that the maximizing approach has its limits. This can be seen in the Austrian literature, in the adaptive approach to rationality that can be found in some of the work on rule following, and in the questioning of the applicability of rationalist or consequentialist approaches to the explanation of social norms. The maximizing approach has often been taken as a fundamental part of the neoclassical program, but some assumption of limited rationality is becoming more common and does not appear to be as disturbing to neoclassicals as was once thought.

Even so, neither the OIE nor the NIE have provided an adequate account of the respective roles, and interrelationships between, consequentialist (rationalist) and non-consequentialist (norm-guided) modes of behaviour. Both traditions raise the issue, and both have insights to offer, but each needs to explore the strengths and weaknesses of rationalist and non-rationalist explanations more fully than has previously been the case.

The points to be made with respect to the issue of evolutionary and design processes are different again; the divisions within each tradition are at least as important as the divisions between them. In the case of the OIE, Veblen's emphasis is on the unintended social consequences of technological innovation, whereas Commons's is on the collective choice processes involved in conflict resolution. In the NIE, those of an Austrian persuasion concentrate almost exclusively on the spontaneous, invisible-hand, development of institutions, but neoclassical analysis incorporates both processes, although with some emphasis on the governmental establishment of property rights.

Game-theoretic work on spontaneous processes initially appeared to support the Austrian view, but more recent developments have shown the fragility of these processes and the necessary role for the organized design and enforcement of social rules. Given that both processes are of obvious social importance, any complete institutional economics should contain an analysis of both. In this, work from the old and the new has relevance. The NIE contains a substantial amount of formal analysis of invisible-hand processes and a large literature on public choice, both of which have been sadly ignored by those in the OIE. In contrast, the OIE contains many suggestive ideas on the operation of courts and legislatures, and on the unintended impact on institutions of intentionally introduced alterations to the technical and material means through which individuals make their living. An awareness of the complexities of social decision processes, and a broader view of the sources and social impacts of unintended consequences are particularly important.

The complementarities between the old and the new are most difficult to see in the area of the normative appraisal of institutions. The predilection of the NIE for individualist and pro-market positions contrasts sharply with the tendency of the OIE to adopt social values and to allocate a much larger role to government. Nevertheless, the normative appraisal of institutions raises problems that bring the two traditions closer on certain points than might at first be thought. The limitations that arise from the adoption of criteria that require, implicitly or explicitly, unanimous approval are widely recognized. The attempt to apply such criteria to the constitutional level mitigates, but does not entirely overcome, the problems of dealing with the conflicts that the redistributive effects of institutional changes will continually be generating. However, if such criteria are not applied, what exactly is to be considered in the social interest and how is totalitarianism, or the exploitation of political power by one group at the expense of others, to be avoided?

Many answers have been given to these questions, but a number of them have the same themes. Both the OIE and the NIE seem to attach considerable importance to creating conditions consistent with economic growth, innovation, and institutional flexibility, although the justification for these positions in terms of social welfare frequently leaves much to be desired. Both also stress the *process* of social decision making, particularly through democratic institutions. Of course, representative democracy is by no means a perfect safeguard against economic inefficiency or the abuse of power, and both old and new institutionalists have suggested methods of improving the operation of democratic institutions in order to alleviate these problems. One alternative that has been proposed – on the ground that markets provide an efficient and non-coercive form of organization – is to limit governmental intervention. This line of argument is exclusive to the NIE, but it is not without its strengths, particularly as a corrective to the over-optimistic picture of government as always acting in the social interest that is too often found in the work of old institutionalists. However, the market does not guarantee efficiency, nor is it free of coercion. Many types of market failures exist and many forms of economic coercion can still be exercised. The old institutionalist critique of markets and of business institutions more generally cannot be so easily dismissed. There is no simple or once-and-for-all solution to the problem of social welfare. The actual performance and the appropriate roles of markets and governments will undoubtedly continue to be analyzed, discussed, and adjusted to meet changing economic and ethical demands. No process, intentionalist or spontaneous, can ensure that the adjustments made or not made will always be to the social advantage.

7.3   Conclusion

Members of the NIE do not see their work as a continuation of the endeavours of old institutionalists such as Veblen or Commons, but as a distinct effort to apply more standard economic approaches to institutional issues. Conversely, old institutionalists have been unimpressed by the NIE, regarding it as a part of a research tradition they rejected long ago. Despite this mutual antagonism, both must address similar issues when attempting to incorporate institutions within economics. Thus it is not surprising that each side has been divided on how to approach these issues, or that these divisions are not altogether unlike those that separate the NIE and the OIE themselves. The NIE, for example, is divided on whether a literary or a formal approach is more appropriate, and on the wholesale applicability of rationalist conceptions and the usefulness of traditional welfare criteria. Many of these concerns are remarkably similar to those previously voiced in the OIE. This is not to suggest that the ideas of the OIE have greater merit. Although the OIE contains many relevant lessons for the NIE, they are not all positive lessons. Most notably, the rapid theoretical advance of the NIE contrasts with the theoretical stagnation that characterizes much of the more recent history of the OIE.

Rather, the point is that the OIE and NIE could speak to each other to a much greater extent than is commonly recognized, and that there could be significant gains from such a conversation, particularly if the similarity of the problems being faced and the areas of complementarity that exist were to be the focus of the discourse. That this potential exists is no guarantee, however, that it will be realized.

Notes

Chapter 1: Definitions and issues

1   Throughout this book, the term "institution" is defined in terms similar to those found in Veblen ([1914] 1964: 7) and in Schotter (1981: 11). An institution is a regularity of behaviour or a rule that is generally accepted by members of a social group, that specifies behaviour in specific situations, and that is either self-policed or policed by external authority. It is important to distinguish between general social rules (sometimes called the institutional environment) and particular organizational forms (sometimes called institutional arrangements). Although organizations can also be thought of as sets of rules, the rules apply only internally. Organizations have constitutions, are collective actors and are also subject to social rules.

2   This concentration was adopted for a number of reasons. First, to include Marxism and historicism would make the discussion unmanageable. Second, almost all issues of interest can be dealt with in the context of the OIE and NIE. Third, the two traditions chosen clearly represent the major more orthodox (NIE) and less orthodox (OIE) traditions of institutionalist thought *in economics.*

3   The term "new institutional economics" is borrowed from Oliver Williamson (1975) but is defined more along the lines of Langlois (1986a). The NIE has also been called "mathematical institutional economics," "theoretical institutional economics," "modern institutional economics" and "neo-institutional economics" (Shubik 1975; Schotter 1981; Coase 1984). Eggertsson (1990) distinguishes between a neoclassically based "neo-institutional economics" based on optimizing models and the "new institutional economics" based on ideas of bounded rationality. However, this distinction is not an easy one to maintain, particularly given the reservations concerning the universal applicability of the optimizing approach that have been expressed even by nominally neoclassical writers. See North (1981) and Chapter 4 of this volume. The term "old" does not imply that the tradition is dead, dying, or old-fashioned. Its use here denotes only the longer tradition of continuous and central concern with institutional issues.

4   Andrew Schotter (1981) provides an Austrian (invisible-hand) interpretation of his own approach.

182

Chapter 2: Formalism and anti-formalism

1   Marshall thought of comparative statics as a poor first approximation to the analysis of the evolving economic system (see Marshall 1920). For discussion of Marshall's use of biological analogy and his concern with long-term evolution, see Levine (1983) and Thomas (1991). Marshall was also an advocate of the detailed study of actual industrial conditions. See O'Brien (1990).

2   Veblen characterizes the Austrian tradition as being based on hedonism. He is aware of the Austrians' concern with process and agrees that their "discussion of marginal utility and subjective value as the outcome of a valuation process must be taken as a genetic study of this range of facts." As Veblen (1898: 72–73) sees it, the failure of the Austrians to go further into the genetic study of institutions is the result of their hedonistic postulates. Veblen, however, does not seem aware of Menger's writings on institutions, and several writers have disputed Veblen's critique of Menger. See Seckler (1975: 145) and Langlois (1986a: 3–5).

3   It should be understood that Veblen uses the term "genetic" to refer to an account or explanation of something that runs in terms of its origins, development, or causal antecedents.

4   The following discussion of Mitchell relies heavily on Rutherford (1987: 67).

5   Commons's full system of categories includes the "Precept" or "the meaning we give to a sensation," the "Concept" or "similarity of attribute," the "Principle" and the "Formula" discussed in the text, and the "Social Philosophy" or "similarity of purpose." Commons then states: "Thus we construct and reconstruct in our minds, by a process called theorizing, five mental tools for investigation and understanding, which, taken together, we name Ideas and their Meanings. Ideas interpreted as meanings are Precepts, Concepts, Principles, Formulae, and Social Philosophies. They are inseparable, and it is on account of their interdependence that we construct a sixth idea which we name Theory" ([1934] 1961: 94–98).

6   As noted above, Veblen was criticized on methodological grounds by Mitchell. Mitchell ([1928] 1936: 412) argued that Veblen did not subject his ideas to careful empirical testing. For Mitchell, Veblen's work was "not accurate in detail," he "paid too little attention to checking his conclusions by patient observation," and failed to establish the relative importance of "the factors he dealt with and the factors he scamped."

7   Mitchell, of course, used large-scale statistical analysis. One can hardly be a participant-observer, in Diesing's sense, of a business cycle. Veblen and Ayres used broad historical reconstruction and interpretation. Neither they nor J. M. Clark used or conducted many case studies of any description.

8   Wisman and Rozansky (1991: 711) argue that the rejection of formalism (and the satisfaction with pattern models) is due to doubts that "suffi-

ciently deterministic trans-cultural and trans-historical regularities can be found so as to enable the formulation of general laws that might permit a high degree of formalism." This seems both to link formalism to the acceptance of universal economic laws, and to imply that most old institutionalists do not accept the existence of cross-cultural generalizations, ideas that are far from obviously the case. Lind (1993: 12) provides more extensive criticism of Wisman and Rozanosky's attempt to link formalism to the acceptance of transtemporal and transspacial regularities. Nevertheless, their argument does point to the old institutionalists' emphasis on institutional detail in determining the precise workings of more general processes.

9   The less formal branch of agency theory is best represented by Jensen and Meckling (1976) and work of a similar nature.

10   Attempts are being made to develop formal models of limited rationality, but considerable difficulties exist. See Lipman (1991).

11   Many writers are interested in chaos theory and other techniques that are being developed and applied to complex dynamic systems. These techniques have interested both neoclassical and old institutionalist economists. See, for example, Anderson, Arrow, and Pines (1988) and Baumol and Benhabib (1989) on the neoclassical side, and Radzicki (1988, 1990), and Dopfer (1991) on the institutionalist. Mirowski argues that chaos theory is not consistent with neoclassical underpinnings (Mirowski 1990), and Carrier (1992) attempts to link nonlinear dynamics with pattern modeling.

12   This passage comes from a letter from Marshall to F. Y. Edgeworth dated 18 August 1902 and quoted by Stone. Marshall also writes, "The keynote of my *Plea* is that the work of the economist is 'to disentangle the interwoven effects of complex causes,' and that general reasoning is essential but a wide and thorough study of facts is equally essential and that a combination of the two sides of the work is *alone* economics *proper*."

Chapter 3: Individualism and holism

1   This list of propositions is a modified version of those provided by Agassi (1960) and Watkins ([1952] 1973). Agassi (1960: 244) defines holism as consisting of (i) "society is the 'whole' which is more than the sum of its parts"; (ii) "'society' affects the individual's aims"; and (iii) "the social set up influences and constrains the individual's behavior." Watkins ([1952] 1973: 150) defines holism as the principle "that the behaviour of individuals should be explained by being deduced from (a) macroscopic laws which are *sui generis* and which apply to the social system as a whole, and (b) descriptions of the positions (or functions) of the individuals within the whole."

2   As with MH, these statements are a modification of those provided by Agassi (1960) and Watkins ([1957] 1973). In Agassi's (1960: 244)

definition of methodological individualism, (i) "only individuals have aims and interests"; (ii) "the individual behaves in a way adequate to his aim, given his circumstances"; and (iii) "the social setup is changeable as a result of individuals' action." Watkins ([1957] 1973: 168) provides the classic definition in his statement that "every complex social situation, institution, or event is the result of a particular configuration of individuals, their dispositions, situations, beliefs, and physical resources and environments. There may be unfinished or half-way explanations of large-scale social phenomena (say, inflation) in terms of other large-scale phenomena (say, full employment); but we shall not have arrived at rock-bottom explanations of such large-scale phenomena until we have deduced an account of them from statements about the dispositions, beliefs, resources and interrelations of individuals."

3   The argument that social theories are reducible is usually stated in terms of the reduction being possible *in principle*. An existing theory may be insufficiently developed to be reducible, or reduction may be too difficult or cumbersome to undertake in practice. Nevertheless, as pointed out by Kincaid (1986: 494), the "in principle" must not "be taken too broadly for fear of trivializing the individualist's claim. The individualist thus must be asserting more than simply that it is logically possible for social science to be done individualistically."

4   The second point implies that a description of individual acts in individualist terms does not uniquely determine their social description. This, however, does not invalidate the notion of *global* supervenience as discussed here. The point is that the *local* supervenience of the social on the individual does not necessarily hold. See Kincaid (1986: 498, n. 2).

5   Nozick (1977) makes the argument that the "methodological individualist wins" if he can explain all with the theory of human action plus evolutionary biology. Institutions are then initially a dependent variable (1977: 359). However, "explanations of current behavior would have to admit (innate) desires or reinforcers for which macro-social reference would be needed" (1977: 360). The idea that institutional history can be traced back to some pre-institutional starting point is also contained in the "myth" of the social contract (Agassi 1960: 255).

6   This discussion of Veblen's methodological approach is carried further in Rutherford (1984).

7   The instrumental or technological versus the ceremonial or institutional dichotomy is a development of Veblen's industry versus business dichotomy. The point here is not that Veblen's work does not contain the dichotomy, but that he usually included an individual level of analysis: the aims and goals of businessmen versus the aims and goals of working men or engineers. For a more extensive discussion of Ayres's system, see Rutherford (1981).

8   This is not only my own position (Rutherford 1983, 1989a, 1990a), but also that of Biddle (1990a), Ramstad (1990), and Vanberg (1989).

9   As discussed in Chapters 5 and 6, various attempts have been made to

supply an evolutionary or invisible-hand explanation for Posner's view of the efficiency of the common law.

10   The rest of this section relies heavily on Rutherford (1989a, 1989b).

11   North (1981: 50) does claim to be able to "predict a good deal of change in ideology in strictly economic terms," but he is far from claiming a complete explanation of ideology or of changes in ideology. See also North (1990: 36–45).

12   A simple prisoners' dilemma game between two individuals with two courses of action, cooperation and non-cooperation, can be found in the matrix provided in Chapter 5, Figure 1c. Direct communication or binding contracts are excluded. On a single play of the game, non-cooperation is the dominant strategy. Regardless of the strategy chosen by the other player, the best option is to defect. Mutual non-cooperation is the result of any single play, although, jointly, the players would do better to cooperate.

Chapter 4: Rationality and rule following

1   Brunner (1987: 373) argues that the operation or processes of socialization and internalization "is hardly disputable," but goes on to state that "REMM emphasizes a biological-genetic heritage," which modifies the effect of socialization and internalization and that "self-interest is a central component" of the biological-genetic endowment.

2   There is, however, a considerable debate over game theory and to what extent it is consistent with standard notions of rationality in economics. See in particular Sugden (1991).

3   Also important is the work of C. S. Peirce. For a discussion of this point, see in particular Daugert (1950).

4   Commons's discussion of habit owes much more to Peirce than to William James. This can be seen in Commons's *Institutional Economics*, particularly Chapter 4, "Hume and Peirce." It should be noted, however, that Commons's interpretations of Peirce are sometimes highly debatable.

5   Apart from J. M. Clark, Rexford Tugwell and Clarence Ayres also discussed the issue of psychology and economics. See Tugwell (1922, 1930a, 1930b) and Ayres (1918, 1921a, 1921b, 1936).

6   In Veblen's work the terms "institution" and "social convention" include, but are not limited to, social norms.

7   In some places Veblen seems to treat the invidious and emulative propensity in man as an instinct, but on other occasions he indicates that it arises from a corruption or distortion of other more beneficent instincts such as the instinct of workmanship. Compare Veblen ([1899b] 1924) and Veblen ([1914] 1964).

8   Dow (1987) claims that Williamson's use of bounded rationality arguments is only selectively applied. For Williamson's response to Dow, see Williamson (1987b).

9   Williamson (1985: 45), however, argues that the maximizing framework
     would not be objectionable *provided* all the relevant information and
     decision costs were included. By contrast, Jon Elster (1984: 59, 135)
     endorses Winter's rejection of maximizing interpretations of satisficing
     models.

10   Vanberg is not claiming that the calculation is *actually* a deliberate or
     conscious one, only that the result may be *consistent* with maximizing
     choice. In his later 1993 paper, Vanberg explicitly adopts an adaptive
     version of rationality.

11   Frank argues that having a *conscience*, which prevents rule violation even
     if it could be done undetected, can be rationalized along these lines. He
     states (1987a: 593) that "it will sometimes be in a selfish person's interest
     to have a utility function that predisposes him not to cheat, even when he
     is *certain* he would not be caught." As noted in the text, this claim relies
     not merely on the individual having a conscience but on his potential
     trading partners being able to tell, with reasonable accuracy, that he is a
     man with a conscience.

12   Akerlof (1976) has been said to demonstrate that "it is possible for an
     institution to persist even though no individual benefits from this. . . .
     Each individual fears violating the norm for fear of being ostracized.
     Those who do the ostracizing do so because they fear that if they do not
     ostracize those who violate the norms of society, then they themselves
     will be ostracized or will have to face social censure" (Basu, Jones, and
     Schlicht 1987: 10).

13   Frank (1987b, 1988) applies this reasoning to emotions, arguing that
     emotions act as commitments, as predispositions to behave in certain
     (non-rational) ways, ways that will sometimes be contrary to our narrow
     self-interest, but that can, nevertheless, confer advantages.

14   It is interesting to note that Hayek and Mitchell agree on the interrela-
     tion of culture and rationality. For Hayek, "mind and culture developed
     concurrently and not successively." He also states "it is probably no more
     justified to claim that thinking man has created his culture than that
     culture created his reason" (1979: 155–156).

15   In recent work within the OIE, the issues surrounding maximization,
     "bounded rationality," and the whole "rationalist conception of action"
     have received surprisingly little attention. For a noteworthy exception,
     see Hodgson (1988).

Chapter 5: Evolution and design

1   An attempt at a reconciliation of Hayek's evolutionary perspective with
     the constitutional contractarianism of Buchanan has been made by
     Vanberg (1983).

2   The most concerted efforts to interpret Veblen by analogy with Darwin
     are to be found in Harris (1934) and Hodgson (1992b). Hodgson argues
     that Veblen was "relatively successful" in applying "the metaphor of

natural selection to economics," but Hodgson provides little detailed analysis of *exactly* how Veblen thought that new institutions are established or come to displace the old. On close examination, Veblen's treatment of institutional change is more than a simple application of the idea of variation and selection to institutions. First, Veblen tends to conflate the processes of variation and selection by having the new technological conditions themselves generate, through habituation, an adaptive response. Thus, in Veblen, variation not only takes place in response to new environmental conditions, but is "disciplined" by those same conditions. Second, although the new ways of thinking that emerge are adapted to the new technology and usually succeed in becoming established, even against the inertia of existing institutions and the opposition of vested interests, Veblen is not clear about exactly how this takes place, and does allow for the possibility that the opposition will be strong enough to resist successfully, possibly even forcing a reversion to an earlier technological state (see note 14). It is, therefore, not always obvious what is selecting what, or what criterion of evolutionary "success" Veblen is applying to institutions. Indeed, institutional change in Veblen might be seen in terms of a political (class) struggle between old and new ideologies (based on different occupational disciplines), the outcome of which is uncertain.

3   It should be recalled that this argument does *not* require adherence to reductionist versions of individualism, but only the adoption of the mildest versions of methodological individualism.

4   It is sometimes argued that standard invisible-hand arguments can deal *only* with the emergence of an institution, and that a functional evolutionary argument is required to explain persistence. This is incorrect. As will be seen shortly, the persistence of an institution (socially beneficial or not) can be explained in individualistic terms.

5   Thus, Hayek can be found making the distinction (which is of crucial importance in his work) between a "spontaneous order" and the spontaneous *origin* of the rules of that order: "At the moment our concern must be to make clear that while the rules on which a spontaneous order rests, may also be of spontaneous origin, this need not always be the case. Although undoubtedly an order originally formed itself spontaneously because the individuals followed rules which had not been deliberately made but had arisen spontaneously, people gradually learned to improve those rules; and it is at least conceivable that the formation of a spontaneous order relies entirely on rules that were deliberately made" (Hayek 1973: 45–46). It is clear, however, that Hayek thought that for the "kind of society with which we are familiar . . . only some of the rules of law (but never all even of these) will be the product of deliberate design, while most of the rules or norms and customs will be spontaneous growths" (Hayek 1973: 46).

6   Not all evolutionary arguments in economics are based on a Darwinian natural selection analogy. Some refer to Lamarck and to processes of

inheritance of acquired characteristics or processes of imitation and cultural transmission. Such processes, however, usually involve the *intention* on the part of the actors involved to perform better. See Nelson and Winter (1982).

7   Heath (1992: 34) adds a further condition that "R is either a structurally complex pattern or part of a set of patterns [R^1 ... R^n] within which the interrelations of [R^1 ... R^A] are complex." This would rule out "trivial explanations of unintended consequences."

8   Hayek's insistence on the unplanned nature of systems of social order often seems to refer specifically to the social system *as a whole*. However, more than this seems to be implied in the depth and rigour of his criticism of design. The fact that societies have not been designed as wholes, does *not* imply that processes of intentional design do not play important, even vital, roles in maintaining the social order.

9   Vanberg (1986) makes a similar point in regard to Hayek's notion of "group selection."

10 It is not clear that this statement is actually at odds with the idea of purposive collective choice, but it is the author's intent to exclude such processes.

11 It might be argued that the individual interactions in collective choice processes are of the nature of cooperative games, while invisible-hand explanations involve non-cooperative games, but it is not clear that this distinction could be maintained.

12 This discussion of Veblen builds upon Rutherford (1984).

13 Veblen presumed the existence of an instinct of idle curiosity. This instinct is sometimes specifically associated with the growth of scientific knowledge, but it is more accurate to regard it as an instinct to build a system of explanation of the world. The instinct is thus as much the source of myth and religion as of science.

14 Veblen does discuss the possibility of a society forsaking new but disruptive technologies and "reverting" to an earlier phase. In his last book he seems to suggest that a state of unresolved conflict between established institutions and new technology may continue for the foreseeable future. See Veblen ([1904] 1975: 398–400, [1915] 1954: 236–237, 1923: 428–445).

15 This discussion of Commons draws on Rutherford (1983).

16 In his earlier work, Commons (1899–1900) did object to log rolling. For the evolution of Commons's views on this and related matters see Chasse (1986).

17 Commons's continuing interest in constitutional reform stemmed from a desire to ensure better representation of interests. For most of his career he favoured proportional representation. In his last book (Commons 1950) he suggested the formation of an "occupational parliament" made up of representatives from all interest groups. See chapter 6.

18 Commons was aware of the importance of war and revolutions in institutional history, but his system relates, for the most part, to the evolution of the Anglo-American system since the time of the Norman conquest of England.

19   Vanberg (1989) discusses this aspect of Commons's work in more detail.
20   An invisible-hand process need not be based on self-interest as narrowly defined. This, however, is the standard approach.
21   The non-cooperative game indicates that communication and formal agreements between the parties are ruled out. This also rules out intentional institutional design from providing a solution to the problems analyzed.
22   It should be stressed that the exact specification of the rules of the game does matter. In addition, as argued in Chapter 3, game theory does not successfully provide a complete reduction of all social rules to individual self-interest and natural givens.
23   This argument requires that Bourgeois–Bourgeois interaction has the same total payoff as Hawk–Dove. If the more complex strategy is also more costly to perform, and the total payoffs lower, then two possible evolutionary equilibria exist. One is Bourgeois–Bourgeois and the other is a mixed population of hawks and doves. The result will depend on the initial proportions of the population playing each strategy (Hirshleifer 1982: 22–23).
24   Otherwise, by backward induction, the defect strategy again becomes dominant.
25   The problem is compounded if the game is extended to include pure cooperators as well. In a population of retaliators, a pure cooperator does just as well. Now, if being a retaliator imposes additional costs owing to the more complex strategy and behavioural repertoire, being a pure cooperator in a population of retaliators will have a higher return. There will be a tendency to move from retaliation to pure cooperation, but in a population of pure cooperators it pays to be a defector (Hirshleifer 1982: 25). The costs of complexity problems are also discussed in Hirshleifer and Coll (1988).
26   Some further analysis has modified the usual PD game by allowing for exit; that is a player, when met by a defect strategy, may refuse to play with that individual again. This can be used to describe a strategy of "prudent morality," a disposition not to retaliate, but to refuse to play again with a player known to be non-cooperative. Given the payoff structure supposed, in which refusing to play gives a higher payoff than mutual defection, the strategy can work well in competition with others, including tit for tat, provided the number of repeat interactions is not too small. See Tullock (1985) and Vanberg and Congleton (1991).
27   Hayek's notion of group selection is discussed in detail by Vanberg (1986) and Hodgson (1991b).
28   In his most recent work, Field (1991) modifies his previous criticism of Posner by claiming that Posner is not attempting to endogenize the legal system *in its entirety*, but in fact treats the "English legal tradition" as exogenous. The evolution of the common law, then, reflects these legal traditions as well as changing relative prices.
29   "Rational ignorance" is the term used by Downs (1957) to describe the idea that as each individual's vote has virtually no influence on the

outcome of an election, rational voters do not spend time or money collecting information. See also Mueller (1989: 205–206).

30 Williamson does credit Commons with beginning the analysis of the transaction. Williamson's most generous comments on Commons can be found in Williamson (1990: 63–64). For an interesting discussion of Williamson and Commons on vertical integration, see Medema (1992).

Chapter 6: Efficiency and reform

1 As far as old institutionalists are concerned, individualism and natural rights philosophy are examples of preconceptions that arose out of economic and social conditions long since gone. See in particular Veblen ([1906] 1961, [1908b] 1961).

2 In the hands of some writers, particularly Ayres, the attempt to find such a non-institutional foundation for values results in a strongly scientistic and naturalistic position. Veblen was, however, much more aware of the difficulties of regarding science as not itself a preconception specific to "the technological circumstances under which it developed" (Samuels 1990: 696). This issue will be discussed in more detail below.

3 There has been a substantial debate over the nature of Veblen's "ideal political economy" and the role played by technical experts within that system. Veblen has been accused of technocratic elitism (Bell 1963; Dobriansky 1957), but this claim has been challenged by Tilman (1972, 1973) and Hodder (1956) who find more anarchistic tendencies in Veblen's thought. Recent debate has centred on Veblen's interest in and involvement with the engineering movement and with the interpretation of Veblen's *The Engineers and the Price System*. See Layton (1962), Stabile (1984, 1986, 1987, 1988), and Tilman (1985, 1988). It is possible to argue that although Veblen had anarchist and syndicalist sympathies, he did not think that a modern industrial economy either could or would be organized along such lines (Rutherford 1992b). It is noteworthy that Veblen ([1904] 1975: 337) states that although socialists protest the existing system, they are "not necessarily adverse to a somewhat rigorous economic organization on new lines of their own choosing."

4 The charge that Veblen's criticisms of the "waste" involved in the existing institutional system were based on subjective appraisals and values was made in a review on *The Theory of the Leisure Class* by Cummings (1899). Veblen's reply is contained in Veblen (1899a).

5 Some have suggested that Veblen posits the existence of a competitive and self-regarding (emulative) instinct. This would then imply two sides to basic human nature variously expressed in different institutional schemes. Veblen clearly argues, however, that the competitive, emulative, and self-regarding propensities were derived later and are not instinctual in nature. Veblen speaks of such propensities arising out of an "inversion" or "self-contamination" of workmanship and parental bent. See Veblen ([1899b] 1924: 270, [1914] 1964: 46, 52–54).

6   Veblen's wartime essays did make some limited suggestions for reform – although probably with an ulterior motive. See Phillips (1987) and Veblen ([1918b] 1954). Veblen did become involved in the attempt to set up a group of academics and engineers at the New School in 1919. For details of Veblen's involvement with the engineers, see Bell (1963), Layton (1962), and Stabile (1986, 1987). For more general discussions of Veblen's position, see also Stabile (1982, 1988) and Tilman (1972, 1973, 1985).

7   The discussion of Ayres that follows is based on Rutherford (1981).

8   The inclusion of idle curiosity as part of workmanship is particularly questionable. Veblen clearly thought of idle curiosity as being just as capable of producing myths and metaphysics as science.

9   Ayres did sometimes lay himself open to attack on the grounds that he valued technological advance above human welfare. An example is the statement: "We sometimes hear it said that the only result of the invention, for example, of airplanes is that people are killing each other on a larger scale than before. If such a proposition were true, it would indeed nullify the technological conception of progress; for if people are indeed being killed on a larger scale than were before, the circumstance must eventually operate to the disadvantage of further airplane building and of technological development generally" (Ayres 1962: 242). This passage was quoted by Henry Hazlitt (1944: 29) in his criticism of Ayres. See also Abba Lerner's (1945) review of *The Theory of Economic Progress* and comments by Mark Lutz (1985: 157).

10   For most of his career, Commons supported the introduction of proportional representation as a way of obtaining a better representation of all interest groups. The idea of the "occupational parliament" was developed only toward the end of Commons's career. See Commons (1896, [1934] 1961: 898–899, 1950: 33).

11   For a more extensive discussion of Commons's approach to reform, see Dugger (1979b), Kennedy (1962), and Harter (1962; 1963).

12   The axioms can be stated as follows (Vickrey 1960; Mueller 1989: 385):

1. Unanimity (the Pareto postulate): If an individual preference is unopposed by any contrary preference of any other individual, this preference is preserved in the social ordering.
2. Nondictatorship: No individual enjoys a position such that whenever he expresses a preference between any two alternatives and all other individuals express the opposite preference, his preference is always preserved in the social ordering.
3. Transitivity: The social welfare function gives a consistent ordering of all feasible alternatives. That is, $(aPbPc) \rightarrow (aPc)$, and $(aIbIc) \rightarrow (aIc)$.
4. Range (unrestricted domain): There is some "universal" alternative u such that for every pair of other alternatives x and y and for every individual, each of the six possible strict orderings of u, x, and y is contained in some admissible ranking of all alternatives for the individual.

5. Independence of irrelevant alternatives: The social choice between any two alternatives must depend only on the orderings of individuals over these two alternatives, and not on their orderings over other alternatives.

13   Mueller (1989: 421) describes the experimental work of Frohlich, Oppenheimer, and Eavey (1987). Most subjects did not choose Rawls's difference principle (maximizing the floor) but instead chose to maximize the average subject to a floor constraint.

14   The problem is how to make a contract binding on future generations. Buchanan argues that each person will accept the established order only if he or she cannot do better by renegotiation. Renegotiation apparently involves undertaking a "detour through anarchy" out of which a new distribution of property would emerge and a new constitutional contract. However, as Gordon points out, this notion of renegotiation gives little practical guide to constitutional reform (Gordon 1976: 586).

15   Wittman, it should be noted, directs his argument "to those who believe that economic markets work well." He does allow for an alternative interpretation: "For those who are unwilling to accept such a view, the arguments can be interpreted as saying that political markets are no more blemished than economic markets" (1989: 1396 n. 3).

Bibliography

Adams, John. 1990. Institutionalism and Social Choice Economics. *Journal of Economic Issues* 24(September):845–859.

Agassi, Joseph. 1960. Methodological Individualism. *British Journal of Sociology* 11(September):244–270.

Agassi, Joseph. 1975. Institutional Individualism. *British Journal of Sociology* 26(June):144–155.

Akerlof, George A. 1976. The Economics of Caste, and of the Rat Race and Other Woeful Tales. *Quarterly Journal of Economics* 90(November):599–617.

Alchian, Armen. 1950. Uncertainty, Evolution and Economic Theory. *Journal of Political Economy* 58(June):211–221.

Alchian, Armen, and Harold Demsetz. 1972. Production, Information Costs, and Economic Organization. *American Economic Review* 62(December):777–795.

Alchian, Armen, and Harold Demsetz. 1973. The Property Rights Paradigm. *Journal of Economic History* 33(March):16–27.

Andersen, Ole Winckler, and Kirstien Bregn. 1992. New Institutional Economics: What Does It Have to Offer? *Review of Political Economy* 4(October):484–497.

Anderson, Philip W., Kenneth J. Arrow, and David Pines, eds. 1988. *The Economy as an Evolving Complex System.* Redwood City, Calif.: Addison–Wesley.

Arthur, W. Brian. 1989. Competing Technologies, Increasing Returns, and Lock-In by Historical Events. *Economic Journal* 99(March):116–131.

Ault, Richard W., and Robert B. Ekelund. 1988. Habits in Economic Analysis: Veblen and the Neoclassicals. *History of Political Economy* 20(Fall):431–445.

Axelrod, Robert. 1984. *The Evolution of Cooperation.* New York: Basic Books.

Axelrod, Robert. 1986. An Evolutionary Approach to Norms. *American Political Science Review* 80(December):1095–1111.

Ayres, Clarence E. 1918. The Epistemological Significance of Social Psychology. *Journal of Philosophy, Psychology, and Scientific Method* (January 17):35–44.

Ayres, Clarence E. 1921a. Instinct and Capacity – I. *Journal of Philosophy* 18(October 13):561–565.

Ayres, Clarence E. 1921b. Instinct and Capacity – II. *Journal of Philosophy* 19(October 27):600–606.

Ayres, Clarence E. 1936. Fifty Years Developments in Ideas of Human Nature and Motivation. *American Economic Review* 26(March):224–236.

Ayres, Clarence E. 1943. The Significance of Economic Planning. In *Develop-*

ment of Collective Enterprise, ed. S. Eldridge et al., pp. 460–481. Lawrence: University of Kansas Press.

Ayres, Clarence E. 1945. Addendum to *The Theory of Economic Progress. American Economic Review* 35(December):937–940.

Ayres, Clarence E. 1952. *The Industrial Economy.* Boston: Houghton Mifflin.

Ayres, Clarence E. 1957. The Pestilence of Moral Agnosticism. *Southwest Review* 42(Spring):116–125.

Ayres, Clarence E. 1958. Veblen's Theory of Instincts Reconsidered. In *Thorstein Veblen: A Critical Reappraisal,* ed. Douglas F. Dowd, pp. 25–37. Ithaca, N.Y.: Cornell University Press.

Ayres, Clarence E. 1961. *Toward a Reasonable Society.* Austin: University of Texas Press.

Ayres, Clarence E. 1962. *The Theory of Economic Progress.* 2d ed. New York: Schocken.

Ayres, Clarence E. 1966. The Nature and Significance of Institutionalism. *Antioch Review* 26(Spring):70–90.

Ayres, Clarence E. 1967. Guaranteed Income: An Instrumentalist View. In *The Guaranteed Income,* ed. R. Theobald, pp. 16 -182. New York: Anchor.

Basu, Kavshik, Eric Jones, and Erkehart Schlicht. 1987. The Growth and Decay of Custom: The Role of the New Institutional Economics in Economic History. *Explorations in Economic History* 24(January):1–21.

Baumol, William J. 1986. Williamson's *The Economic Institutions of Capitalism. Rand Journal of Economics* 17(Summer):279–286.

Baumol, William J., and J. Benhabib. 1989. Chaos: Significance, Mechanism and Economic Applications. *Journal of Economic Perspectives* 3(Winter):77–105.

Becker, Gary. 1976. *The Economic Approach to Human Behavior.* Chicago: University of Chicago Press.

Bell, Daniel. 1963. Veblen and the New Class. *American Scholar* 32(Autumn):616–638.

Berle, Adolph A., and Gardiner C. Means. [1932] 1947. *The Modern Corporation and Private Property.* New York: Macmillan.

Biddle, Jeff. 1990a. Purpose and Evolution in Commons's Institutionalism. *History of Political Economy* 22(Spring):19–47.

Biddle, Jeff. 1990b. The Role of Negotiational Psychology in J. R. Commons's Proposed Reconstruction of Political Economy. *Review of Political Economy* 2(March):1–25.

Binger, Brian R., and Elizabeth Hoffman. 1989. Institutional Persistence and Change: Questions of Efficiency. *Journal of Institutional and Theoretical Economics* 145(March):67–84.

Binmore, Ken. 1988. Modelling Rational Players: Part I. *Economics and Philosophy* 3(October):179–214.

Binmore, Ken. 1987. Modelling Rational Players: Part II. *Economics and Philosophy* 4(April):9–55.

Boehm, Stephan. 1992. Smith, Menger, and Hayek on Institutions and Unintended Consequences. Paper presented at the Allied Social Science Association Meetings, New Orleans, January.

Boettke, Peter J. 1989. Evolution and Economics: Austrians as Institutionalists. *Research in the History of Economic Thought and Methodology* 6:73–89.

Boland, Lawrence. 1979. Knowledge and the Role of Institutions in Economic Theory. *Journal of Economic Issues* 12(December):957–972.

Boland, Lawrence. 1982. *The Foundations of Economic Method.* London: George Unwin & Allen.

Brunner, Karl. 1987. The Perception of Man and the Conception of Society: Two Approaches to Understanding Society. *Economic Inquiry* 15(July):367–388.

Brunner, Karl, and William H. Meckling. 1977. The Perception of Man and the Conception of Government. *Journal of Money, Credit and Banking* 9(February):60–85.

Buchanan, James M. 1975. *The Limits of Liberty – Between Anarchy and Leviathan.* Chicago: University of Chicago Press.

Buchanan, James M. 1976. Taxation in Fiscal Exchange. *Journal of Public Economics* 6(July/August):17–29.

Buchanan, James M. 1978. *Freedom in Constitutional Contract: Perspectives of a Political Economist.* College Station: Texas A&M University Press.

Buchanan, James M. 1979. *What Should Economists Do?* Indianapolis: Liberty Press.

Buchanan, James M. 1987. *Economics: Between Predictive Science and Moral Philosophy.* College Station: Texas A&M University Press.

Buchanan, James M. 1988. Political Economy 1957–1982. In *Ideas, Their Origins, and Their Consequences*, pp. 119–130. Washington D.C.: Thomas Jefferson Center Foundation.

Buchanan, James M., and Gordon Tullock. 1965. *The Calculus of Consent: Logical Foundations of Constitutional Democracy.* Ann Arbor: University of Michigan Press.

Burns, Arthur F., and Wesley C. Mitchell. 1946. *Measuring Business Cycles.* New York: National Bureau of Economic Research.

Carrier, David. 1992. A Methodology for Pattern Modelling: Nonlinear Macroeconomic Dynamics. *Journal of Economic Issues* 26(March):221–242.

Chandler, Alfred D. 1977. *The Visible Hand.* Cambridge, Mass.: Harvard University Press.

Chasse, John Dennis. 1986. J. R. Commons and the Democratic State. *Journal of Economic Issues* 20(September):759–784.

Chasse, John Dennis. 1991. The American Association for Labor Legislation: An Episode in Institutional Policy Analysis. *Journal of Economic Issues* 25(September):799–828.

Clark, John M. [1917] 1967. Business Acceleration and the Law of Demand: A Technical Factor in Economic Cycles. Reprinted in *Preface to Social Economics*, pp. 237–354. New York: Augustus M. Kelley.

Clark, John M. [1918] 1967. Economics and Modern Psychology. Reprinted in *Preface to Social Economics*, pp. 92–169. New York: Augustus M. Kelley.

Clark, John M. 1921. Soundings in Non-Euclidean Economics. *American Economic Review* 11(March):132–147.

Clark, John M. 1923. *Studies in the Economics of Overhead Costs*. Chicago: University of Chicago Press.

Clark, John M. [1926] 1969. *The Social Control of Business*. New York: Augustus M. Kelley.

Clark, John M. [1927] 1967. The Relation between Statics and Dynamics. In *Economic Essays Contributed in Honor of John Bates Clark*, ed. Jacob H. Hollander, pp. 46–70. Freeport, N.Y.: Books for Libraries Press.

Clark, John M. 1929. Government Control of Industry. *World Tomorrow* 12(February):74–76.

Clark, John M. [1935] 1965. *The Economics of Planning Public Works*. New York: Augustus M. Kelley.

Clark, John M. 1940. Towards a Concept of Workable Competition. *American Economic Review* 30(June):241–256.

Clark, John M. 1957. *Economic Institutions and Human Welfare*. New York: Alfred A. Knopf.

Clark, John M. 1961. *Competition as a Dynamic Process*. Washington, D.C.: Brookings Institution.

Coase, Ronald H. 1937. On the Nature of the Firm. *Economica* 4(November):386–405.

Coase, Ronald H. 1974. The Choice of Institutional Framework: A Comment. *Journal of Law and Economics* 17(October):493–496.

Coase, Ronald H. 1984. The New Institutional Economics. *Journal of Institutional and Theoretical Economics* 140(March):229–231.

Coase, Ronald H. 1988. *The Firm, the Market, and the Law*. Chicago: University of Chicago Press.

Coase, Ronald H. 1992. The Institutional Structure of Production. *American Economic Review* 82 (September): 713–719.

Coats, A. W. 1954. The Influence of Veblen's Methodology. *Journal of Political Economy* 62(December):529–537.

Coats, A. W. 1986. Review of Richard N. Langlois, ed., *Economics as Process: Essays in the New Institutional Economics*. *Kyklos* 39(4):628–630.

Cohen, G. A. 1982. Reply to Elster on Marxism, Functionalism, and Game Theory. *Theory and Society* 11(July):483–495.

Cohen, Michael D., and Robert Axelrod. 1984. Coping with Complexity: The Adaptive Value of Changing Utility. *American Economic Review* 74(March):30–42.

Coleman, James S. 1990. *Foundations of Social Theory*. Cambridge, Mass.: Harvard University Press.

Commons, John R. 1896. *Proportional Representation*. Boston and New York: Thomas Crowell.

Commons, John R. 1899–1900. A Sociological View of Sovereignty. *American Journal of Sociology* 5(July-November):1–15, 155–171, 347–366; 6(January-May):544–552, 683–695, 814–825; 7(July):68–89.

Commons, John R. 1909. American Shoemakers, 1648–1895. A Sketch of Industrial Evolution. *Quarterly Journal of Economics* 24(November):39–84.

Commons, John R. [1924] 1968. *The Legal Foundations of Capitalism.* Madison: University of Wisconsin Press.

Commons, John R. 1925. Law and Economics. *Yale Law Journal* 34(February):371–382.

Commons, John R. 1931. Institutional Economics. *American Economic Review* 21(December):648–657.

Commons, John R. 1932. The Problem of Correlating Law, Economics and Ethics. *Wisconsin Law Review* 8(December):3–26.

Commons, John R. [1934] 1961. *Institutional Economics: Its Place in Political Economy.* Madison: University of Wisconsin Press.

Commons, John R. 1939. Twentieth Century Economics. *Journal of Social Philosophy* 5(October):29–41.

Commons, John R. 1950. *The Economics of Collective Action.* New York: Macmillan.

Cross, John G. 1983. *A Theory of Adaptive Economic Behavior.* Cambridge: Cambridge University Press.

Cummings, John. 1899. *The Theory of the Leisure Class. Journal of Political Economy* 7(September):425–455.

Currie, Gregory. 1984. Individualism and Global Supervenience. *British Journal of the Philosophy of Science* 35(December):345–358.

Daugert, Stanley M. 1950. *The Philosophy of Thorstein Veblen.* New York: Columbia University Press.

David, Paul A. 1985. CLIO and the Economics of QWERTY. *American Economic Review* 75(May):332–337.

De Alessi, Louis. 1983. Property Rights, Transactions Costs, and X Efficiency: An Essay in Economic Theory. *American Economic Review* 75(March):64–81.

De Alessi, Louis. 1990. Form, Substance, and Welfare Comparisons in the Analysis of Institutions. *Journal of Institutional and Theoretical Economics* 146(March):5–23.

Demsetz, Harold. 1967. Towards a Theory of Property Rights. *American Economic Review* 57(May):347–359.

Demsetz, Harold. 1969. Information and Efficiency: Another Viewpoint. *Journal of Law and Economics* 12(April):1–22.

Diesing, Paul. 1971. *Patterns of Discovery in the Social Sciences.* Chicago: Aldine Atherton.

Dixit, Avinash, and Barry Nalebuff. 1991. *Thinking Strategically.* New York: Norton.

Dobriansky, Lev E. 1957. *Veblenism: A New Critique.* Washington, D.C.: Public Affairs Press.

Dopfer, Kirk. 1991. The Complexity of Economic Phenomena: Reply to Tinbergen and Beyond. *Journal of Economic Issues* 25(March):39–76.

Dore, R. P. 1973. Function and Cause. In *The Philosophy of Social Explanation*, ed. A. Ryan, pp. 65–81. Oxford: Oxford University Press.

Dow, Gregory K. 1987. The Function of Authority in Transaction Cost Economics. *Journal of Economic Behavior and Organization* 8(March):13–38.

Dow, Gregory K. 1993. Why Capital Hires Labor: A Bargaining Perspective. *American Economic Review* 83(March):118–134.

Downs, Anthony. 1957. *An Economic Theory of Democracy.* New York: Harper & Row.

Dray, W. H. 1967. Holism and Individualism in History and Social Science. *The Encyclopedia of Philosophy,* vol. 4, pp. 53–58. New York: Macmillan Free Press.

Dugger, William M. 1979a. Methodological Differences between Institutional and Neoclassical Economics. *Journal of Economic Issues* 13(December):899–909.

Dugger, William M. 1979b. The Reform Method of John R. Commons. *Journal of Economic Issues* 13(June):369–381.

Dugger, William M. 1983. The Transaction Cost Analysis of Oliver Williamson: A New Synthesis? *Journal of Economic Issues* 17(March):95–114.

Dugger, William M. 1989a. Austrians vs. Institutionalists: Who Are the Real Dissenters. *Research in the History of Economic Thought and Methodology* 6:115–123.

Dugger, William M., ed. 1989b. *Radical Institutionalism: Contemporary Voices.* Westport, Conn.: Greenwood Press.

Dyer, Alan W. 1986. Veblen on Scientific Creativity: The Influence of Charles S. Peirce. *Journal of Economic Issues* 20(March):21–41.

Eggertsson, Thrainn. 1990. *Economic Behavior and Institutions.* Cambridge: Cambridge University Press.

Einhorn, Hillel J., and Robin M. Hogarth. 1978. Confidence in Judgment: Persistence of the Illusion of Validity. *Psychological Review* 85(September):395–416.

Eklund, Robert B., and Robert D. Tollison. 1982. *Mercantilism as a Rent Seeking Society.* College Station: Texas A&M University Press.

Elster, Jon. 1982. Marxism, Functionalism, and Game Theory. *Theory and Society* 11(July):453–482.

Elster, Jon. 1983. *Explaining Technical Change.* Cambridge: Cambridge University Press.

Elster, Jon. 1984. *Ulysses and the Sirens.* Cambridge: Cambridge University Press.

Elster, Jon. 1989a. *The Cement of Society.* Cambridge: Cambridge University Press.

Elster, Jon. 1989b. Social Norms and Economic Theory. *Journal of Economic Perspectives* 3(Fall):99–117.

Elster, Jon. 1989c. *Solomonic Judgements.* Cambridge: Cambridge University Press.

Elster, Jon, and John E. Roemer, eds. 1991. *Interpersonal Comparisons of Well-Being.* Cambridge: Cambridge University Press.

Endres, A. M. 1984. Institutional Elements in Carl Menger's Theory of Demand: A Comment. *Journal of Economic Issues* 18(September):897–903.

Enke, S. 1951. On Maximizing Profits: A Distinction between Chamberlin and Robinson. *American Economic Review* 41(September):566–578.

Etzioni, Amitai. 1987. On Thoughtless Rationality (Rules of Thumb). *Kyklos* 40(4):496–514.

Ferguson, Adam. [1767] 1966. *An Essay on the History of Civil Society.* Edinburgh: Edinburgh University Press.

Field, Alexander. 1979. On the Explanation of Rules Using Rational Choice Models. *Journal of Economic Issues* 13(March):49–72.

Field, Alexander. 1981. The Problem with Neoclassical Institutional Economics: A Critique with Special Reference to the North/Thomas Model of Pre-1500 Europe. *Explorations in Economic History* 18(April):174–198.

Field, Alexander. 1984. Microeconomics, Norms and Rationality. *Economic Development and Cultural Change* 32(July):683–711.

Field, Alexander. 1991. Do Legal Systems Matter?. *Explorations in Economic History* 28(January):1–35.

Frank, Robert H. 1987a. If Homo Economicus Could Choose His Own Utility Function, Would He Want One with a Conscience. *American Economic Review* 77(September):593–604.

Frank, Robert H. 1987b. Shrewdly Irrational. *Sociological Forum* 2(Winter):21–41.

Frank, Robert H. 1988. *Passions within Reason.* New York: W. W. Norton.

Frank, Robert H. 1992. Melding Sociology and Economics: James Coleman's *Foundations of Social Theory. Journal of Economic Literature* 30(March):147–170.

Friedman, Milton. 1953. *Essays in Positive Economics.* Chicago: Chicago University Press.

Frohlich, Norman, Joe A. Oppenheimer, and Cheryl L. Eavey. 1987. Laboratory Results on Rawls's Distributive Justice. *British Journal of Political Science* 17(January):1–21.

Furubotn, Eirik G., and Rudolf Richter. 1991. The New Institutional Economics: New Views on Antitrust. *Journal of Institutional and Theoretical Economics* 147(March):1–6.

Galbraith, John Kenneth. 1971. *The New Industrial State.* 2d ed. Boston: Houghton Mifflin.

Gilbert, M. 1989. Rationality and Salience. *Philosophical Studies* 57(September):61–77.

Goldberg, Victor. 1974. Institutional Change and the Quasi-Invisible Hand. *Journal of Law and Economics* 17(October):461–492.

Goodman, John C. 1978. The Economic Theory of the Evolution of Common Law. *Journal of Legal Studies* 7(June):393–406.

Gordon, Wendell. 1980. *Institutional Economics.* Austin: University of Texas.

Gordon, H. Scott. 1976. The New Contractarians. *Journal of Political Economy* 84(May/June):573–590.

Gordon, H. Scott. 1981. The Political Economy of F. A. Hayek: Review Article. *Canadian Journal of Economics* 14(August):470–487.

Granovetter, Mark. 1985. Economic Action and Social Structure: The Problem of Embeddedness. *American Journal of Sociology* 91(November):481–510.

Gruchy, Allan G. 1939a. The Economics of the Natural Resources Committee. *American Economic Review* 19(March):60–73.

Gruchy, Allan C. 1939b. The Concept of National Planning in Institutional Economics. *Southern Economic Journal* 6(October):121–144.

Gruchy, Allan G. 1947. *Modern Economic Thought: The American Contribution.* New York: Prentice Hall.

Gruchy, Allan G. 1972. *Contemporary Economic Thought: The Contribution of Neo-Institutional Economics.* Clifton, N.J.: Augustus M. Kelley.

Gruchy, Allan G. 1987. *The Reconstruction of Economics.* Westport, Conn.: Green-wood Press.

Hargraves Heap, Shaun. 1989. *Rationality in Economics.* Oxford: Basil Blackwell.

Harris, Abram L. 1934. Economic Evolution: Dialectical and Darwinian. *Journal of Political Economy* 42 (February):34–79.

Harsanyi, John G. 1968. Individualistic and Functionalistic Explanations in the Light of Game Theory: The Example of Social Status. In *Problems in the Philosophy of Science,* ed. I. Lakatos and A. Musgrave, pp. 305–348. Amsterdam: North Holland.

Harter, Lafayette G., Jr. 1962. *John R. Commons: His Assault on Laissez-Faire.* Corvallis: Oregon State University.

Harter, LaFayette G., Jr. 1963. John R. Commons: Conservative or Liberal. *Western Economic Journal* 1 (Spring):226–232.

Hayek, F. A. 1945. The Use of Knowledge in Society. *American Economic Review* 35 (September):519–530.

Hayek, F. A. 1960. *The Constitution of Liberty.* Chicago: University of Chicago Press.

Hayek, F. A. 1967. *Studies in Philosophy, Politics, and Economics.* London: Routledge & Kegan Paul.

Hayek, F. A. 1973. *Law, Legislation and Liberty Vol. 1: Rules and Order.* London: Routledge & Kegan Paul.

Hayek, F. A. 1978. *New Studies in Philosophy, Politics, and the History of Ideas.* London: Routledge & Kegan Paul.

Hayek, F. A. 1979. *Law, Legislation, and Liberty Vol. 3: The Political Order of a Free People.* London: Routledge & Kegan Paul.

Hazlitt, Henry. 1944. John Dewey on *The Theory of Economic Progress. Saturday Review of Literature* (October 14):29–32.

Heath, Eugene. 1992. Rules, Function, and the Invisible Hand: An Interpretation of Hayek's Social Theory. *Philosophy of the Social Sciences* 22 (March):28–45.

Heiner, Ronald A. 1983. The Origin of Predictable Behaviour. *American Economic Review* 73 (September):560–595.

Heiner, Ronald A. 1986. Imperfect Decisions and the Law: On the Evolution of Legal Precedent and Rules. *Journal of Legal Studies* 15 (June):227–262.

Heiner, Ronald A. 1990. Rule Governed Behaviour in Evolution and Human Society. *Constitutional Political Economy* 1 (Winter):19–46.

Hickerson, Steven R. 1987. Instrumental Valuation: The Normative Compass of Institutional Economics. *Journal of Economic Issues* 71 (September):1117–1143.

Hickman, C. Addison. 1975. *J. M. Clark.* New York: Columbia University Press.

Hill, Forest G. 1967. Veblen, Berle, and the Modern Corporation. *American Journal of Economics and Sociology* 26 (July):279–295.

Hill, Lewis E. 1989. Cultural Determinism or Emergent Evolution: An Analysis of the Controversy Between Clarence Ayres and David Miller. *Journal of Economic Issues* 23 (June):465–471.

Hirshleifer, Jack. 1982. Evolutionary Models in Economics and Law. *Research in Law and Economics* 4:1–59.

Hirshleifer, Jack, and Juan C. M. Coll. 1988. What Strategies Can Support the

Evolutionary Emergence of Cooperation? *Journal of Conflict Resolution* 33(June):367–398.

Hodder, H. J. 1956. The Political Ideas of Thorstein Veblen. *Canadian Journal of Economics and Political Science* 22(August):347–357.

Hodgson, Geoffrey M. 1988. *Economics and Institutions: A Manifesto for Modern Institutional Economics*. Philadelphia: University of Pennsylvania Press.

Hodgson, Geoffrey M. 1991a. Economic Evolution: Intervention Contra Pangloss. *Journal of Economic Issues* 25(June):519–533.

Hodgson, Geoffrey M. 1991b. Hayek's Theory of Cultural Evolution: An Evaluation in the Light of Vanberg's Critique. *Economics and Philosophy* 7(April):67–82.

Hodgson, Geoffrey. 1992a. Carl Menger's Theory of the Evolution of Money: Some Problems. *Review of Political Economy* 4 (October): 396–412.

Hodgson, Geoffrey. 1992b. Thorstein Veblen and Post-Darwinian Economics. *Cambridge Journal of Economics* 16 (September): 285–301.

Hume, David. [1739] 1951. *A Treatise on Human Nature*, ed. L. A. Selby-Bigge. Oxford: Oxford University Press.

Hutchison, T. W. 1973. Some Themes from *Investigations into Method*. In *Carl Menger and the Austrian School of Economics*, ed. J. R. Hicks and W. Weber, pp. 15–37. Oxford: Oxford University Press.

Jacquemin, Alexis. 1987. *The New Industrial Organization*. Cambridge, Mass.: MIT Press.

James, William. 1893. *Psychology*. New York: Holt.

Jensen, Michael C., and William H. Meckling. 1976. Theory of the Firm: Managerial Behaviour, Agency Costs, and Ownership Structure. *Journal of Financial Economics* 3(October):305–360.

Kahneman, Daniel, P. Slovic, and Amos Tversky, eds. 1982. *Judgement Under Uncertainty: Heuristics and Biases*. Cambridge: Cambridge University Press.

Kahneman, Daniel, Jack L. Knetsch, and Richard H. Thaler. 1986a. Fairness and the Assumptions of Economics. *Journal of Business* 59(October):285–300.

Kahneman, Daniel, Jack L. Knetsch, and Richard H. Thaler. 1986b. Fairness as a Constraint on Profit Seeking: Entitlements in the Market. *American Economic Review* 76(September):728–741.

Kaplan, Abraham. 1964. *The Conduct of Inquiry*. San Francisco: Chandler.

Kauper, Thomas E. 1980. The Goals of American Antitrust Policy: The Current Debate. *Zeitschrift für die gesamte Staatswissenschaft* 136(September):408–434.

Kayaalp, Orhan. 1989. Reconciling Economic Postulates: Does "Adaptive" Egoism Satisfice? *The Journal of Behavioral Economics* 18(Winter): 289–306.

Kennedy, W. F. 1962. John R. Commons, Conservative Reformer. *Western Economic Journal* 1(Fall):29–42.

Kincaid, Harold. 1986. Reduction, Explanation, and Individualism. *Philosophy of Science* 53(December):492–513.

Kindleberger, Charles P. 1983. Standards as Public, Collective, and Private Goods. *Kyklos* 36(3):377–396.

Koopmans, Tjalling C. 1947. Measurement Without Theory. *Review of Economics and Statistics* 29(August):161–172.

Landes, William M., and Richard A. Posner. 1975. The Independent Judiciary in an Interest-Group Perspective. *Journal of Law and Economics* 18 (December):875–901.

Langlois, Richard N. 1986a. The New Institutional Economics: An Introductory Essay. In *Economics as a Process: Essays in the New Institutional Economics*, ed. R. Langlois, pp. 1–25. Cambridge: Cambridge University Press.

Langlois, Richard N. 1986b. Rationality, Institutions and Explanation. In *Economics as a Process: Essays in the New Institutional Economics*, ed. R. Langlois, pp. 225–255. Cambridge: Cambridge University Press.

Langlois, Richard N. 1989. What Was Wrong with the Old Institutional Economics (and What Is Still Wrong with the New)? *Review of Political Economy* 1 (November):270–298.

Langlois, Richard N., 1990. Bounded Rationality and Behavioralism: A Clarification and Critique. *Journal of Institutional and Theoretical Economics* 146 (December):691–695.

Langlois, Richard N., and Laszlo Csontos. 1993. Optimization, Rule Following, and the Methodology of Situational Analysis. In *Rationality, Institutions, and Economic Methodology*, ed. U. Maki, B. Gustafsson, and C. Knudsen, pp. 113–132. London: Routledge.

Layton, Edwin T., Jr. 1962. Veblen and the Engineers. *American Quarterly* 14 (Spring):64–72.

Leathers, Charles G. 1989. New and Old Institutionalists on Legal Rules: Hayek and Commons. *Review of Political Economy* 1 (November):361–380.

Leathers, Charles G. 1990. Veblen and Hayek on Instincts and Evolution. *Journal of the History of Economic Thought* 12 (Fall):162–178.

Lerner, Abba. 1945. Review of Ayres: *The Theory of Economic Progress. American Economic Review* 35 (March):160–165.

Levine, A. L. 1983. Marshall's Principles and the 'Biological Viewpoint': A Reconsideration. *Manchester School of Economics and Social Studies* 51 (September):276–293.

Levinthal, Daniel. 1988. A Survey of Agency Models of Organizations. *Journal of Economic Behavior and Organization* 9 (March):153–185.

Lewis, D. K. 1969. *Convention: A Philosophic Study*. Cambridge, Mass.: Harvard University Press.

Libecap, Gary. 1986. Property Rights in Economic History: Implications for Research. *Explorations in Economic History* 23 (3):227–252.

Liebhafsky, Herbert H. 1986. Peirce on the *Summum Bonum* and the Unlimited Community; Ayres on "The Criterion of Value." *Journal of Economic Issues* 20 (March):5–20.

Lind, Hans. 1993. The Myth of Institutionalist Method. *Journal of Economic Issues* 27 (March):1–17.

Lindenberg, Siegwert. 1990. Homo Socio–Oeconomicus: The Emergence of a General Model of Man in the Social Sciences. *Journal of Institutional and Theoretical Economics* 146 (December):727–748.

Lipman, Barton L. 1991. How to Decide How to Decide How to . . .: Modeling Limited Rationality. *Econometrica* 59 (July): 1105–1125.

Lloyd, Christopher. 1986. *Explanation in Social History.* Oxford: Basil Blackwell.

Lukes, Steven. 1968. Methodological Individualism Reconsidered. *British Journal of Sociology* 19(March):119–129.

Lutz, Mark A. 1985. Pragmatism, Instrumental Value Theory, and Social Economics. *Review of Social Economy* 43(October):140–172.

McFarland, Floyd B. 1985. Thorstein Veblen versus the Institutionalists. *Review of Radical Political Economy* 17(Winter):95–105.

Maki, Uskali. 1987. Review of Richard N. Langlois, ed., *Economics as a Process: Essays in the New Institutional Economics. Economics and Philosophy* 3(October):367–373.

Mandelbaum, Maurice. [1955] 1973. Societal Facts. Reprinted in *Modes of Individualism and Collectivism,* ed. J. O'Neill, pp. 221–234. London: Heinemann.

Mandelbaum, Maurice. [1957] 1973. Societal Laws. Reprinted in *Modes of Individualism and Collectivism,* ed. J. O'Neill, pp. 235–247. London: Heinemann.

Margolis, Howard. 1982. *Selfishness, Altruism, and Rationality.* Cambridge: Cambridge University Press.

Markham, Jesse W. 1968. Clark, John Maurice. In *International Encyclopedia of the Social Sciences,* ed. David L. Stills, vol. 2, pp. 508–11. New York: Macmillan and the Free Press.

Marris, Robin. 1988. Review of Oliver E. Williamson, *The Economic Institutions of Capitalism. Economic Journal* 98(March):184–186.

Marshall, Alfred. 1920. *Principles of Economics.* 8th ed. London: Macmillan.

Mayhew, Anne. 1987. Culture: Core Concept under Attack. *Journal of Economic Issues* 21(June):587–603.

Maynard Smith, J. 1982. *Evolution and the Theory of Games.* Cambridge: Cambridge University Press.

Meckling, William H. 1976. Values and the Choice of the Model of the Individual in the Social Sciences. *Schweizerische Zeitschrift Für Volkswirtschaft und Statistik* 112(December):545–560.

Medema, Steven G. 1992. Transactions, Transaction Costs, and Vertical Integration: A Reexamination. *Review of Political Economy* 4(July): 291–316.

Mellor, D. H. 1982. The Reduction of Society. *Philosophy* 57(January):51–75.

Menger, Carl. [1871] 1950. *Principles of Economics.* Glencoe, Ill.: Free Press.

Menger, Carl. [1883] 1985. *Investigations into the Method of the Social Sciences with Special Reference to Economics.* New York: New York University Press.

Mirowski, Philip. 1981. Is There a Mathematical Neoinstitutional Economics? *Journal of Economic Issues* 15(September):593–613.

Mirowski, Philip. 1983. An Evolutionary Theory of Economic Change: A Review Article. *Journal of Economic Issues* 17(September):757–768.

Mirowski, Philip. 1986. Institutions as a Solution Concept in a Game Theory Context. In *The Reconstruction of Economic Theory,* ed. P. Mirowski, pp. 241–263. Boston: Kluwer Academic.

Mirowski, Philip. 1989. *More Heat Than Light: Economics as Social Physics, Physics as Nature's Economics.* Cambridge: Cambridge University Press.

Mirowski, Philip. 1990. From Mandelbrot to Chaos in Economic Theory. *Southern Economic Journal* 57(October):289–307.

Mirowski, Philip. 1991. The When, the How and the Why of Mathematical Expression in the History of Economic Analysis. *Journal of Economic Perspectives* 5(Winter):145–157.

Mises, Ludwig von. 1949. *Human Action: A Treatise on Economics*. London: William Hodge.

Mitchell, Wesley C. 1910a. The Rationality of Economic Activity: I. *Journal of Political Economy* 18(February):97–113.

Mitchell, Wesley C. 1910b. The Rationality of Economic Activity: II. *Journal of Political Economy* 18(March):197–216.

Mitchell, Wesley C. [1912] 1950. The Backward Art of Spending Money. Reprinted in *The Backward Art of Spending Money and Other Essays*, pp. 3–19. New York: Augustus M. Kelley.

Mitchell, Wesley C. 1914. Human Behaviour and Economics: A Survey of Recent Literature. *Quarterly Journal of Economics* 29(November):1–47.

Mitchell, Wesley C. [1916] 1950. The Role of Money in Economic Activity. Reprinted in *The Backward Art of Spending Money and Other Essays*, pp. 149–176. New York: Augustus M. Kelley.

Mitchell, Wesley C. [1918] 1950. Bentham's Felicific Calculus. Reprinted in *The Backward Art of Spending Money and Other Essays*, pp. 177–202. New York: Augustus M. Kelley.

Mitchell, Wesley C. [1925] 1950. Quantitative Analysis in Economic Theory. Reprinted in *The Backward Art of Spending Money and Other Essays*, pp. 20–41. New York: Augustus M. Kelley.

Mitchell, Wesley C. 1927. *Business Cycles: The Problem and Its Setting*. New York: National Bureau of Economic Research.

Mitchell, Wesley C. [1928] 1936. Letter to J. M. Clark. Reprinted in *Preface to Social Economics*, J. M. Clark, pp. 410–416. New York: Farrar and Rhinehart.

Mitchell, Wesley C. 1929. Thorstein Veblen, 1857–1927. *New Republic* 60(September):66–68.

Mitchell, Wesley C. [1931] 1950. Economics 1904–1929. Reprinted in *The Backward Art of Spending Money*, pp. 386–415. New York: Augustus M. Kelley.

Mitchell, Wesley C. [1935] 1950. The Social Sciences and National Planning. Reprinted in *The Backward Art of Spending Money and Other Essays*, pp. 83–102. New York: Augustus M. Kelley.

Mitchell, Wesley C. [1936] 1950. Intelligence and the Guidance of Economic Evolution. Reprinted in *The Backward Art of Spending Money and Other Essays*, pp. 103–136. New York: Augustus M. Kelley.

Mitchell, Wesley C. 1944a. Facts and Values in Economics. *Journal of Philosophy* 41(April):212–219.

Mitchell, Wesley C. 1944b. The Role of Money in Economic History. *Journal of Economics History* 4(December):61–67.

Mitchell, Wesley C. 1950. *The Backward Art of Spending Money and Other Essays*. New York: Augustus M. Kelley.

Mueller, Dennis C. 1986. Rational Egoism versus Adaptive Egoism as Fundamental Postulate for a Descriptive Theory of Human Behavior. *Public Choice* 51(1):3–23.

Mueller, Dennis C. 1989. *Public Choice II.* Cambridge: Cambridge University Press.

Munkirs, John R. 1988. The Dichotomy: Views of a Fifth Generation Institutionalist. *Journal of Economic Issues* 22(December):1035–1044.

Neale, Walter C. 1990. Absolute Cultural Relativism: Firm Foundation for Valuing and Policy. *Journal of Economic Issues* 24(June):333–344.

Nelson, Richard R., and Sidney G. Winter. 1982. *An Evolutionary Theory of Economic Change.* Cambridge, Mass.: Harvard University Press.

Nisbitt, R. E., and L. Ross. 1980. *Human Inference: Strategies and Shortcomings of Social Judgement.* Englewood Cliffs, N.J.: Prentice Hall.

North, Douglass C. 1978. Structure and Performance: The Task of Economic History. *Journal of Economic Literature* 16(September):963–978.

North, Douglass C. 1981. *Structure and Change in Economic History.* New York: Norton.

North, Douglass C. 1984. Three Approaches to the Study of Institutions. In *Neoclassical Political Economy,* ed. D. Colander, pp. 33–40. Cambridge, Mass.: Ballinger.

North, Douglass C. 1986. The New Institutional Economics. *Journal of Institutional and Theoretical Economics* 142(March):230–237.

North, Douglass C. 1990. *Institutions, Institutional Change and Economic Performance.* Cambridge: Cambridge University Press.

North, Douglass C., and Robert Thomas. 1973. *The Rise of the Western World: A New Economic History.* Cambridge: Cambridge University Press.

Nozick, Robert. 1974. *Anarchy, State, and Utopia.* New York: Basic Books.

Nozick, Robert. 1977. On Austrian Methodology. *Synthese* 36(November):353–392.

O'Brien, D. P. 1990. Marshall's Industrial Analysis. *Scottish Journal of Political Economy* 37(February):61–84.

O'Driscoll, Gerald P., and Mario J. Rizzo. 1985. *The Economics of Time and Ignorance.* Oxford: Basil Blackwell.

Olson, Mancur. 1971. *The Logic of Collective Action.* Rev. ed. Cambridge, Mass.: Harvard University Press.

Olson, Mancur. 1982. *The Rise and Decline of Nations.* New Haven, Conn.: Yale University Press.

Opp, Karl-Dieter. 1985. Sociology and Economic Man. *Journal of Institutional and Theoretical Economics* 141(June)213–243.

Parsons, Talcott. 1968. *The Structure of Social Action.* New York: Free Press.

Perlman, Mark. 1986. Subjectivism and American Institutionalism. In *Subjectivism, Intelligibility and Economic Understanding,* ed. I. Kirzner, pp. 268–280. London: Macmillan.

Perrow, Charles. 1986. Economic Theories of Organization. *Theory and Society* 15:11–45.

Petr, Jerry L. 1984. Fundamentals of an Institutionalist Perspective on Economic Policy. *Journal of Economic Issues* 18(March):1–17.

Phillips, Ron J. 1987. Veblen and the "Wobblies": A Note. *Review of Radical Political Economy* 19(Spring):98–103.

Polanyi, Karl. 1944. *The Great Transformation.* New York: Rinehart.

Popper, Karl. 1961. *The Poverty of Historicism.* London: Routledge & Kegan Paul.

Posner, Richard A. 1977. *Economic Analysis of Law*. 2d ed. Boston: Little, Brown.

Posner, Richard A. 1981. *The Economics of Justice*. Cambridge, Mass.: Harvard University Press.

Posner, Richard A. 1987. The Law and Economics Movement. *American Economic Review* 77 (May):1–13.

Pressler, Jonathan. 1987. Rights and Social Choice: Is There a Paretian Libertarian Paradox. *Economics and Philosophy* 3 (April):1–22.

Priest, George L. 1977. The Common Law Process and the Selection of Efficient Rules. *Journal of Legal Studies* 6 (January):65–82.

Prisching, M. 1989. Evolution and Design of Social Institutions in Austrian Theory. *Journal of Economic Studies* 16(2):47–62.

Rachels, James. 1977. John Dewey and the Truth about Ethics. In *New Studies in the Philosophy of John Dewey*, ed. S. M. Cahn, pp. 149–171. Hanover, N.H.: University Press of New England.

Radzicki, Michael J. 1988. Institutional Dynamics: An Extension of the Institutionalist Approach to Socioeconomic Analysis. *Journal of Economic Issues* 22(September):633–665.

Radzicki, Michael J. 1990. Institutional Dynamics, Deterministic Chaos, and Self Organizing Systems. *Journal of Economic Issues* 24(March):57–102.

Raines, J. Patrick, and Charles G. Leathers. 1991. Endogenous Habit Formation in Veblen's Evolutionary Theory: The Case of Financial Institutions. Paper presented at the Meetings of The History of Economics Society, College Park, Md., June.

Ramstad, Yngve. 1986. A Pragmatist's Quest for Holistic Knowledge: The Scientific Methodology of John R. Commons. *Journal of Economic Issues* 20(December):1067–1105.

Ramstad, Yngve. 1989. "Reasonable Value" versus "Instrumental Value": Competing Paradigms in Institutional Economics. *Journal of Economic Issues* 23(September):761–777.

Ramstad, Yngve. 1990. The Institutionalism of John R. Commons: Theoretical Foundations of a Volitional Economics. *Research in the History of Economic Thought and Methodology* 8:53–104.

Rawls, John A. 1971. *A Theory of Justice*. Cambridge, Mass.: Belknap Press.

Roemer, John E. 1982. Methodological Individualism and Deductive Marxism. *Theory and Society* 11 (July):513–520.

Romer, Thomas. 1988. Nobel Laureate: On James Buchanan's Contributions to Public Economics. *Journal of Economic Perspectives* 2 (Fall):165–179.

Ross, Dorothy. 1991. *The Origins of American Social Science*. Cambridge: Cambridge University Press.

Rowley, Charles K., and Alan T. Peacock. 1975. *Welfare Economics*. London: Martin Robertson.

Rubin, Paul H. 1977. Why Is the Common Law Efficient? *Journal of Legal Studies* 6(January):51–61.

Rubin, Paul H. 1982. Evolved Ethics and Efficient Ethics. *Journal of Economic Behavior and Organization* 3 (June/September):161–174.

Rutherford, Malcolm. 1980. Veblen on Owners, Managers, and the Control of Industry. *History of Political Economy* 12(Fall):434–440.

Rutherford, Malcolm. 1981. Clarence Ayres and the Instrumental Theory of Value. *Journal of Economic Issues* 15(September):657–673.

Rutherford, Malcolm. 1983. John R. Commons's Institutional Economics. *Journal of Economic Issues* 17(September):721–744.

Rutherford, Malcolm. 1984. Thorstein Veblen and the Processes of Institutional Change. *History of Political Economy.* 16(Fall):331–348.

Rutherford, Malcolm. 1987. Wesley Mitchell: Institutions and Quantitative Methods. *Eastern Economic Journal* 13(March):63–73.

Rutherford, Malcolm. 1989a. Some Issues in the Comparison of Austrian and Institutional Economics. *Research in the History of Economic Thought and Methodology* 6:159–172.

Rutherford, Malcolm. 1989b. What Is Wrong with the New Institutional Economics (and What Is Still Wrong with the Old)? *Review of Political Economy* 1(November):299–318.

Rutherford, Malcolm. 1990a. Introduction to *Institutional Economics: Its Place in Political Economy,* by J. R. Commons, pp. xii–xxxvii. New Brunswick, N.J.: Transaction.

Rutherford, Malcolm. 1990b. Rational Expectations in the Light of Modern Psychology. *Research in the History of Economic Thought and Methodology* 7:127–140.

Rutherford, Malcolm. 1990c. Science, Self-Correction and Values: From Peirce to Institutionalism. In *Social Economics: Retrospect and Prospect,* ed. J. Lutz, pp. 391–406. Boston: Kluwer Academic.

Rutherford, Malcolm. 1992a. On Trusts and Technostructures: Veblen, Berle and Means, and Galbraith. *International Journal of Social Economics* 19 (10/11/12):268–278.

Rutherford, Malcolm. 1992b. Thorstein Veblen and the Problem of the Engineers. *International Review of Sociology* (3):125–150.

Rutherford, Malcolm. 1993. Review Essay on William Dugger, ed. *Radical Institutionalism. Research in the History of Economic Thought and Methodology* 11:221–228.

Samuels, Warren J. 1990. The Self-referentiability of Thorstein Veblen's Theory of the Preconceptions of Science. *Journal of Economic Issues* 24(September): 695–718.

Samuels, Warren J., and A. Allan Schmid, eds. 1981. *Law and Economics: An Institutional Perspective.* Boston: Martinus Nijhoff.

Sandmo, Agnar. 1990. Buchanan on Political Economy: A Review Article. *Journal of Economic Literature* 28(March):50–65.

Saraydar, Edward. 1989. The Conflation of Productivity and Efficiency in Economics and Economic History. *Economics and Philosophy* 5(April):55–67.

Schaffer, Mark E. 1989. Are Profit Maximizers the Best Survivors? *Journal of Economic Behavior and Organization* 12(August):29–45.

Schelling, Thomas C. 1960. *The Strategy of Conflict.* New York: Oxford University Press.

Schelling, Thomas C. 1978. *Micromotives and Macrobehavior*. New York: W. W. Norton.

Schlicht, Ekkehart. 1990. Rationality, Bounded or Not, and Institutional Analysis. *Journal of Institutional and Theoretical Economics* 146(December):703–719.

Schmid, A. Allan. 1978. *Property, Power, and Public Choice*. New York: Praeger.

Schofield, Norman. 1985. Anarchy, Altruism and Cooperation: A Review. *Social Choice and Welfare* 2(December):207–219.

Schotter, Andrew. 1981. *The Economic Theory of Social Institutions*. Cambridge: Cambridge University Press.

Schotter, Andrew. 1983. Why Take a Game Theoretical Approach to Economics? Institutions, Economics and Game Theory. *Economie Appliquée* 36(4):673–695.

Seckler, David. 1966. The Naivete of John R. Commons. *Western Economic Journal* 4(Summer):261–267.

Seckler, David. 1975. *Thorstein Veblen and the Institutionalists*. Boulder: Colorado Associated University Press.

Sen, Amartya, 1970. The Impossibility of a Paretian Liberal. *Journal of Political Economy* 78(January/February):152–157.

Shubik, Martin. 1975. The General Equilibrium Model is Incomplete and Not Adequate for the Reconciliation of Micro and Macroeconomic Theory. *Kyklos* 28(3):545–573.

Simon, Herbert A. 1955. A Behaviorial Model of Rational Choice. *Quarterly Journal of Economics* 69(February):99–118.

Simon, Herbert A. 1957. *Administrative Behavior: A Study of Decision Making Processes in Administrative Organization*. 2d ed. New York: Macmillan.

Simon, Herbert A. 1959. Theories of Decision-Making in Economic and Behaviorial Sciences. *American Economic Review* 49(June):253–283.

Simon, Herbert A. 1976. From Substantive to Procedural Rationality. In *Method and Appraisal in Economics*, ed. S. Latsis, pp. 129–148. Cambridge: Cambridge University Press.

Smith, Adam. [1776] 1976. *An Inquiry into the Nature and Causes of the Wealth of Nations*. Chicago: Chicago University Press.

Stabile, Donald R. 1982. Thorstein Veblen and His Socialist Contemporaries: A Critical Comparison. *Journal of Economic Issues* 16(March):1–28.

Stabile, Donald R. 1984. *Prophets of Order*. Boston: South End Press.

Stabile, Donald R. 1986. Veblen and the Political Economy of the Engineer: The Radical Thinker and Engineering Leaders Came to Technocratic Ideas at the Same Time. *American Journal of Economics and Sociology* 45(January):41–52.

Stabile, Donald R. 1987. Veblen and the Political Economy of Technocracy: The Herald of Technological Revolution, Developed an Ideology of 'Scientific' Collectivism. *American Journal of Economics and Sociology* 46(January):35–48.

Stabile, Donald R. 1988. Veblen's Analysis of Social Movements: Bellamyites, Workers and Engineers. *Journal of Economic Issues* 22(March):211–226.

Stanfield, J. Ron. 1989. Of Paradigms and Discipline. *Research in the History of Economic Thought and Methodology* 6:173–179.

Stone, Richard. 1966. *Mathematics in the Social Sciences and Other Essays*. Cambridge, Mass.: MIT Press.

Sugden, Robert. 1985. Liberty, Preference, and Choice. *Economics and Philosophy* 1(October):213–239.

Sugden, Robert. 1986. *The Economics of Rights, Co-operation and Welfare*. Oxford: Basil Blackwell.

Sugden, Robert. 1989. Spontaneous Order. *Journal of Economic Perspectives* 3(Fall):85–97.

Sugden, Robert. 1991. Rational Choice: A Survey of Contributions from Economics and Philosophy. *Economic Journal* 101(July):751–785.

Sugden, Robert, and Albert Weale. 1979. A Contractual Reformulation of Certain Aspects of Welfare Economics. *Economica* 46(May):111–123.

Taylor, Michael. 1976. *Anarchy and Cooperation*. London: Wiley.

Taylor, Michael. 1982. *Community, Anarchy and Liberty*. Cambridge: Cambridge University Press.

Taylor, Michael. 1987. *The Possibility of Cooperation*. Cambridge: Cambridge University Press.

Thomas, Brinley. 1991. Alfred Marshall on Economic Biology. *Review of Political Economy* 3(1):1–14.

Tilman, Rick. 1972. Veblen's Ideal Political Economy and Its Critics. *American Journal of Economics and Sociology* 31(July):307–317.

Tilman, Rick. 1973. Thorstein Veblen: Incrementalist and Utopian. *American Journal of Economics and Sociology.* 32(April):155–169.

Tilman, Rick. 1984. Dewey's Liberalism versus Veblen's Radicalism: A Reappraisal of the Unity of Progressive Social Thought. *Journal of Economic Issues* 18(September):745–769.

Tilman, Rick. 1985. The Utopian Vision of Edward Bellamy and Thorstein Veblen. *Journal of Economic Issues* 19(December):879–898.

Tilman, Rick. 1988. A Comment on Stabile's Interpretation of Veblen and the Engineers. *Journal of Economic Issues* 22(December):1247–1249.

Tilman, Rick. 1990. New Light on John Dewey, Clarence Ayres, and the Development of Evolutionary Economics. *Journal of Economic Issues* 24(December):963–979.

Tool, Marc R. 1977. A Social Value Theory in Neoinstitutional Economics. *Journal of Economic Issues* 11(December):823–846.

Tool, Marc R. 1979. *The Discretionary Economy*. Santa Monica: Goodyear.

Tool, Marc R. 1986. *Essays in Social Value Theory: The Neoinstitutional Alternative*. New York: M. E. Sharpe.

Tugwell, Rexford G. 1922. Human Nature in Economic Theory. *Journal of Political Economy* 30(June):317–345.

Tugwell, Rexford G. 1930a. Human Nature and Social Economy – I. *Journal of Philosophy* 27(August 14):449–457.

Tugwell, Rexford G. 1930b. Human Nature and Social Economy – II. *Journal of Philosophy* 27(August 28):479–492.

Tugwell, Rexford G. 1932. The Principle of Planning and the Institution of Laissez-Faire. *American Economic Review* 22(March):75–92.

Tugwell, Rexford G. 1935. When Corporations Save. In *The Battle for Democracy*, pp. 187–192. New York: Columbia University Press.

Tugwell, Rexford G., Thomas Munro, and Roy E. Stryker. 1930. *American Economic Life and the Means of Its Improvement.* New York: Harcourt, Brace.

Tullock, Gordon. 1985. Adam Smith and the Prisoners' Dilemma. *Quarterly Journal of Economics* 100(Supplement):1073–1081.

Ullmann-Margalit, Edna. 1977. *The Emergence of Norms.* Oxford: Oxford University Press.

Ullmann-Margalit, Edna. 1978. Invisible Hand Explanations. *Synthese* 39(October):263–291.

Vanberg, Viktor. 1983. Libertarian Evolutionism and Contractarian Constitutionalism. In *Philosophical and Economic Foundations of Capitalism*, ed. S. Pejovich, pp. 77–87. Lexington, Mass.: Lexington Books, D. C. Heath.

Vanberg, Viktor. 1986. Spontaneous Market Order and Social Rules: A Critical Examination of F. A. Hayek's Theory of Cultural Evolution. *Economics and Philosophy* 2(April):75–100.

Vanberg, Viktor. 1988. Rules and Choice in Economics and Sociology. *Jahrbuch für Neue Politische Oeconomie* 7:1–22.

Vanberg, Viktor. 1989. Carl Menger's Evolutionary and John R. Commons' Collective Action Approach to Institutions: A Comparison. *Review of Political Economy* 1(November):334–360.

Vanberg, Viktor. 1993. Rational Choice, Rule-Following and Institutions: An Evolutionary Perspective. In *Rationality, Institutions and Economic Methodology*, ed. U. Maki, B. Gustafsson, and C. Knudsen, pp. 171–200. London: Routledge.

Vanberg, Viktor, and Congleton, Roger. 1991. Rationality, Morality and Exit. *American Political Science Review* 86 (June):418–431.

Veblen, Thorstein. [1898] 1961. Why is Economics Not an Evolutionary Science? Reprinted in *The Place of Science in Modern Civilisation*, pp. 56–81. New York: Russell & Russell.

Veblen, Thorstein. [1899a] 1954. Mr. Cummings's Strictures on *"The Theory of the Leisure Class."* Reprinted in *Essays in Our Changing Order*, ed. L. Ardzrooni, pp. 16–31. New York: Viking Press.

Veblen, Thorstein. [1899b] 1924. *The Theory of the Leisure Class.* London: George Allen & Unwin.

Veblen, Thorstein. [1900] 1961. The Preconceptions of Economic Science, III. Reprinted in *The Place of Science in Modern Civilisation*, pp. 148–179. New York: Russell & Russell.

Veblen, Thorstein. [1901] 1961. Industrial and Pecuniary Employments. Reprinted in *The Place of Science in Modern Civilisation*, pp. 279–323. New York: Russell & Russell.

Veblen, Thorstein. [1904] 1975. *The Theory of Business Enterprise.* Clifton, N.J.: Augustus M. Kelley.

Veblen, Thorstein. [1906] 1961. The Place of Science in Modern Civilisation. Reprinted in *The Place of Science in Modern Civilisation*, pp. 1–31. New York: Russell & Russell.

Veblen, Thorstein. [1907] 1961. The Socialist Economics of Karl Marx and His

Followers, II. Reprinted in *The Place of Science in Modern Civilisation,* pp. 431–456. New York: Russell & Russell.

Veblen, Thorstein. [1908a] 1961. The Evolution of the Scientific Point of View. Reprinted in *The Place of Science in Modern Civilisation,* pp. 32–55. New York: Russell & Russell.

Veblen, Thorstein. [1908b] 1961. Professor Clark's Economics. Reprinted in *The Place of Science in Modern Civilisation,* pp. 180–230. New York: Russell & Russell.

Veblen, Thorstein. [1909] 1961. The Limitations of Marginal Utility. Reprinted in *The Place of Science in Modern Civilisation,* pp. 231–251. New York: Russell & Russell.

Veblen, Thorstein. [1914] 1964. *The Instinct of Workmanship and the State of the Industrial Arts.* New York: Augustus M. Kelley.

Veblen, Thorstein. [1915] 1954. *Imperial Germany and the Industrial Revolution.* New York: Augustus M. Kelley.

Veblen, Thorstein. 1918a. *The Higher Learning in America.* New York: B. W. Huebsch.

Veblen, Thorstein. [1918b] 1954. Farm Labor and the I.W.W. Reprinted in *Essays in Our Changing Order,* ed. L. Ardzrooni, pp. 319–336. New York: Viking Press.

Veblen, Thorstein. [1919] 1964. *The Vested Interests and the Common Man.* New York: Augustus M. Kelley.

Veblen, Thorstein. [1921] 1965. *The Engineers and the Price System.* New York: Augustus M. Kelley.

Veblen, Thorstein. [1923] 1954. *Absentee Ownership.* New York: Augustus M. Kelley.

Vickrey, William. 1960. Utility, Strategy, and Social Decision Rules. *Quarterly Journal of Economics* 74(November):507–535.

Vining, Rutledge. 1949. Methodological Issues in Quantitative Economics. *Review of Economics and Statistics* 31(May):77–86.

Walker, Donald A. 1979. The Institutionalist Economic Theory of Clarence Ayres. *Economic Inquiry* 17(October):519–538.

Waller, William T. 1982. The Evolution of the Veblenian Dichotomy: Veblen, Hamilton, Ayres, and Foster. *Journal of Economic Issues* 16(September):757–771.

Watkins, J. W. N. [1952] 1973. Ideal Types and Historical Explanation. Reprinted in *Modes of Individualism and Collectivism,* ed. J. O'Neill, pp. 143–165. London: Heinemann.

Watkins, J. W. N. [1955] 1973. Methodological Individualism: A Reply. Reprinted in *Modes of Individualism and Collectivism,* ed. J. O'Neill, pp. 179–184. London: Heinemann.

Watkins, J. W. N. [1957] 1973. Historical Explanation in the Social Sciences. Reprinted in *Modes of Individualism and Collectivism,* ed. J. O'Neill, pp. 166–178. London: Heinemann.

Wieser, Friedrich von. [1927] 1967. *Social Economics.* New York: Augustus M. Kelley.

Wilber, Charles K., and Robert S. Harrison. 1978. The Methodological Basis of

Institutional Economics: Pattern Model, Storytelling, and Holism. *Journal of Economic Issues* 12(March):61–89.

Wilber, Charles K., and Kenneth P. Jameson. 1983. *An Inquiry into the Poverty of Economics.* Notre Dame: University of Notre Dame.

Williamson, Oliver E. 1975. *Markets and Hierarchies: Analysis and Antitrust Implications.* New York: Free Press.

Williamson, Oliver E. 1985. *The Economic Institutions of Capitalism.* New York: Free Press.

Williamson, Oliver E. 1987a. Corporate Finance and Corporate Governance. Berkeley Business School, Economic Analysis and Policy Working Paper No. EAP–26.

Williamson, Oliver E. 1987b. Transaction Cost Economics: The Comparative Contracting Perspective. *Journal of Economic Behavior and Organization* 8(December):617–625.

Williamson, Oliver E. 1990. A Comparison of Alternative Approaches to Economic Organization. *Journal of Institutional and Theoretical Economics* 146(March):61–71.

Winter, Sidney G. 1964. Economic 'Natural Selection' and the Theory of the Firm. *Yale Economic Essays* 4:225–272.

Wisman, Jon D., and Joseph Rozansky. 1991. The Methodology of Institutionalism Revisited. *Journal of Economic Issues* 25 (September): 709–737.

Wittman, Donald. 1989. Why Democracies Produce Efficient Results. *Journal of Political Economy* 97(November/December):1395–1424.

Wrong, Dennis H. 1961. The Oversocialized Conception of Man in Modern Sociology. *American Sociological Review* 26(April):183–193.

Index

Adams, John, 127
adaption
  change based on, 8
  in old institutional economics, 61–2,
    66, 79
  in Veblen, 58, 98
adaptive rationality
  difference from maximizing rational-
    ity, 55
  with evolutionary perspective, 75–6
  in new institutional economics, 78–9
  in old institutional economics, 66–7,
    78
  in organization of the firm, 124
Agassi, Joseph, 32, 35, 37
agency capture, 149, 162, 167
agency theory
  case-by-case maximizing, 67–8
  formal methods used in, 20, 24
  functionalism in, 124
  less formal branch of, 184n9
  in new institutional economics, 2, 20
Akerlof, George, 54, 73
Alchian, Armen A., 2, 43, 81, 123, 124,
  168
analytic description (Mitchell), 11
Andersen, Ole Winckler, 2
Anderson, Philip W., 175
anti-formalism, 4, 20–4, 174, 177
Arrow, Kenneth J., 154, 175
Arthur, W. Brian, 168
artificial selection (Commons), 109
Ault, Richard W., 4, 55, 58, 69, 72, 78
Austrian economics
  deductive methods, 8, 23–4
  distinction between spontaneous and
    designed institutions, 99
  formal and non-formal methodology,
    23–4
  formation of social norms and
    common law, 85
  institutional development, 83
  invisible-hand process, 91–3
  in new institutional economics, 3, 173,
    175

reductionism and anti-reductionism,
  48–9
spontaneous process, 82–3, 85, 89–90,
  99, 132, 175–6
unintended consequences, 83, 90–91
Axelrod, Robert, 47, 53, 73, 75, 78, 114
Ayres, Clarence
  components of men's action, 78
  guaranteed income schemes, 148
  instrumentalism, 66–7, 91
  instrumental value theory, 138–144
  technological continuum, 40–1, 100–
    1, 139–44, 176
  value judgements, 130

bargaining transactions (Commons),
  102, 109
Basu, Kavshik, 25–6, 48, 49, 73, 132,
  165–6
Baumol, William, 23, 175
Becker, Gary, 78
behaviour
  adopting rules of, 72
  consequences of patterns of
    (Mitchell), 41–2
  culturally significant patterns of
    (Ayres), 139
  generated by norms and standards
    (Veblen), 38–9
  incorporated in social norms, 53
  institutions' effect on (Williamson),
    49
  J. M. Clark's interpretation, 60
  maximizing and non-maximizing, 54–
    5
  Mises, 48
  norm-guided, 63, 76–7, 79–80
  rule-governed (Heiner), 70–7
behaviourism, 55–6
Benhabib, J., 175
Berle, Adolph, 109
best existing practices (Commons), 145
Biddle, Jeff, 15, 150
Binger, Brian R., 132, 165
Binmore, Ken, 75